FACETS OF
EMOTION
RECENT RESEARCH

FACETS OF
EMOTION
RECENT RESEARCH

EDITED BY

KLAUS R. SCHERER
University of Geneva
and
University of Giessen

88-1261

 LAWRENCE ERLBAUM ASSOCIATES, PUBLISHERS
1988   Hillsdale, New Jersey   Hove and London

Lawrence Erlbaum Associates, Inc., Publishers
365 Broadway
Hillsdale, New Jersey 07642

Library of Congress Cataloging-in-Publication Data

Facets of emotion.

  Bibliography: p.
  Includes indexes.
  1. Emotions.   2. Emotions — Cross-cultural studies.
I. Scherer, Klaus R. [DNLM: 1. Emotions. BF 531 F138]
BF531.F33 1988   152.4   88-3879
ISBN 0-8058-0141-3
ISBN 0-8058-0142-1 (pbk.)

Printed in the Unites States of America
10 9 8 7 6 5 4 3 2 1

CONTENTS

PREFACE

We are presently witnessing a renaissance of research on emotion. In the last 10 years, an increasing number of empirical studies dealing with many different aspects of emotion has appeared. Given the fact that emotion researchers are spread over many subdisciplines of psychology as well as over many neighboring disciplines, there has not been any single publication outlet used to disseminate theoretical ideas and research findings. On the contrary, research reports are scattered over many different journals and edited books. This situation is frustrating for both readers and authors. It is increasingly difficult to perceive links between different research approaches and to identify research programs. This fragmentation of the publication of relevant research obviously has rather negative effects in terms of the integration of research findings from different approaches.

Our research group has been particularly suffering from this dispersion of publication opportunities. Because we have been working in a number of different areas related to emotion research, our work has appeared in a large number of outlets. Consequently, it is difficult to demonstrate that while concerns may be different in each individual project, there are interesting links as far as both methodology and theoretical approach are concerned.

This volume of research papers from our research group is intended to counteract the tendency toward dispersion. Rather than submitting the various research reports to journals, we have opted for the original publication of these reports in the form of an edited research monograph. One concern has been publication delay which with some journals is now approaching several years. However, more importantly, we want to provide the reader interested in emotion research with the opportunity to examine different research approaches, thematic questions, and the results of several studies within the confines of a single volume. With the exception of one chapter (Chapter 2, Wallbott & Scherer, which has been prepublished in *Social Science Information*), none of the chapters in this volume has been published previously.

A major intent of this volume is to introduce a number of new methodological tools for research on emotion (for example, facet theory, nonmetrical regression for patterns, voice resynthesis, and other methods) as well as to reassert the utility of some classical tools of social science research for studies of emotion (e.g., properly constructed questionnaires).

In addition we present a number of theoretical notions that seem relevant to a systematic study of the emotion process (such as component process theory, a taxonomy of appraisal and coping dimensions, contextual and situational approaches, and interchannel comparison). It is hoped that the results presented in this volume can serve as hypotheses for further work in this area. In the Appendix several sets of research materials are reprinted to encourage use in student research projects.

Klaus R. Scherer

EMOTIONAL EXPERIENCE IN EVERYDAY LIFE

One of the major drawbacks to emotion research is the difficulty of studying actual emotions. Researchers in this area have often commented on the fact that it is unethical and impractical to induce strong emotions in the laboratory and virtually impossible to study natural emotions in the field (given that many emotions are rather private affairs). The scarcity of research on emotion may be partly due to the difficulty of actually getting hold of the phenomenon. The few laboratory studies that have been conducted have often been accused of a high degree of artificiality. Consequently, one of the major difficulties for theorizing in this area is that one usually has to base one's theoretical inferences on personal introspection and/or cultural lore.

One potential solution is the use of self-report techniques, in particular questionnaires to elicit descriptions of emotional experiences from a large number of people. These methods are well proven in many different areas of psychology where one has to rely on verbal report of internal processes that one cannot measure otherwise with present methodology. Strangely enough, in the area of emotion research, these methods have long been considered of little use. Although it is true that there are many potential snares, in the form of reporting bias, stereotyping, social desirability, memory lapses, and so on, it is equally true that we could not possibly study many of the aspects of emotion unless we were to use self-report. Given the difficulty of gaining access to settings where one could objectively observe different types of emotions, asking people about such experiences remains the only possible approach.

A more extensive justification of the use of self-report, in particular questionnaire methods, has been provided in a recent volume describing a large cross-cultural survey of emotional experiences in different European countries (Chapter 1 in Scherer, Wallbott, & Summerfield, 1986). This collaborative effort of psychologists from several European countries has been rather useful in investigating, in an actuarial fashion, the types of emotional experiences that people live through day by day. An attempt has been made to categorize the information provided on the antecedents of emotion, that is, the situations eliciting emotional response, on the physiological and expressive reactions to emotional arousal, and on subjective feeling state and attempts made to control the emotional reaction.

One of the most surprising findings in this large survey was the high degree of universality of emotional antecedents and reactions across the European cultures studied. The commonalities in emotional experiences between the students studied in eight European countries were much larger than the differences we had expected on the basis of common stereotypes, such as those relating to the "hot-blooded Southerners" and the "cool Northerners."

One of the suggestions made to account for this unversality is that in spite of the national differences in Europe, the prevailing culture may be similar enough to render it unlikely to find large-scale cultural differences in a phenomenon that is commonly supposed to be highly determined by biological factors.

In order to test this assumption, we decided to use the same procedure as in the European study in two different cultures: the United States and Japan. The former, in spite of its very close ties to European culture, has developed quite a number of different traditions, particularly in terms of interpersonal interaction patterns that might be relevant for emotional experience. Japan is a culture that is often used as a comparison case against which to measure Western behavior.

In Chapter 1, we report data comparing Japanese and American respondents to a representative sample of the European respondents studied earlier. The results are fascinating. We find both a large degree of universality, particularly as far as emotion-eliciting situations are concerned, and interesting differences in emotional reactions. The pattern of findings invites a number of speculations concerning the origin of the differences found, including socioeconomic factors, life-style, cultural and religious values, and cultural control rules for affect display and subjective feeling states. We have to underline the word *speculation* — so far we dispose of very few tools for the systematic comparison of cultural differences in terms of a grid of variables or dimensions that could be used to independently assess the determining factors.

We will need many more intercultural studies, as well as close collaboration with anthropologists and sociologists, to better understand the factors that determine differences in emotional experiences across cultures. We also need many more different cultures with different value systems, socioeconomic conditions, and life-styles to understand the range and variability of emotional experience.

To this end, we started another major intercultural study of emotional experiences, briefly called the "ISEAR project" (International Study on Emotion Antecedents and Reactions). This study is ongoing. At the time of publication of this volume we have studied about 3,000 subjects in more than 30 countries on all five continents. This massive effort was possible only because of the enthusiastic collaboration of a large number of researchers from several disciplines all over the world. Chapter 2 describes the pattern of data for 27 of the countries for which the data have been analyzed so far. Whereas in the European studies as well as in the cross-cultural comparison among Japan, the U.S., and Europe (reported in Chapter 1), open-ended questionnaires were used, the ISEAR questionnaires used answer alternatives based on the results of the earlier studies. Despite the reduction in the richness of detail due to the use of precoded questions, the results are again intriguing. As before, we are able to replicate the patterns of findings from the earlier studies and thus strongly support most of the hypotheses we formulated earlier (Scherer, 1986b).

The overall impression now gained is that there is indeed a very strong universality in emotional experience, both in terms of antecedent situations and in terms of physiological, expressive, and subjective feeling reactions. However, as one might have expected on the basis of the comparison of European, Japanese, and American data, we discover additional differences with the addition of further non-Western cultures. Most interesting, we find a relationship between the gross national product (GNP) of a country and the intensity and duration of emotional experience—a negative correlation. Obviously, gross national product is a very uninteresting psychological indicator. It is probably correlated with the "real" factors determining the differences in emotional reactivity.

At the present state of our knowledge, we can do little more than speculate about the findings reported in Part I of this volume. We believe that the results on emotional experiences across the world that are reported here provide a rich source for further theorizing about the elicitation of emotion and the process of emotional behavior. We hope that they will stimulate a more systematic and hypothesis-based approach to intercultural comparison of emotional experience.

1 EMOTIONAL EXPERIENCE IN CULTURAL CONTEXT: A COMPARISON BETWEEN EUROPE, JAPAN, AND THE UNITED STATES[1]

KLAUS R. SCHERER
University of Geneva and University of Giessen

HARALD G. WALLBOTT
University of Giessen

DAVID MATSUMOTO
Wright Institute, Berkeley

TSUTOMU KUDOH
University of Osaka

INTRODUCTION

A major problem in emotion research is gaining access to the phenomenon. Whereas different kinds of cognitive processes can be studied in the laboratory as well as in natural settings, there are both ethical and practical limits to emotion induction, in and out of the laboratory. Consequently, even though emotions are ubiquitous and almost everyone has extensive firsthand experience with a wide range and intensity of emotions, we have very little actuarial information on the incidence and the nature of emotional experiences in everyday life. No doubt empirical data on the patterns of emotional experience in representative groups would be most useful for emotion psychologists both with respect to direction and focus of future studies and for the difficult task of hypothesis generation in an era where there is little theoretical background to build on.

In 1979 a group of European researchers (see acknowledgement note) began to use an anonymous questionnaire method to gather preliminary data on everyday emotional experiences. Although the validity of questionnaires as instruments to collect *objective* data has been criticized, there

[1] The European data reported in this chapter have been collected in collaboration with H. Ellgring, Max-Plank-Institute of Psychiatry, Munich; A.B. Summerfield, University of London; P. Ricci-Bitti and D. Giovannini, University of Bologna; B. Rimé, University of Louvain; J. Cosnier, University of Lyon; V. Aebischer, LEPS, Paris; E. Baenninger-Huber, University of Zürich; E. Babad, Hebrew University of Jerusalem; and A. J. Fernandez and J. M. Dols, Autonoma University of Madrid. The authors would like to thank Ursula Hess and Erin Nishimura for their aid during data collection and coding.

is often no other way to gather information about the *subjective* experience of emotion—both feeling and perceived reactions—than by asking subjects (see Wallbott & Scherer, 1985a, for a methodological discussion). Furthermore, because the evaluation or appraisal of emotional stimuli is often considered primary in the elicitation and differentiation of emotions (Arnold, 1960; Lazarus, 1966, 1984; Scherer, 1981b, 1984a, 1986a), subjects' verbal reports concerning their assessment of the antecedent situations are necessary. Given the reticence of people to talk about their emotional experiences, the use of anonymous questionnaires appears to be a promising method.

The questionnaire method is also rather suitable for use in cross-cultural research. For example, while the importance of intercultural comparison is generally acknowledged, especially for addressing issues concerning biological versus cultural determinants of emotional processes, the number of cross-cultural studies addressing these issues is small; a reasonably extensive body of data exists only in the area of facial expressions of emotion (see Ekman, 1982; Izard, 1977). The comparison of questionnaire data across cultures can help pinpoint the areas in which more involved behavioral and observational measurement might yield interesting cross-cultural differences.

In the concluding chapter to the monograph publication of the results of the European studies mentioned above (Scherer, Wallbott, & Summerfield, 1986), Scherer (1986b) cautioned against broad generalizations of the data, given the fact that for most of the issues investigated no specific a priori hypotheses nor informal expectations had been advanced. The major patterns of results were therefore formulated as specific areas for further work. In addition, although there were a number of interesting cross-cultural differences, there was also a surprisingly large degree of correspondence among the reported emotional experiences in the various European countries (including Israel; for details compare Scherer, Summerfield, & Wallbott, 1983; Scherer, Wallbott, & Summerfield, 1986). Although one may interpret these data to mean that the emotions are primarily biologically based and only superficially subjected to cultural regulation, another argument could be that a comparison of Western European countries—in spite of the stereotypical notions about North–South differences—does not provide a strict test of cultural differences because these countries may be too similar in terms of cultural background.

The purposes of this study were twofold: (a) to further test the hypotheses that have been advanced on the basis of the earlier European studies; and (b) to provide a somewhat stronger test of the cultural differences versus universality hypothesis by including not only the United Stated but also Japan, a culture that is traditionally considered to be rather different from Western cultures. Because in our earlier work many different hypotheses concerning antecedents, reactions, and control of emotions have been postulated, we describe the respective hypotheses together with the appropriate section of the results in order to allow the reader to compare predictions and outcomes more readily.

METHOD

Subjects

Subjects from the United States were 165 university students participating in partial fulfillment of class requirements; these data were collected in Milwaukee and Berkeley. Subjects from Japan were 174 university students, also participating in partial fulfillment of class requirements; these data were collected in Osaka. To make the European sample collected earlier comparable, a random sample of $N = 171$ was drawn from a total of 779 subjects gathered in different countries of Europe (West Germany, Great Britain, Italy, Spain, Switzerland, France, Belgium, Israel) using the same questionnaire (see following section). All subjects were from a variety of social classes and fields of study, with their ages ranging from 18 to 35.

Questionnaire

We were interested in three issues concerning the emotions: (a) the antecedents and determinants of emotion; (b) the reactions of the subjects in these situations; and (c) the amount of control and coping attempts they used to regulate their reactions. Specific questions were designed to structure the subjects' descriptions of their experiences and to obtain as exhaustive a report as possible. In order not to bias the answer alternatives and to avoid prompting effects, we used an open-ended free response format throughout (except for three intensity ratings, where 9-point scales were used). Obtaining information on the determinants and antecedents meant we had to collect detailed descriptions of what really happened, who was involved in the situation, where the situation took place, when the situation happened, and how long it lasted. To provide data concerning symptoms and reactions subjects reported on their nonverbal reactions (i.e., facial expression, gestures, body posture changes, changes in voice and speech, etc.), their physiological symptoms and sensations, and their verbal utterances. Subjects also rated the overall intensity of their feelings. Finally, subjects rated the efforts they used to control their nonverbal, verbal, and physiological reactions.

Subjects were instructed to describe situations or events that led them to experience four different emotions, which were labeled as "joy/happiness," "sadness/grief," "fear/anxiety," and "anger/rage," using the appropriate terms in the respective language. (While we do not deny the existence of a potential problem of semantic equivalence of emotion terms in different languages, we believe that the problem is minor in the case of these four major emotions.) Subjects were told they they should recall not only situations in which emotional arousal was very obvious but also events in which they were emotionally aroused without anybody noticing it. The order of the emotions was randomized across subjects.

The main questionnaire was followed by a personal information sheet eliciting information about the subject's national, linguistic, and academic background (see Appendix A).

Procedure

Subjects were tested in groups. The complete task of answering the questionnaires took between 30 minutes and 2 hours, depending on the length of descriptions given and the time subjects needed to think about, formulate, and write down their descriptions. Before and again after the task subjects were assured that all information they gave would be handled anonymously and that no information in whatever form would be published or used if it might allow easy identification of the subject.

Coding of Questionnaire Items

Codes were developed for all open-ended questions, especially for the antecedents of emotional experiences and for the reported reactions and symptoms.

Antecedent Codes.   An attempt was made to code themes applicable to all four emotions (e.g., "relationships with friends" or "achievement-related situations"; for details of the code development see Ellgring & Baenninger-Huber, 1986). Some categories specific to only one emotion, however, had to be introduced (see Appendix B). Reliability for antecedent coding was calculated using two coders in each of the participating European countries, who coded 20 questionnaires each. Overall, this realiability within and across countries are about 80%. The persons employed to code the Japanese and the U.S. questionnaires were trained on the basis of 80 sample situations to which an expert code had been assigned by several European coders. For later statistical analyses codings were grouped into larger, less specific categories.

Physiological Symptoms and Nonverbal Reactions.   The open-ended reports on physiological symptoms and nonverbal reactions required a quite extensive coding system. Using a modality approach we distinguished between vocal and nonvocal reactions, with further classifications for facial expression, gaze, and body part movements, and more specific subcategories within each of these modalities. Physiological symptoms were also classified using a hierarchical system with different modalities (skin symptoms, temperature symptoms, stomach symptoms, etc.), with more specific subclassifications. The total code included about five hundred single categories (for a detailed description see Scherer et al., 1986). Reliability studies here resulted in an average reliability of about 70%, which becomes larger when specific codes are combined according to modalities.

Coding of Other Responses.   Other parts of the questionnaire required simpler coding systems, inasmuch as only a few categories were necessary for classification:

- Location of the event (inside, known: inside, unknown: outside).
- Other persons involved (group size: alone, dyad, small group, large group; familiarity with persons involved: familiar, unfamiliar).
- Duration of feeling (under 5 minutes, up to 1 hour, up to a day, longer than 1 day).
- Verbal behavior (saying nothing; affect exclamation; short utterance; long utterance; discussion).

Data obtained via scales (intensity of feeling, amount of control of verbal behavior and of reactions/symptoms) were used as reported by the subjects themselves.

RESULTS

It should again be noted that the data presented are based on subjective recall of situations and reactions. To what extent such reports reflect objective events depends on a number of factors. The initial storage of emotional events in memory as well as recall and report may be influenced by factors like ego-involvement or defense mechanisms. Furthermore, general inference tendencies, such as the "availability," "representativeness," and "vividness" heuristics may interfere (see Nisbett & Ross, 1980; Scherer & Tannenbaum, 1986; Tversky & Kahneman, 1974). Certain situations may be more "available" than others, depending on the subject's state when reporting or on situational factors. Subjects may report situations and reactions they consider as being "representative" for certain emotions. Some situations may be more "vivid" than others and thus more easily recalled.

While these potential sources of influence on the situations available for self-report are acknowledged, we believe not that the reports themselves are purposively falsified or inaccurate, given subjects' motivation in such studies (see Magnusson & Stattin, 1981), but that they largely reflect the respondents' subjective experience of emotion-eliciting situations and emotional reactions.

In order to sequentially discuss antecedents, reactions, and control attempts, we follow the order of the questions as they occurred in the questionnaire.

Relative Incidence of Different Emotions

Although we have no direct data concerning the relative incidence of joy, fear, anger, and sadness, subjects' responses to "How long ago did the situation happen?" allow us to speculate about the incidences of these emotions. It is not unlikely that the further back in time subjects need to go to recall a situation (in which a particular emotion has been experienced with an intensity high enough to remain in long-term memory), the less frequently this type of emotion occurs. On the basis of the European data, the following rank ordering of emotions in terms of most frequent to least frequent had been suggested: anger > joy > sadness > fear (Scherer, 1986b). Our data, however, indicate that this detailed ranking cannot be maintained, inasmuch as no significant linear trend was found within each of the cultures. Post-hoc comparisons did show, though, that anger and joy situations were significantly more recent than fear and sadness situation (see Table 1.1).

TABLE 1.1
How Long Ago

(means)	Europe	Japan	USA	mean	df	F	p	Newman-Keuls
Joy	3.83	3.26	3.48	3.52	2/502	13.38	.0000	JAP<USA<EUR
Sadness	4.07	3.31	3.93	3.78	2/492	22.16	.0000	JAP<EUR=USA
Fear	4.03	3.30	3.85	3.73	2/487	18.56	.0000	JAP<EUR=USA
Anger	3.68	3.19	3.42	3.43	2/497	10.12	.0000	JAP<USA<EUR
Average	3.80	3.16	3.61	3.44	2/507	31.55	.0000	JAP<USA<EUR

Across emotions:

df	3/687	3/670	3/645	3/2010	
F	3.61	n.s.	7.57	10.00	
p	.0131		.0001	.0000	
Newman-Keuls				Joy=Anger<Fear=Sad	
			Joy=Anger<Fear=Sad		
	Anger<Sad				

Post-hoc analyses also indicated several interesting cultural differences. Across emotions, the situations reported by Europeans are longest ago, followed by the United States and Japan. This pattern was also repeated within each of the emotions separately. These data suggest that the Japanese need not go back into the past as far as the Europeans and Americans to find emotional situations with sufficient intensity for recall. These differences are particularly noticeable for sadness and fear.

The Nature of Antecedent Events

Although we had no formal hypotheses, we did expect that events that were important in Europe for certain emotions would be important in Japan and the United States as well. We also expected little difference in the rank order of antecedent events per emotion because there were few differences among the European countries in terms of the relative frequency of the various event classes. The data, however, show that the nature and pattern of antecedent events across our three cultures were quite different (see Table 1.2), with the major differences arising from the Japanese sample, the American and European samples being somewhat similar. In many cases certain types of situations that are very important in Europe and the United States are not very frequent in Japan. Yet some situations that frequently determine emotions in Japan are also important antecedents in Europe and the United States. Let us look at these differences in more detail.

Joy/Happiness. Cultural pleasures, birth of a new family member, and body-centered "basic pleasures," which were important antecedents for joy in Europe and the United States, are less frequently sources for joy in Japan. The relative insignificance of bodily pleasure seems to underline the stereotypical notion of the Japanese as a sober, hardworking, and at times somewhat ascetic people. Our finding that the birth of a new family member was less a source of joy for the Japanese subjects may be related to the observation that to older children, the birth of younger siblings threatens an already strong parent–child bond. Thus in Japanese society the birth of a younger sibling may represent an event that separates older children from their parents' care and love, much more so than in other cultures.

Achievement-related joy situations were also much more frequent in the United States and Europe than in Japan. As we shall see later, achievement seems to be equally important in the United States and Japan, but in Japan there is oftentimes more pressure for achievement, (for example, success in examinations) — and possibly higher expectations for success — both by the person and the social environment. Also in Japan there

TABLE 1.2
Major Antecedents Reported for the Four Emotions[a]

(in %)	Europe	Japan	USA	Chi2	p
JOY					
News	9.9	4.6	10.3	4.61	.1000
Relationships	29.4	33.3	23.6	3.91	.1415
Social Institutions	4.7	.6	10.3	16.57	.0003
Temporary meetings	19.6	13.2	17.6	2.66	.2646
Birth	8.3	.6	6.1	11.69	.0029
Body	12.8	2.9	16.4	17.68	.0001
Achievement	16.0	13.8	26.1	9.49	.0087
SADNESS					
News	9.5	2.3	14.5	16.25	.0003
Relationships	27.1	36.2	20.0	11.14	.0038
Temporary separation	6.5	2.3	12.7	14.09	.0009
Permanent separation	8.9	2.3	12.1	12.04	.0024
Death	22.2	5.2	22.4	24.49	.0000
Body	10.1	5.2	10.3	3.76	.1525
FEAR					
Relationships	4.6	9.8	3.6	6.53	.0381
Death	6.5	6.9	4.2	1.25	.5346
Body	7.2	4.6	3.0	3.16	.2063
Strangers	14.9	5.2	20.0	16.84	.0002
Achievement	11.7	16.7	18.8	3.41	.1821
Supernatural	3.9	4.6	6.7	1.50	.4734
Risky situations	11.2	5.2	14.5	8.37	.0152
Traffic	20.0	14.4	11.5	4.88	.0871
Novel situations	14.5	17.2	13.3	1.07	.5848
ANGER					
Relationships	38.5	29.3	58.2	30.13	.0000
Strangers	19.9	52.3	14.5	69.20	.0000
Achievement	6.7	10.3	8.5	1.49	.4739
Injustice	20.9	4.0	20.6	25.15	.0000
Inconvenience	8.5	9.8	6.1	1.60	.4496

[a] (listed only if at least 5% in at least one sample)

are implicit and subtle rules that inhibit joy reactions to personal success, (while supporting such reactions to group-oriented achievements).

Sadness/Grief. For sadness experiences we find significant differences among the cultures of almost every class of antecedent event. Most striking is the difference for sadness experiences provoked by the death of a family member or a close friend. Whereas both in Europe and in the United States such events account for about 1/5 of all sadness experiences, only one in twenty sadness situations in Japan is due to death. This striking difference may be traced back to differences in Japanese religious activities, particularly to the Shinto-Buddhist rules of veneration of ancestors, and the different connotations death may have for the Japanese. Japanese, of course, mourn the loss of loved ones much the same way as people in other countries do. In the Japanese culture, however, while a person may die, the person's soul always remains with and is protected by his or her family. Thus the emotion of sadness in response to death is often replaced by the consciousness that the deceased is always with the family.

We find other cultural differences in emotions due to problems with relationships and temporary or permanent separation, with Japan and the United States at the extreme ends and Europe in the middle. Sadness due to relationship problems is particularly common in Japan. In contrast, the Japanese seem less frequently saddened by both temporary and permanent separation, particularly in comparison with Americans. A possible interpretation is that separations from persons with whom one is involved in a close relationship are most frequent in the United States, less frequent in Europe, and least frequent in Japan. This could be due both to more restricted geographical mobility in Japan and at least some parts of Europe (particularly outside of the big cities) and to differences in the closeness and permanence of relationships. While in the United States, particularly in California and certainly in Berkeley (i.e., for half of our U.S. sample), the breaking up of relationships and the forming of new ones are rather frequent phenomena, this may be much less the case in Japan and the small-town cultures of Europe. This would explain why sadness would tend to be based on events that happen *within* the relationships rather than due to a separation in the latter two cultures.

Another difference appears in the results for world news. Whereas the Japanese subjects are rarely saddened by world events, European and especially American subjects are. It is highly unlikely that this is due to a differential incidence of world news relevant for the different samples, although it may be the case that the number of hijackings, hostage crises, and crime reports are somewhat more copious for the American population than for Japan and Europe. Another possibility is that Americans tend toward higher empathy with the victims of catastrophes of various sorts. The general level of national participation and awareness in cases such as hostage crises (e.g., flying flags, candles in the windows) may provide some indication for this. This finding may also be influenced by the Japanese's heavy reliance on immediate personal relationships, given their group orientation, thus making the influence of the happenings of people outside their group less immediate.

Fear/Anxiety. The largest cultural differences in the antecedents for fear arose in three antecedent categories: stranger fear, risky situations, and relationships. For the American subjects stranger fear was the most frequent category, followed by fear of failure in achievement situations. For the Europeans, too, it is a rather sizable category, second only to fear of traffic accidents. For the Japanese subjects, however, fear of strangers is almost insignificant, dwarfed by fear of novel situations, fear of failure in achievement situations, and fear of traffic. These findings are most likely related to the differential incidence of threatening events in each of our cultures. The incidence of crime is likely to be higher in U.S. urban areas than in many European countries and certainly than in Japan. In the original European study we found that this category differs rather widely depending on whether subjects live in a major metropolitan area or in small university towns (see Scherer et al., 1986). Given the relatively low incidence of crime and stranger aggression in Japanese society, it would seem reasonable to expect that this situation be less the cause of fear than in the United States or Europe.

Another interesting difference is the low incidence of fear following involvement in risky situations in Japan. In most of the situations reported this is related to events encountered during the pursuit of a rather risky activity, such as certain sports. Most likely Japanese students engage more rarely in risky activities than their European and particularly American counterparts, especially when alone or individually rather than when they are in groups.

One category for which there is a much higher anxiety incidence for the Japanese students is relationship-produced fear, for example, fear of hurting or angering one's parents or lover. This finding probably reflects the Japanese's constant monitoring and regulation of social relationships, particularly vis-à-vis social transgressions. Japanese are often overly concerned with the people around them, and this constant monitoring may easily be much more an antecedent of fear or, more specifically, anxiety, than in our other two cultures.

Anger/Rage.   The Japanese were again radically different from the Europeans and the Americans in their anger antecedents. In general, Japanese students are much more readily angered by strangers than by problems in relationships with known others, whereas the opposite is true for Europeans and particularly for Americans. The U.S. students experience almost 60% of their anger situations due to some kind of problem in their relationships. Anger due to the behavior of strangers, however, is limited to about 15%, in Europe 20%. But in Japan, more than half of the anger situations were produced by the behavior of strangers. One speculation to account for these findings might be that the social norms for behavior in relationships with relatives, friends, and acquaintances are more highly structured and readily obeyed in Japan, making it less likely that a breach of these norms leads to anger outbursts. Even in situations where a social transgression has been made in Japan, oftentimes the situation dictates

TABLE 1.3
Frequency of Antecendents Across Emotions[a]

mean	Europe	Japan	USA	F	df	p	Newman-Keuls
News	.26	.10	.33	9.25	2/507	.0001	USA = EUR > JAP
Relations	1.00	1.09	1.06			n.s.	
Institutions	.11	.03	.16	6.94	2/507	.0011	USA = EUR > JAP
Temporary	.28	.16	.35	7.00	2/507	.001	USA = EUR > JAP
Permanent	.10	.02	.15	7.66	2/507	.0005	USA = EUR > JAP
Death/birth	.38	.13	.35	12.11	2/507	.0000	USA = EUR > JAP
Body	.32	.14	.32	7.10	2/507	.0009	USA = EUR > JAP
Strangers	.38	.59	.38	7.53	2/507	.0006	JAP > USA = EUR
Achievement	.42	.71	.64	7.01	2/507	.001	JAP = USA > EUR
Risky situations	.11	.06	.15	4.23	2/507	.0151	USA > JAP
Supernatural	.04	.05	.07			n.s.	
Traffic	.20	.14	.12	2.45	2/507	.0875	
Novel situations	.15	.17	.13			n.s.	
Inconvenience	.09	.10	.06			n.s.	
Injustice	.21	.04	.21	13.13	2/507	.0000	USA = EUR > JAP

[a] (summed per subject: NEWS = JNEWS + SNEWS + FNEWS + ANEWS, etc.)

that one not get angry, or at least not show his or her anger (see results on emotion control attempts in a later section). Because relationships in the United States and Europe lack such firmly prescribed rules for the obligations of partners, relationships can more easily lead to anger, particularly if the solution of terminating the relationship is a viable one.

Another major difference concerns situations of injustice. Whereas these provoke anger in about 20% of the cases in both Europe and the United States, they account for only 4% of the Japanese anger situations. This could be due to the possibility that in Japan the rules of justice are more strictly applied in behavior, giving less rise to anger because of infrequent violations of the justice principle. Also, in actual anger-provoking situations of injustice, the actual expression of anger in Japanese society is often considered immature. Although our data do not allow us to address this point directly, the issue should be of major interest to researchers studying the social psychology of justice.

Because many classes of antecedents (e.g., relationships, achievement) were found as being important for all of the emotions, we examined these categories collapsing across emotions. We calculated the number of instances subjects mentioned these categories across all emotions (see Table 1.3). As one might expect, significant differences usually arose between the Japanese on the one hand and Americans and Europeans on the other. The Japanese mentioned significantly fewer news, separation, birth/death, and body-related but more stranger-related situations than subjects in the other countries. In only one category, achievement-related situations, did the Japanese respond more like the Americans, both differing significantly from the Europeans. These data imply that achievement-related tasks represent a much more ego-involving and thus emotion-producing issue in Japan and the United States than in Europe. This is not surprising, inasmuch as in both Japan and the United States a high value is placed on success in school, and particularly in college entrance examinations, both in terms of social desirability and as part of self-esteem. Achievement has played a more ambiguous role in many European countries, particularly in the sixties and seventies. The only category for which no differences were found is relationships—attesting to the universal significance of social relationships in human life.

The Ecology of Emotional Experience

We asked subjects to report the place where the emotions occurred and who else was involved in the situation. As predicted from the European data, more than half of the emotional situations in all cultures occurred inside familiar places, except for fear situations, which more often took place outside or in unfamiliar surroundings (see Table 1.4). There were again some noticeable differences for Japan. For example, joy occurs very

TABLE 1.4
Where Did It Happen?–Location of the Event

(in %)	Europe	Japan	USA	mean		
JOY						
Inside, familiar	56.6	64.1	51.7	57.5		
Inside, unfamiliar	18.2	5.3	21.9	15.1	Chi2	= 19.86
Outside	25.2	30.6	26.5	27.4	p	= .0005
SADNESS						
Inside, familiar	69.9	51.2	77.0	66.0		
Inside, unfamiliar	14.7	21.7	11.9	6.1	Chi2	= 24.63
Outside	15.3	27.1	11.1	17.8	p	= .0001
FEAR						
Inside, familiar	39.6	26.2	47.0	37.6		
Inside, unfamiliar	11.8	15.6	7.3	11.6	Chi2	= 16.49
Outside	48.7	58.1	45.7	50.8	p	= .0024
ANGER						
Inside, familiar	67.8	79.6	79.7	75.7		
Inside, unfamiliar	12.3	.6	7.4	6.8	Chi2	= 21.77
Outside	19.9	19.8	12.8	17.5	p	= .0002
Mean across emotions:						
Inside, familiar	58.5	55.3	63.9			
Inside, unfamiliar	14.3	10.8	12.1			
Outside	27.3	33.9	24.0			

rarely *inside* unfamiliar places in Japan (5%) compared to about 20% in Europe and the United States. For sadness, in contrast, the Japanese are more likely to experience the emotion inside unfamiliar places and outside, compared to Europeans and particularly Americans. These findings are most likely attributable to traditional interaction patterns in the society.

For fear there is a lower incidence inside familiar places in Japan compared to the two other cultures, and a somewhat lower incidence in Europe compared to the United States. We are tempted to link this with the relative likelihood that aggression or threats are directed toward people inside their homes. For the Japanese in particular, fear situations occur more frequently than in the other two cultures outside and inside unfamiliar places.

For anger, again there is one significant difference for the Japanese subjects, who almost never seem to experience anger inside unfamiliar places. Again, it is difficult to disentangle the frequency factor (i.e., the possibility that Japanese more rarely go inside buildings like other people's homes with which they are not familiar), or the role of politeness rules, which may suppress not only the expression but also the experience of anger.

We also asked subjects to report on the number of persons present and the degree of familiarity with these persons (Table 1.5). As in the original European data, all of the emotions except fear occur mostly in dyads and to a somewhat lesser extent in small groups. Only fear is frequently experienced when alone. Emotions in large groups are very rare and, in the present data, absent in the case of the Japanese students. As before, the findings differentiated the Japanese data from the European and American: Japanese students experienced the emotions more frequently in dyads than in small groups compared to Europeans and Americans, where the rank order is in the same direction but much less strong. Thus, one might hypothesize that emotions are somewhat more private, restricted to a close relationship or to a dyadic encounter, as compared to a group phenomenon.

As far as familiarity of the other people present is concerned, these are familiar others in about ¾ of all cases for all emotions except fear, where there is a 50/50 split between familiar and unfamiliar others. As far as cultural differences go, there is a marginally significant difference in the direction of the Japanese experiencing emotions somewhat more frequently with familiar others, particularly in comparison with Americans.

Characteristics of the Subjective Feeling State

Duration of Emotional Experience.   Emotion duration is a highly interesting variable, given the theoretical need to distinguish between moods

TABLE 1.5
Other Persons Involved in the Situation

Group Size

(in %)	Europe	Japan	USA	mean		
JOY						
Alone	11.6	10.9	20.2	14.2		
Dyad	47.7	60.3	43.6	50.5		
Small group	36.8	28.7	32.5	32.7	Chi2 =	19.79
Large group	3.9	—	3.7	2.5	p =	.0030
SADNESS						
Alone	18.0	20.0	23.9	20.6		
Dyad	44.9	55.3	40.5	46.9		
Small group	33.8	24.7	34.4	31.0	Chi2 =	14.94
Large group	3.3	—	1.2	1.5	p =	.0207
FEAR						
Alone	31.2	31.7	33.5	32.1		
Dyad	33.8	47.3	32.9	38.0		
Small group	29.2	21.0	28.0	26.1	Chi2 =	17.81
Large group	5.7	—	5.5	3.7	p =	.0067
ANGER						
Alone	7.9	4.1	6.1	6.0		
Dyad	43.3	60.0	57.1	53.5		
Small group	44.1	35.9	34.4	38.1	Chi2 =	17.24
Large group	4.7	—	2.5	2.4	p =	.0084
Mean across emotions:						
Alone	17.2	16.7	20.9			
Dyad	42.4	55.7	43.5			
Small group	36.0	27.6	32.3			
Large group	4.4	—	3.2			

Familiarity

(in %)	Europe	Japan	USA	mean		
JOY						
Unfamiliar	19.0	12.6	31.9	21.2	Chi2 =	19.41
Familiar	81.0	87.4	68.1	78.8	p =	.0001
SADNESS						
Unfamiliar	26.0	22.9	26.4	25.1	Chi2 =	.64
Familiar	74.0	77.1	73.6	74.9	p =	.7266
FEAR						
Unfamiliar	53.5	43.1	55.5	50.7	Chi2 =	5.89
Familiar	46.5	56.9	44.5	49.3	p =	.0527
ANGER						
Unfamiliar	23.4	18.2	18.4	20.0	Chi2 =	1.83
Familiar	76.6	81.8	81.6	80.0	p =	.4012
Mean across emotions:						
Unfamiliar	30.5	24.2	33.1			
Familiar	69.5	75.8	66.9			

and emotions (see Ekman, 1984). In the original European study we found very stable and highly significant differences in duration between the different emotions and a set of detailed predictions were developed, which we cite verbatim:

• Fear is predicted to last from a few seconds up to a maximum of an hour. The assumption underlying this hypothesis is that fear is an emergency response par excellence which is usually provoked by an immediate stimulus event requiring flight or submission to the aversive consequences. It is likely, then, that this very high intensity emotion will be rather short-lived and could not be endured for longer periods of time. Obviously, this is not true for anxiety. (For a discussion of the conceptual differences between fear and anxiety see Gaylin, 1979, pp. 16–19.)

• Anger is predicted to last from a few minutes up to a maximum of a few hours. The assumption is that this emotion is fairly transient, since it is mostly related to discrete events that require either coping or internal adaptation. It would seem unlikely that anger will persist if the person is no longer exposed to its object or constantly reminded of it.

• Joy is predicted to last from about an hour to a maximum of a day. It is expected that joy is a more lasting emotion because of the significant concerns relating to the self or to salient relationships.

• Sadness is predicted to last from about a day to several days, given the fact that in most cases important relationship concerns underlie the occurrence of this emotion, and that extensive "grief work" is required to adapt to the changed situation.

The data from the present study show that these predictions are rather well supported (Table 1.6); the rank order of the emotions in terms of duration — fear < anger < joy < sadness — is exactly as predicted. Furthermore, the parametric predictions in terms of the expected length in terms of minutes, hours, and days are also supported — grosso modo — by the results, with the possible exception of joy, which frequently seems to last longer than a day. These data support the notion that there is a definite time course for each emotion (see Scherer, 1986b, pp. 180–181). These data allow for interesting speculations concerning deviations from this "normal" time course in affective disorders or stress response (see Scherer, 1986c).

There were, however, some significant intercultural differences, with the American subjects deviating from the pattern of the European and Japanese students. American students, particularly for fear and anger, report consistently longer durations for their emotional feelings (see Table 1.6). In the next section we discuss these findings in more detail.

TABLE 1.6
Duration of Emotion

(means)	Europe	Japan	USA	mean	df	F	p	Newman-Keuls
Joy	3.12	3.31	3.41	3.28	2/501	2.87	.0574	— —
Sadness	3.41	3.31	3.59	3.44	2/498	2.67	.0702	— —
Fear	2.20	2.34	2.55	2.33	2/495	3.39	.0344	USA > EUR
Anger	2.61	2.85	3.14	2.87	2/498	8.13	.0003	USA > EUR = JAP
Average	2.78	2.89	3.13	2.93	2/507	11.18	.0000	USA > EUR = JAP

Across emotions:

df	3/698	3/676	3/648	3/2030
F	45.09	22.09	29.30	89.65
p	.0000	.0000	.0000	.0000

Newman-Keuls   Fear < Anger < Joy = Sad
                      Fear < Anger < Joy = Sad
                Fear < Anger < Joy = Sad
          Fear < Anger < Joy = Sad

(1 = under five minutes, 2 = up to one hour, 3 = up to one day, 4 = several days)

Intensity of Emotional Feelings.   It was hypothesized that anger would be experienced less intensely than the other emotions (see Wallbott & Scherer, 1985a, for a discussion of possible mediating factors for this finding). The data from this study suggest that, as predicted, anger is the emotion with the lowest overall intensity (Table 1.7). This finding is supported by recent results obtained by Dore and Kirouac (1986), who found

TABLE 1.7
Intensity of Emotion

(means)	Europe	Japan	USA	mean	df	F	p	Newman-Keuls
Joy	7.33	7.34	7.77	7.48	2/495	4.10	.0172	USA > EUR = JAP
Sadness	7.37	7.24	7.61	7.41	2/492	1.79	.1685	— —
Fear	7.38	6.83	7.33	7.18	2/488	4.19	.0158	JAP < EUR = USA
Anger	6.97	6.71	7.54	7.07	2/495	9.37	.0001	USA > EUR = JAP
Average	6.93	6.86	7.42	7.07	2/507	8.08	.0003	USA > EUR = JAP

Across emotions:

df	3/684	3/675	3/644	3/2011
F	n.s.	4.42	n.s.	6.04
p		.0044		.0004

Newman-Keuls   Anger = Fear < Joy = Sad

                          — —
          Anger < Joy = Sad
          Fear < Joy

    — —

that descriptions of anger-eliciting situations were judged as being of lower intensity than sadness situations, followed by fear and joy/happiness situations with the highest intensity. Contrary to what we expected, however, fear intensity was also somewhat lower than joy and sadness, particularly in Japan. In contrast, the American students differ from the Europeans and Japanese on joy and anger, where they reported consistently higher intensities. The lower fear intensities in Japan might be due to the fact that the fear of crime, which seems to lead to fairly high fear intensities, is less pronounced there, and that there might still be more of a feeling of being safe in a network of social support. It is difficult to see why American subjects report higher intensities throughout, particularly for joy and anger. These findings may be attributable to either a higher emotionality or emotional responsivity on the part of the American subjects.

Verbal Expression of Emotion. We predicted that joy and anger would be associated with more extensive verbal responses than sadness and fear, since joy and anger are often elicited by others and are often experienced in social settings that would encourage a greater degree of verbalization, contrary to sadness and fear. The present findings again support this hypothesis (Table 1.8), with anger and joy being significantly more verbal in comparison to sadness and particularly fear. The only significant intercultural difference is found for joy. Here the Japanese students seem to be much more verbal than either the American or European students.

Nonverbal Expressions of Emotion. We used an open-ended format to

TABLE 1.8
Amount of Verbal Behavior

(means)	Europe	Japan	USA	mean	df	F	p	Newman-Keuls
Joy	2.24	2.62	2.31	2.43	2/480	10.56	.0000	JAP>EUR=USA
Sadness	1.94	2.15	2.13	2.07	2/479	2.30	.1009	— —
Fear	1.77	1.99	1.90	1.89	2/477	2.34	.0970	— —
Anger	2.33	2.39	2.35	2.36	2/492	.18	.8323	— —
Average	1.91	2.23	2.07	2.07	2/507	13.76	.0000	JAP>USA>EUR

Across emotions:				
df	3/655	3/675	3/625	3/1963
F	9.88	14.69	8.53	29.36
p	.0000	.0000	.0000	.0000

Newman-Keuls

Joy = Anger > Sad > Fear

Joy = Anger = Sad > Fear

Joy > Anger > Sad = Fear

Joy = Anger > Sad = Fear

collect information about the type of nonverbal behavior the respondents remembered to have shown. As one would expect with such a response format, the actual frequency of reported behavior patterns was rather low (about one reaction coded per emotion on the average). Because precoded answer alternatives were not used, subjects were not reminded of behavior patterns that do not come readily to mind; or, subjects may have been too lazy to write extensive descriptions of their nonverbal behavior. Another important possibility is that they did not readily find a convenient verbal label to use as a description of what happened.

Given the low response frequency, and the fact that no detailed predictions for nonverbal behavior had been made on the basis of the earlier studies, mainly because it was difficult to infer the specific nature of a nonverbal act from the questionnaire descriptions, we differentiated only fairly gross types of behavior, such as facial or vocal symptoms (discrete acts) or quality changes, without further specification. These data also show a pattern similar to the qualitative summary presented earlier (Scherer, 1986b, pp. 182–183). For example, as one might expect, we found laughing and smiling, and a little bit of crying for joy, and a lot of crying for sadness. Joy leads to approach behavior and expansiveness in nonverbal gesturing, whereas fear often leads to freezing of nonverbal behavior. Expressive hand movements can be found for all emotions except sadness, which seems to indicate the very passive nature of this emotion, with generally reduced nonverbal activity.

As in our earlier study (see Scherer, Wallbott, & Summerfield, 1986), the most important nonverbal channels for emotional expression were the face and voice. In order to analyze intercultural differences, we combined the codes to major modalities or channels (Table 1.9). Gaze reactions are very rarely mentioned overall and will thus not be considered. Across all emotions the Japanese students reported many fewer body part reactions (mostly hand and arm gestures) and whole body reactions than the Europeans and Americans. These data indicate that the Japanese were less expressive in terms of gross motor activity and gesturing. Across all emotions, American subjects were somewhat more expressive in body part reactions (e.g., gesturing) than the Europeans and, of course, the Japanese, although this finding was statistically weaker.

Except for the case of joy, the Japanese also report fewer voice reactions than the Americans and Europeans, indicating that their emotional expressions tend to be generally more silent than in the other two cultures. There were, however, no differences in facial reactions between the Japanese students and the other two cultures for each of the emotions separately. But across all emotions we found that American subjects reported significantly more facial reactions than the Europeans, again suggesting a high degree of expressiveness.

TABLE 1.9
Combined Nonverbal Reaction Modalities

(mean no. mentioned)	Europe	Japan	USA	Chi2	p
JOY					
Voice reactions	.19	.16	.13	2.99	.5600
Face reactions	.48	.60	.62	14.11	.0284
Gaze reactions	.02	.02	.03	.70	.7036
Body part react.	.19	.12	.29	15.19	.0042
Whole body react.	.09	.05	.12	6.00	.1989
SADNESS					
Voice reactions	.19	.12	.16	3.64	.4569
Face reactions	.44	.35	.55	14.92	.0049
Gaze reactions	.03	.04	.04	.13	.9367
Body part react.	.09	.01	.12	16.84	.0021
Whole body react.	.04	— —	.06	9.97	.0409
FEAR					
Voice reactions	.16	.02	.13	18.40	.0010
Face reactions	16	.21	.21	6.81	.1463
Gaze reactions	.04	.04	.06	1.24	.5382
Body part react.	14	—	.24	40.51	.0000
Whole body react.	.14	— —	.14	27.28	.0001
ANGER					
Voice reactions	.33	.21	.30	8.97	.1752
Face reactions	.29	.32	.33	2.91	.8197
Gaze reactions	.04	.09	.07	3.60	.1651
Body part reactions	.20	.12	.29	19.45	.0035
Whole body react.	.08	— —	.09	17.20	.0018
SUMMED ACROSS EMOTIONS					
Voice reactions	.85	.51	.73	19.37	.0358
Face reactions	1.39	1.48	1.72	16.46	.1709
Gaze reactions	.12	.18	.20	4.71	.7880
Body part reactions	.71	.24	.93	62.26	.0000
Whole body react.	.37	.05	.41	44.81	.0000

The general picture emerging from these data indicates that the Japanese students have a comparatively low degree of emotional expressiveness, manifesting their reaction mostly in the face except for instances of joy and anger, where there are some voice reactions (although much lower, particularly in anger than in the other two cultures). These findings are most likely attributable to Japanese people's tendency to control emotional reactions in social situations (cf. Ekman, 1973). Americans were highly expressive compared to the other two cultures, particularly in the visual domain, facial expression, and gesturing. Unfortunately, our data do not allow us to differentiate between different sources of these differences, that is, differential physiologically based response tendencies, culturally prescribed display rules for expressive behavior, or differential reporting tendencies. There can be little doubt, however, that factors related to the communication of emotion in terms of signaling function and the cultural frame provided for this are likely to play a major role.

Physiological Reactions to Emotional Arousal.   Our data obviously cannot provide direct evidence relevant to the continuing debate concerning whether emotions are differentiated in terms of specific physiological response patterns. Nevertheless, it is still of interest to compare the findings from physiological studies with self-report of perceived physiological symptoms. Although there are reports of fairly low accuracy in the self-perception of physiological changes, (e.g., Pennebaker, 1982), these are difficult to evaluate because emotions induced in many of the laboratory studies are neither very intense nor very specific. Because it is possible that only fairly extreme physiological changes are accurately monitored and labeled by lay persons, it would seem that such studies do not yet settle the issue. In any case, it would certainly strengthen the argument for physiological differentiation of emotion if one were to find very similar patterns in self-report as in studies using physiological assessment.

In the concluding chapter in the monograph on the earlier studies, Scherer proposed a prediction table for differential physiological reactions for the four emotions studies, based on claims in the literature as well as the results of the European questionnaire study (Table 1.10). A + stands for a predicted increase, a − for a predicted decrease of the respective symptom group, with ? indicating that no prediction is ventured at this point. (The *A* and *J* characters in parentheses will be explained in the following paragraphs.)

Because we again had the problem of low response frequency in our physiological categories, we have combined a number of the more specific codes that we used in coding the responses (Table 1.11), rendering both the prediction and the data less specific than one might wish. Even at this degree of specificity, however, there is clear differentiation for the four emotions under study.

We first examined whether the American and Japanese data separately support the predictions. Given the low response rates, we considered

TABLE 1.10
Predictions of Physiological Changes for Emotions

Symptoms	Joy	Sadness	Fear	Anger
Cardiovascular activity	+ A	?	+ A	+
Striated muscle tone	+ A	− A	+ JA	+ A
Gastric disturbance	0	+ A	+ A	+ A
Skin temperature	+ J	0	−	+ JA

TABLE 1.11
Physiological Symptoms and General Sensations[a]

(in %)	Europe	Japan	USA	Chi2	p
JOY					
Pleasant rest	19.1	2.9	15.8	23.23	.0000
Pleasant arousal	13.4	4.0	14.5	12.06	.0024
Feeling warm	7.4	5.2	8.5	1.50	.4718
Blood pressure	9.1	1.1	4.8	11.50	.0032
Stomach troubles	4.6	— —	6.7	11.14	.0038
Muscle symptoms	9.1	— —	9.1	16.85	.0002
SADNESS					
Unpleasant rest	14.4	14.4	17.0	.58	.7468
Unpleasant arousal	5.6	— —	9.1	15.58	.0004
Stomach troubles	13.1	— —	22.4	41.91	.0000
Muscle symptoms	17.7	— —	20.0	37.82	.0000
FEAR					
Unpleasant arousal	14.4	3.4	16.4	16.66	.0000
Feeling cold	8.9	— —	4.8	15.68	.0004
Perspiration	7.1	4.6	6.7	1.06	.5901
Blood pressure	18.9	— —	16.4	35.25	.0000
Stomach troubles	20.5	— —	21.2	42.14	.0000
Muscle symptoms	37.6	16.1	38.2	25.74	.0000
ANGER					
Unpleasant arousal	14.9	15.5	8.5	4.48	.1064
Feeling warm	9.8	4.0	10.9	6.21	.0448
Blood pressure	6.7	1.1	4.8	6.81	.0333
Stomach troubles	9.4	— —	18.8	35.72	.0000
Muscle symptoms	19.8	— —	20.6	40.55	.0000

[a] (listed only if at least 5% in at least one sample)

response categories with frequency $> = 10\%$ to be of interest. Using this criterion we entered either a *J* or *A* into the prediction table (Table 10) where the number of respondents mentioning the respective symptom indicated more than chance fluctuation. The American data support a large number of the predictions, whereas the Japanese data provide support in only three cases. This, however, is due to the fact that the Japanese report substantially fewer physiological symptoms across all emotions. The fact that the Japanese respondents only rarely indicated physiological responses formed the basis for our strongest intercultural difference.

The same pattern is true for the report of unspecific sensations, such as pleasant or unpleasant arousal or rest states. While the American and the European students are very similar in this respect (Table 1.11), the Japanese students, except in the case of anger, report such sensations much more infrequently.

In general we found that Japanese students report fewer physiological symptoms, whereas the European and American data are very parallel. These data are most likely not attributable to strong biological differences between the Japanese and the Europeans and Americans; it is also difficult to see how culturally prescribed display rules or feeling rules might affect the incidence of such physiological reactions. Thus we believe that these results are due to a differential reporting tendency, which in fact may be related to display rules in the sense of attempting to control the appearance of arousal (see results on emotion control in the next section).

The Control of Emotional Reactions.   As predicted earlier (Scherer, 1986b), the respondents indicated that they attempted to control sadness, fear, and anger in the verbal, nonverbal, and physiological modalities, whereas they did not try to do so for joy (Table 1.12). This suggests that the negative emotions are much more culturally regulated than the positive emotions. Within the three negative emotions there is also a rank ordering in terms of the severity of control for verbal behavior, although these differences do not quite reach significance for the control of reactions: anger is controlled most, with sadness and fear following. We found a striking and significant difference in a post hoc comparison for anger. As in our earlier studies (see Scherer et al., 1986), we found that anger is strongly controlled in the verbal modality. This is not surprising, since anger is the most socially relevant of the four emotions, with a high amount of verbalization (see above), and given the possibility of an escalation of conflict upon verbal anger display.

In line with the stereotypical notions about Japanese society we had expected very strong differences for Japan in this respect. For joy, sadness, and fear, however, there are no significant differences at all between the three cultures. For anger there is a significant difference, but it separates Europe on the one hand from America and Japan on the other, control of anger being significantly higher in all modalities for the latter two cultures. It seems, then, that anger is only moderately controlled in Europe, particularly in the verbal channel (much less in the nonverbal and physiological areas), whereas it seems to be very strongly sanctioned in Japan and the United States.

CONCLUSIONS

The most immediate impression produced by the pattern of data in this study is the surprising degree of confirmation of the predictions based on earlier results. As far as self-report of emotional experience is concerned, the following findings were replicated in two European studies

TABLE 1.12
Control of Symptoms/Reactions and of Verbal Behavior

Symptoms/Reactions

(means)	Europe	Japan	USA	mean	df	F	p	Newman-Keuls
Joy	1.58	2.07	2.13	1.89	2/496	2.23	.1086	— —
Sadness	3.49	4.28	3.85	3.87	2/485	2.46	.0866	— —
Fear	3.78	3.26	3.64	3.56	2/479	1.07	.3440	— —
Anger	3.52	4.42	4.39	4.10	2/492	4.43	.0124	EUR < USA = JAP
Average	2.93	3.37	3.41	3.20	2/507	3.61	.0277	EUR < USA = JAP

Across emotions:

df	3/684	3/666	3/639	3/1997	
F	21.59	21.36	16.20	52.43	
p	.0000	.0000	.0000	.0000	

Newman-Keuls   Joy < Fear = Anger = Sad
                            Joy < Fear = Anger = Sad
                  Joy < Fear < Anger = Sad
         Joy < Fear = Anger = Sad

Verbal Behavior

(means)	Europe	Japan	USA	mean	df	F	p	Newman-Keuls
Joy	1.92	1.66	2.13	1.90	2/495	1.56	.2107	— —
Sadness	3.99	4.25	4.39	4.21	2/472	.56	.5734	— —
Fear	3.50	3.50	3.63	3.54	2/460	.06	.9377	— —
Anger	4.45	5.14	5.57	5.05	2/494	5.61	.0030	EUR < USA = JAP
Average	3.19	3.49	3.76	3.45	2/507	4.09	.0173	USA > EUR

Across emotions:

df	3/665	3/667	3/626	3/1966	
F	20.53	42.17	34.03	9070	
p	.0000	.0000	.0000	.0000	

Newman-Keuls   Joy < Fear < Sad < Anger
                            Joy < Fear < Sad < Anger
                  Joy < Fear < Sad < Anger
         Joy < Fear = Sad = Anger

(Scherer et al., 1983; Scherer et al., 1986) as well as in the American and Japanese samples investigated in the present study:

- Anger and joy situations recalled by the subjects tend to be more recent than sadness and fear situations.
- The differences in the nature of the respective eliciting situations tend to be rather stable. Furthermore, there is some replication for the rank ordering of the relative importance of subcategories of antecedent situations for each emotion (even though there are major differences for Japan, see following sections).

- There are clear differences in the average duration of the respective emotions: fear < anger < joy < sadness. Not only this rank order but also the magnitudes of average duration are well replicated.
- The intensity of subjectively experienced anger tends to be lower than that of fear, joy, and sadness.
- Anger and joy produce more verbalization, and may thus represent somewhat more "social" emotions as compared to sadness and fear.
- There seem to be highly differentiated patterns of self-perceived nonverbal reactions and physiological symptoms for the four emotions studied here. The amount of replication is all the more impressive given that open-ended questions without prompting were used.
- The effort to control the emotion is lower in joy than for the three negative emotions.

Although only self-report of subjective experience has been studied here, the strong degree of convergence of the data from many different cultures might well be considered as supporting the notion of universal, biologically based differences between individual emotions. At the same time, however, the importance of social-interactional factors in both the elicitation of and the reaction to certain emotional states cannot be emphasized too strongly.

These social factors, while present in all of the national samples studied, become more pronounced when intercultural differences are examined. Whereas the earlier studies of eight European countries yielded surprisingly few cultural differences, the comparison between Japan, the United States, and Europe suggests some rather pronounced differences. Many of these distinguish Japanese experiences from European and American, which tend to be more similar. This is particularly true for the nature of antecedent situations: Japanese subjects reported less body-related joy, fewer death- and separation-induced sadness episodes, less stranger-induced fear but much more stranger-induced anger, and fewer anger episodes produced by perceived injustice. The origins of these differences can only be guessed at the present time. Possible causes implicate cultural values, norms, and interactional practices but also demographic and socioeconomic factors, as well as the frequency of certain types of events, such as crime.

Apart from elicitation factors, differential reaction patterns are another major domain of intercultural differences. Here we find a spread between all three cultures on a continuum from low to high emotionality/expressiveness. Whereas Americans are very high on this dimension, especially as far as the intensity of the subjective feeling and the expressive nonverbal response is concerned, the Japanese are very low, both in terms of nonverbal behavior and, surprisingly, frequency of physiological symptoms.

Again, the reasons for these differences are far from obvious. As far as nonverbal expressive behavior is concerned one might argue that cultural "display rules" for emotional expression (Ekman, 1973; Wundt, 1905) are at the root of the phenomenon. Such an explanation would bring the findings in line with our stereotypes concerning the "inscrutable Oriental," hiding emotions between an impassive or politely smiling face, on the one hand, and the free expression, if not accentuation, of emotion that seems to have become popular in at least some United States youth subcultures after the sixties. Although normative pressure to control the public display of emotion may certainly play a role in explaining the phenomenon, it is clearly not sufficient.

If the control of expressive behavior on public display were the decisive factor, we would expect corresponding differences for the perceived intensity of control attempts. This is not the case, however. On the contrary, we find almost no intercultural differences for this variable, except for anger. Here, interestingly, the Americans and Japanese, who are at the opposite ends of the emotionality/expressiveness continuum, are more like each other in reporting stronger control attempts than Europeans. Furthermore, a mere *display* control explanation could not account for the stronger felt intensity in the Americans and the very low incidence of physiological symptoms in the Japanese. Although the former could be explained by a feedback amplification notion (e.g., proprioceptive somatic system feedback increasing intensity of feeling; see Gellhorn, 1967; Tomkins, 1963), the latter could not. One could argue that the low level of nonverbal and physiologic responding in the Japanese is due not to conscious display control attempts but rather to deep-seated unconscious regulation of affect that might after all have been produced by appropriate cultural socialization practices. Even if this were the case, however, it would be hard to argue that such tendencies are not related to an "emotionality" dimension.

The difficulties in accounting for the intercultural differences found, ranging from not finding an explanation at all to finding too many, almost always accompanied by an uneasy feeling about the amount of speculation involved, show one of the major drawbacks of intercultural research. We believe that in the long run only an interdisciplinary approach can help to overcome these problems. The issues raised in the discussion of the data from this study show clearly that emotion is not an exclusively psychological phenomenon. Sociologists, anthropologists, economists, historians, and political scientists, as well as physiologists and medical scientists, could contribute significantly to our understanding of the patterns of emotional experiences found in these studies. Their contribution could render more plausible a number of explanations that are little more than vague hunches at the present time. This would also help to settle a major problem of intercultural questionnaire studies—the role of differential response tendencies. It could be argued, of course, that all of the differences we find are due, for example, to the reticence of Japanese students to report the death of relatives or their physiological symptoms on a questionnaire, albeit anonymous. Unfortunately, the problem of response bias is present whenever we ask a person to report information, quite independent of the form questioning takes (Nisbett & Wilson, 1977).

As we have pointed out, subjective experience cannot be studied in any other way than by asking the person to report the information. We believe that the anonymous questionnaire method is highly preferable to personal interviewing as far as the intimate sphere of emotions is concerned. We believe that we would not have been able to elicit many of the situations reported by our subjects, which are not always very flattering to themselves, had it not been for the anonymity of the questionnaire method. We believe that the differentiation of the data pattern and the convergence of differential findings across many cultures render it difficult to interpret these results as reflections of cultural stereotypes of emotional experience.

The open-ended questionnaire format used has been very complicated and time-consuming for subjects and researchers alike. However, it was a necessary first step to collect a store of information without biasing the data through prompting or preconceived categorization. We now have sufficient data and patterns of results that are stable enough to move to a research stage where precoded questionnaires can be used where the categories are based on the empirical results of the studies so far. These precoded questionnaires, which are more economical and require much less effort and motivation from the subjects, can now be used in a large-scale intercultural study comparing a greater number of very diverse cultures as well as a greater number of different emotions. A major effort of this sort, involving researchers in more than 20 countries on all continents, is now under way (Wallbott & Scherer, 1986a; compare Chapter 2). We hope that the combined results of these questionnaire studies on subjective experience can provide a rich basis for hypothesis formation in the psychology of emotion, which may help in the design of field and laboratory studies on *objective* antecedents and correlates of different emotion states.

2 HOW UNIVERSAL AND SPECIFIC IS EMOTIONAL EXPERIENCE? EVIDENCE FROM 27 COUNTRIES ON FIVE CONTINENTS

HARALD G. WALLBOTT
University of Giessen

KLAUS R. SCHERER
University of Geneva and University of Giessen

ARE EMOTIONAL EXPERIENCES AND REACTIONS UNIVERSAL AND SPECIFIC TO DISCRETE EMOTIONS?

In 1872 Charles Darwin published his work on "The expression of the emotions in men and animals," claiming that emotional reactions, particularly facial and vocal expression, are innate and thus universal as well as specific for at least some basic, discrete emotions like joy, sadness, fear, and anger. His work, now considered as a milestone in the psychology of emotion (Ekman, 1973), gave rise to a long debate between "universalists" and proponents of the "culture specific view" of emotional expression. Whereas universalists like Tomkins (Tomkins & McCarter, 1964), Izard (1977), or Ekman (1972) argued for innate "emotional programs" (as illustrated by discrete facial expression patterns) that are universal and differentiate emotions, a number of cultural relativists such as Landis (1924), Klineberg (1938), or Birdwhistell (1970) shared the view that emotional experiences and reactions differ depending on cultural factors. Although there is increasing evidence that at least the recognition of facial expressions of emotion is universal (Ekman, 1972; Ekman & Friesen, 1982; Izard, 1977, 1980), there has been little cross-cultural research on other modalities of emotion responses.

Yet, research on emotion should consider at least the following aspects: the nature of the emotion-eliciting situation, the reactions shown by a person when confronted with the emotion-eliciting situation (in particular physiological symptoms), nonverbal reactions like facial or vocal expression, the subjective experience or feeling state of the person, and the regulation attempts used to control or manage the situation and the emotional reactions (Wallbott & Scherer, 1985a). To demonstrate universality and discreteness of emotion it is necessary to study all these aspects in terms of the differences between various emotions and between countries or cultures.

Research on specific stimulus conditions eliciting specific emotions is almost nonexistent. With respect to differential reaction and symptom patterns for specific emotions, research has been mainly centered around emotional facial expression. Recent work (Ekman, Friesen, & Ancoli, 1980) has shown that differential reaction patterns seem to exist at least for the "basic" or "primary" emotions. Research on differential reaction patterns in other nonverbal reaction modalities is more scarce. Riskind (1984) has shown that some emotional states may be accompanied by typical bodily postures. Research on vocal expression, summarized by Scherer (1981a; 1986a), reveals specificity in recognition studies, but there is not yet sufficient evidence for claiming specificity in acoustic patterning.

Differential physiological symptom patterns are a matter of hot debate. Whereas some researchers still hold the notion of "general arousal," that is, physiological activity being the same irrespective of the emotion experienced, others claim to have found differential patterns, though in these studies usually only the emotions anger and fear have been compared (Ax, 1953; Stemmler, 1984). Recently, Ekman, Levenson, and Friesen (1983) have reported evidence that other emotions may also be accompanied by distinctive physiological patterns. Control and regulation processes, finally, have been rarely studied, although sociologists have often pointed to the importance of affect control processes in interaction and communication (Elias, 1977; Hochschild, 1979). Thus the perennial issues of universality and specificity can hardly be considered settled. In many ways, empirical research on these issues has hardly even started. How can we gain access to the phenomena?

The general question asked in this chapter is whether different emotions are elicited by different situation patterns, whether they are accompanied by different expressive and physiological reactions, and whether different coping or control strategies are used with different emotions. We have argued elsewhere (Scherer, 1986b; Wallbott & Scherer, 1985a) that it is difficult, if not impossible, to study most emotional processes by using either laboratory techniques of emotion induction or field observation. Emotion induction in the laboratory is often inefficient because it results, at best, in rather weak emotional experiences. It is difficult, on the other hand, to have access to strong emotions experienced outside the laboratory. In addition, the objective measurement of emotional responses such as physiological reactions is often difficult or impossible to undertake in real-life situations.

We have argued that a questionnaire approach to the study of emotional processes asking subjects to describe emotional situations and the reactions experienced may be a suitable way to study not only emotion-eliciting situations but also emotional reactions. Recall and self-presentation processes may certainly bias the results from such question-naires, and "subjective" experiences, not objective measurements of situa-tions and reaction characteristics, are collected. Yet, many aspects of emo-tion response can be studied in this way, and our experiences with a ques-tionnaire approach to the study of emotional processes leads us to con-sider this technique as a viable method. In a series of studies we have used a free-response questionnaire in which subjects were asked to report situa-tions eliciting one of the basic emotions (joy, sadness, fear, and anger), and their nonverbal and physiological reactions and self-control attempts, as well as perceived characteristics of the emotional experience, such as its duration or intensity.

The first study, with about 600 respondents, was conducted in five Euro-pean countries (Scherer, Summerfield, & Wallbott, 1983). In a second study (Scherer, Wallbott, & Summerfield, 1986; Wallbott & Scherer, 1985a), about 800 respondents from eight European countries (West Germany, Great Britain, France, Switzerland, Belgium, Italy, Spain, Israel) partici-pated. Finally, a weighted sample of the European respondents (N = 177) was compared to samples from the United States (N = 165) and Japan (N = 174) to test whether the surprising uniformity in emotional ex-periences found between European samples would hold up when com-paring a European sample to samples from non-European cultures (com-pare Chapter 1).

The results obtained in these three studies allow us to present specific hypotheses for differences between emotions (the four emotions studied) with respect to situation and reaction characteristics. In this chapter we test these hypotheses by using a larger sample of respondents from more countries (this time not restricted to mainly European countries but in-volving samples from all over the world). We focus on the relative con-tributions to the variance in the data of intercultural differences (the universality issue) and emotion category differences (the specificity issue) respectively. Differences between individual country samples are not discussed in detail, mainly because it is difficult, if not impossible, to state hypotheses on that issue at the present time.

Hypotheses Based on Past Research

In our previous studies four emotions (joy, sadness, fear, anger) were in-vestigated. Three further emotions, disgust, shame, and guilt, were add-ed in this study. Hypotheses on different aspects of the emotion-eliciting situation and emotional experiences and reactions can be formulated only with regard to the original four emotions of joy, sadness, fear, and anger. As the results of the previous studies do not necessarily totally coincide, we always state the "weakest" hypotheses concerning differences between emotions.

Characteristics of the Emotional Experience

In this section we study the duration of the emotional experience reported, its intensity, and how long ago in the past the event occurred. The last aspect may be considered to provide an indirect answer to the question of how often the different emotions were experienced in everyday life. We argue that emotional situations reported to have happened further in the past indicate that the respective emotion is experienced less frequently (see Scherer, 1986b).

Concerning the frequency of emotional experiences the data from the previous studies led to the following hypothesis (Chapter 1):

$$\text{anger} = \text{joy} > \text{fear} = \text{sadness}$$

Though the post hoc analysis in Scherer, Wallbott, and Summerfield (1986) resulted in the more clear-cut succession anger > joy > sadness > fear, we can at least hypothesize that anger and joy will be more recent (and thus more frequently experienced) emotions compared to fear and sadness, where incidents that happened much further in the past are reported.

For the intensity of emotional experiences we propose the following "weak" hypothesis (from Chapter 1):

$$\text{joy} = \text{sadness} > \text{fear} = \text{anger}$$

We should expect sadnesss and joy to be reported as being of higher experienced intensity than other emotions, especially anger.

The hypothesis for the duration of emotional experiences derived from the previous studies is based on very stable results across studies (from Chapter 1):

$$\text{sadness} = \text{joy} > \text{anger} > \text{fear}$$

Thus, sadness and joy should be reported as being of longer duration than anger and fear, the latter being the most short-lived emotional experiences.

Control of Emotional Reactions

In the previous studies we asked subjects to report separately the degree of control for reactions/symptoms and verbal behavior. In this study we asked only one question concerning control (hiding) of affect in general. Here the results from the previous studies have to be based on the average of the two questions on control, which results in the following hypothesis (from Scherer et al., 1986):

$$\text{anger} = \text{sadness} = \text{fear} > \text{joy}$$

From the results one would expect that joy as a positive emotion is reported to be controlled least, while the negative emotions, especially anger, would tend to be controlled to a much greater degree. (The open expression of anger is often discouraged by social norms and thus calls for a higher degree of control.)

Nonverbal Reactions, Physiological Symptoms, and Speech Activity

In the previous studies data on perceived nonverbal reactions, physiological symptoms, and the speech activity accompanying emotional experiences were obtained by coding free responses of subjects to open questions. In this study, lists of symptoms and reactions (developed on the basis of our earlier results) were given to subjects, who had to check off which reactions or symptoms they had experienced. In this study the number of possible reactions/symptoms to be reported is limited to some major categories. But as the selection of these alternatives was governed by the results of the free reports, as in the previous studies, hypotheses can be formulated concerning which reactions/symptoms we would expect to be specific for certain emotions. These predictions are summarized in Table 2.1.

With respect to nonverbal reactions, laughing/smiling should be characteristic of joy, crying of sadness, and distinctive voice reactions of anger. We would expect joy and anger in general to be accompanied by more nonverbal reactions than sadness and, especially, fear. This may be because joy and anger are "active" emotions, compared to the more "passive" emotions of sadness and fear. Physiological symptoms will probably be mentioned most often for the experience of fear, which according to our previous results is a more "internalized" emotion (that is, gives rise to few nonverbal reactions, but many physiological symptoms) compared to anger and joy, which should be more "externalized" (more reactions, fewer symptoms).

For physiological symptoms, we would expect skin temperature sensations to differentiate the four emotions strongly, with joy being experienced as "warm," anger as "hot," and sadness and fear as "cold." Gastric disturbances should differentiate negative emotions from positive emotions, while striated muscle tone symptoms and cardiovascular symptoms

TABLE 2.1
Predictions for Emotion-Specific Nonverbal and Verbal Reactions,
and Physiological Symptoms Reported

Nonverbal reactions and speech behavior specific to:

Joy	Sadness	Fear	Anger
Laughing/smiling	Crying		
	Changes in facial expression	Changes in facial expression	Changes in facial expression
Changed voice quality	Changed voice quality and voice reactions	Changed voice quality and voice reactions	Changed voice quality and voice reactions
Gestures			Gestures
Movements toward other people			
Speech activity			Speech activity
	Silence	Silence	

Physiological symptoms specific to:

Joy	Sadness	Fear	Anger
Feeling of pleasant rest/warmth		Feelings of coldness	Feelings of hotness
	Stomach symptoms	Stomach symptoms	Stomach symptoms
	Muscle symptoms	Muscle symptoms	Muscle symptoms
		Perspiration	
		Heart rate/blood pressure changes	

should be important concomitants for all emotions, with the possible exception of sadness (Scherer, 1986b). Muscle activity and cardiovascular symptoms may indicate "general arousal" processes accompanying all types of emotional experience, while some of the other symptoms (especially temperature sensations) may differentiate specific emotions.

Evaluation of the Emotion-Eliciting Situation

In the previous studies aspects of the eliciting situation were classified using an a posteriori coding scheme to code general characteristics of the situation such as "relationship aspects," "news," or "achievement situations," and characteristics of the persons involved in the situation such as their familiarity with the person experiencing the emotion. In this study we asked subjects to report on evaluative aspects of the situation such as its intrinsic pleasantness or expectedness, as well as their self-perception of their coping potential. These questions were motivated by an attempt to obtain data pertinent to the theoretical model of emotion proposed by Scherer (1981b; 1984a; 1986a). This "component process model" of emotion postulates successive evaluations of a given situation with respect to its novelty, intrinsic pleasantness, goal/need conduciveness, the coping potential of the person experiencing the situation, and the norm/self compatibility of events and reactions. The sequence of outcomes of these "stimulus evaluation checks" is seen to determine the affective state of a person, which is then labeled as an emotion such as joy or sadness. If different emotions are indeed the results of different outcome combinations of stimulus evaluations, an examination of the subjective perception of situation properties by subjects should allow at least a preliminary assessment of the nature of the evaluation process and of the plausibility of the hypotheses put forward by Scherer (1986a). Because the questions concerning the subjective evaluation of the emotion-eliciting events had to be rather general, given the restrictions on time and space in this intercultural study, they cannot be seen as sufficiently precise operationalizations of the stimulus evaluation checks. Thus, no detailed formal predictions for these questions were proposed.

Range of Prediction

As mentioned previously, the hypotheses proposed here (except those for the stimulus evaluation check outcomes) can be formulated only for the four emotions joy, sadness, fear, and anger, which were investigated in our previous studies. For the emotions added in this study no data exist so far. We added disgust in this study because recent research (Ekman, 1984) suggests that disgust may also be a "primary" and universal emotion, which should imply distinctive situation and reaction patterns for this emotion, too. Shame and guilt were added to investigate whether the social and interactional aspects that are of prime importance for these emotions (see Izard, 1977; Scherer, 1986a) might limit the universality of experience. We do not state hypotheses on the cause of the emotional experiences, that is, the agent responsible for the situation, because relevant data from the previous studies do not exist.

METHOD

The Questionnaire

Given the experience gained with the previous open-answer questionnaire format and the opportunity to test specific hypotheses derived from the earlier studies, we decided to use a questionnaire with closed-answer alternatives in this study. The aim in constructing this questionnaire was to cover all aspects of the emotion process. At the same time we also wanted to construct an instrument that would be manageable for subjects, that is, would allow them to answer the questions on seven emotions in a reasonable amount of time (a maximum of 2 hours). It was decided to limit the questions concerning each emotion to two pages and to provide subjects with a limited number of answer alternatives for each question. The choice of answer alternatives was based on the response categories that were found to occur most frequently in the earlier free-response studies.

The first version of the questionnaire was written in English and then sent out to all participants in the project. After pilot studies in each country, the comments and suggestions of participants were collected, and a revised, final version was developed. This final English-language version was translated into the respective countries' languages by the participants and a translation back into English was obtained from a person in each country unfamiliar with the project. By this process of translation and translation back we wanted to assure ourselves that the respective versions of the questionnaire in the different countries reflected the meaning originally intended in the English-language version.

The version finally used is reproduced in Appendix C. The items for all seven emotions were identical, with the labels for the respective emotions inserted on the top of the first page. The order of emotions was randomized across subjects in each participating country.

After reading the instructions (see Appendix C), subjects were asked to report some background information, specifically their age, sex, field of study (all subjects were students — see next section), their religion (and whether they were practicing the religion or not), the country they had grown up in and the country of their origin, as well as their native language (to assure that only subjects who were native citizens of the respective country were included in the sample), and their father's and mother's occupation (to allow rough comparisons of socioeconomic status of subjects between country samples).

Subjects were either paid for their participation in the study or received course credits, depending on local norms. The appropriateness of payment or course credit was determined by the local researchers in the respective countries. The task of filling in the questionnaires took subjects between 30 and 120 minutes. Questionnaires were given out during courses and lectures. Given the somewhat intimate reports asked for, total anonymity of responses was assured to subjects in all countries.

Subjects

Before starting the project it was decided to use only students as subjects, as the task of remembering and describing emotional situations in some detail calls for a rather high degree of introspective ability and articulateness. Though it would have been interesting to study nonstudent populations using such an approach, it was decided to restrict subject populations to students. This was also in the interests of the comparability of findings with earlier results and across cultures, inasmuch as the previous studies were conducted with students and sample characteristics should be more comparable between cultures if only student populations were used. (In general, it is virtually impossible to assure total comparability of samples in cross-cultural studies, given educational and socioeconomic differences between countries and cultures).

Some constraints with respect to sample characteristics were introduced before starting the study. Each collaborator in the different participating countries was to collect a sample of about 80 to 100 subjects, with ideally a 50/50 male–female subject distribution (with a maximally skewed distribution admitted of 30/70). About 50% of subjects were to be studying psychology (given that most collaborators are psychologists), with the other 50% distributed evenly between the other social sciences, the natural sciences, and medicine. None of the subjects were to be younger than 18 years or older than 35 years.

The data base of this report consists of samples from 27 countries from all five continents, with a total of 2,235 subjects. Table 2.2 presents the characteristics of the 27 country samples. In all countries it was possible to collect samples that were comparable with respect to sex distribution and age range. Given the different university systems in the different countries, and the varying accessibility to students from other faculties for the collaborators in the different countries, the distribution of student subjects across faculties is in some cases not in line with our original requirements concerning sample composition. Nevertheless, the total sample approximates to the sample characteristics originally proposed.

RESULTS

It should again be noted that the data presented are based on subjective recall of situations and reactions. To what extent such reports reflect objective events depends on a number of factors. The initial storage of emotional events in the memory, as well as recall and report, may be influenced by factors such as ego involvement or defense mechanisms. General inference tendencies, such as the "availability," "representativeness," and "vividness" heuristics, may also interfere (see Nisbett & Ross, 1980; Scherer & Tannenbaum, 1986; Tversky & Kahneman, 1974). Certain situations may be more "available" than others, depending on the subject's state. Subjects

TABLE 2.2
Major Characteristics of the 27 Country Samples

Country	N of subjects	% male	% female	Average age (years)	Faculties (%)		
					Psy-chology	Social Sciences	Natural Sciences
CENTRAL EUROPE							
Austria	69	41	59	21.4	100	-	-
France	72	19	81	20.3	99	1	-
Netherlands	71	34	66	21.4	100	-	-
West Germany	117	38	62	23.2	47	22	31
NORTHERN EUROPE							
Finland	76	33	67	23.5	43	38	19
Norway	36	61	39	24.3	-	-	100
Sweden	84	44	56	26.5	42	58	-
SOUTHERN EUROPE							
Greece	71	49	51	22.5	48	38	14
Italy	98	51	49	21.1	51	49	-
Portugal	88	24	76	21.2	39	15	47
Spain	78	50	50	21.0	49	27	24
EASTERN EUROPE							
Bulgaria	73	42	58	22.2	48	10	42
Poland	87	49	51	21.6	44	29	28
AFRICA							
Botswana	82	68	32	22.8	1	91	7
Malawi	75	51	49	22.2	-	-	100
Nigeria	77	65	35	23.4	100	-	-
Zimbabwe	99	53	47	22.3	40	60	-
Zambia	119	67	33	22.3	6	57	37
NEAR EAST							
Israel	49	33	67	23.6	4	71	24
Lebanon	68	31	69	20.7	51	8	39
FAR EAST							
Hong Kong	83	54	46	20.7	5	58	36
India	68	53	47	23.4	100	-	-
Japan	199	50	50	20.9	33	46	21
OCEANIA							
Australia	95	29	71	22.3	38	27	34
New Zealand	61	36	64	24.0	47	38	15
SOUTH AMERICA							
Brazil	59	29	71	22.0	2	67	32
NORTH AMERICA							
U.S.A.	81	54	46	19.4	11	26	63
Average	83	45	55	22.1	44	36	20

Data in some cases do not add up to 100% because of missing data.

may report situations and reactions they consider "representative" for certain emotions. Some situations may be more "vivid" than others and thus more easily recalled. Although these potential sources of influence on self-report are acknowledged, we do not believe that the reports themselves are purposively falsified or inaccurate; they largely reflect the respondents' subjective experience of emotion-eliciting situations and emotional reactions.

We focus here on the question of whether different patterns of situational evaluations, nonverbal and verbal reactions, physiological symptoms experienced, and control attempts can be detected between the seven emotions studied. In view of this aim and given the richness of the data base we restrict data analyses to an analysis of variance approach with additional post hoc comparisons between emotions (by the Newman–Keuls test), comparing each variable (each questionnaire item) separately for differences between emotions. Country differences are not discussed in detail but are mentioned only in cases where they are larger than the differences between emotions.

All results reported are based on an analysis of variance approach with each questionnaire item as a dependent variable and the two factors, "emotion" (with seven emotions, joy, sadness, fear, anger, disgust, shame, guilt) and "country" (the 27 country samples collected) as independent variables. When analyzing the questionnaire items with either multiple-answer possibilities (reactions, symptoms, verbal behavior) or items that could not be considered as in an interval or at least as in an ordinal scale (coping attempts, agent responsible), each answer alternative was treated as a separate item with answer alternatives 0 and 1, and analyses of variance were run on these 0/1 data. For items that included the answer alternative of "not applicable" (0), the ANOVAS were run excluding cases where this alternative had been mentioned. (We are aware of the fact that treating each item or its answer alternatives respectively as an interval scale and analyzing it via an ANOVA approach may not seem conservative to experienced statisticians; but given the type of data collected this approach seemed to be best suited to provide a first overall view of the data.)

To determine the relative contribution of the two factors "emotion" and "country" on each item, "etas" are reported throughout (the squared eta indicating the amount of variance for each item contributed by the two factors). Interaction effects between the factors "country" and "emotion" are not reported here, as they had very low F and p values.

In presenting the results we follow the distinction put forward in the hypotheses section and present results on ecological features of emotional experiences, data on control attempts, reports on nonverbal, verbal, and physiological concomitants of emotional experiences, and the subjective evaluation of emotion-eliciting situations separately. In the discussion section an attempt is made to integrate the findings with respect to the question of emotion-specific elicitation and reaction patterns and the question of the universality of emotional experiences.

The Characteristics of Emotional Experience

The hypothesis that anger (and to a lesser degree joy) should be a more frequent emotional experience and that more recent situations should therefore be reported is fully supported by the data. The respective means and the post hoc comparison indicated that anger situations were most recent, followed by joy, sadness, and fear. It is interesting that disgust situations were nearly as recent as anger situations, indicating that this emotion was also experienced frequently. Shame and guilt, on the contrary, were similar to joy, sadness, and fear. Two groups of emotions can thus be distinguished: anger and disgust on the one hand, and joy, sadness, fear, shame, and guilt on the other. Country differences for this variable are about as important as differences between emotions (compare the respective etas in Table 2.3). Thus, the recall or the frequency of experience of certain emotions is to some degree determined by cultural factors.

As far as the duration of emotional experiences is concerned, we had expected sadness to be longest, followed by joy, anger, and fear (the shortest in duration). This hypothesis was fully supported by the means and the post hoc comparison. Among the three additional emotions studied, disgust and shame were rather short-lived emotions comparable to fear, while guilt was longer lasting (differentiating shame and guilt, which in other respects are similar to one another). For the duration of emotional experiences, differences due to the emotions far exceed those due to country, which implies that the differences found in our studies are a stable phenomenon, pointing to general and universal differences in the duration of emotional experiences.

The predictions for experienced intensity from the past studies were that sadness and joy should be reported as being of higher intensity, especially in relation to anger. Though this was supported by the means, the differences between the four emotions were too small to reach statistical significance in the post hoc comparison. As in the other studies, this may be explained by a ceiling effect, because subjects may have reported only situations of high intensity (see Scherer, 1986b). It was interesting that disgust and, especially, shame and guilt were reported as being of lower intensity than the other four emotions. One wonders whether social norms and self-serving mechanisms prohibit the report of situations where these emotions are experienced with high intensity, or whether these emotions are generally not experienced as intensely as the other four. Though for the intensity of experiences the eta for emotion

TABLE 2.3

Differences Between Emotions in Characteristics of Experience and Control

Variable	Joy	Fear	Anger	Sad-ness	Disgust	Shame	Guilt	F	df (X/6)	Newman-Keuls Post-hoc	eta EMOT.	eta COUN.
How long ago	2.8	3.1	2.5	3.0	2.6	3.0	2.8	80.5	14916	F>S=SH>J=G>D>A	.17	.21
Duration	3.4	2.5	2.8	3.6	2.6	2.7	3.1	344.4	14916	S>J>G>A>SH>D=F	.34	.19
Intensity	3.1	3.1	3.0	3.2	2.7	2.5	2.6	189.2	14916	S>J=F>A>D>SH=G	.26	.19
Control	1.3	1.9	1.6	1.9	1.7	2.3	2.1	454.9	14447	SH>G>S=F>D>A>J	.39	.07

All comparisons between emotions significant below the .001-level; How long ago = answer to questionnaire item 2; Duration = answer to item 3; Intensity = answer to item 4; Control = answer to item 6; answer alternatives for these analysis interpreted as interval scale values; for Control answer alternative "0 = not applicable" excluded from the analysis.

exceeds the eta for country, the country factor is quite important. Compared to other variables (especially reactions and symptoms, see the following section), cultural differences for frequency, intensity, and duration were relatively large. Either the intensity of emotional experiences in fact differs in different countries or culturally determined factors influence the reporting of this aspect.

Nonverbal Reactions, Speech Behavior, and Physiological Symptoms

For physiological symptoms, nonverbal reactions, and speech behavior the degree of variance due to country is generally much lower than the amount due to emotion. This general result implies that emotional reaction patterns may be to a large degree universal. We report the results for each reaction/symptom in turn (for details see Table 2.4).

Let us first consider the overall *number* of nonverbal reactions and physiological symptoms reported. Previous studies have indicated that fear is the most "physiological" emotion and that anger and joy are more "active" in terms of nonverbal behavior than sadness and fear. Both hypotheses were strongly supported by the present data. The largest amount of physiological symptoms is reported for fear and the smallest for guilt and disgust. Most nonverbal reactions were mentioned for anger, followed by joy and sadness, and many fewer reactions for fear, disgust, shame, and guilt. The quotient "number of reactions reported/number of symptoms reported," which indicates dominance of both reaction modalities (>1 = more reactions than symptoms = "externalizing"; <1 = more symptoms than reaction = "internalizing") also replicates past results, in that joy and anger are relatively more externalized than the other emotions, while shame, guilt, and fear especially are the most "internalized."

Given the predominance of *physiological symptoms* in fear, it is not surprising that physiological symptoms differentiate it from the other emotions. For fear, a higher incidence of breathing symptoms, stomach symptoms, feelings of cold, heartbeat changes, perspiration, and muscle tensions were reported. The other emotion showing a very distinctive pattern of symptoms was joy, for which, more than for any other emotion, feelings of warmth and muscle relaxation were reported and the symptoms of "a lump in the throat," stomach problems, feelings of coldness, and tense muscles were relatively absent.

Symptoms can be categorized into those that indicate more general arousal and emergency preparation of the organism (and therefore accompany more or less all emotions), and symptoms specific to certain emotions. Our data indicate that the general indicators of *arousal* processes

TABLE 2.4

Differences in Physiological Symptoms, Nonverbal Reactions, and Speech Behavior Between Emotions

Variable	Joy	Fear	Anger	Sad-ness	Disgust	Shame	Guilt	F	df (X/6)	Newman-Keuls post hoc	eta EMOT.	eta COUN.
PHYSIOLOGICAL SYMPTOMS												
Lump in throat	.12	.29	.26	.53	.22	.24	.27	194.6	15320	S>F>G=A>Sh=D>J	.26	.13
Breathing	.19	.46	.36	.25	.18	.20	.17	163.6	15320	F>A>S>Sh>all oth.	.23	.16
Stomach	.02	.20	.10	.17	.18	.10	.14	79.9	15320	F>D=S>G>A=SH>J	.17	.13
Feeling cold	.02	.35	.09	.23	.16	.11	.13	216.6	15320	F>S>D>G=SH>A>J	.27	.12
Feeling warm	.65	.02	.02	.01	.01	.02	.01	2902.1	15320	J>all others	.72	.06
Feeling hot	.15	.15	.31	.09	.11	.37	.17	177.7	15320	SH>A>all oth. >D=S	.25	.11
Heartbeat	.40	.67	.49	.28	.24	.37	.28	234.3	15320	F>A>J>SH>S=G>D	.29	.15
Muscles tense	.10	.51	.43	.28	.26	.24	.22	232.3	15320	F>A>S>D>SH=G>J	.28	.18
Muscles relaxed	.29	.02	.02	.06	.03	.03	.03	395.3	15320	J>S>all others	.36	.09
Perspiring	.11	.37	.21	.15	.14	.25	.17	118.6	15320	F>SH>A>G>S=D>J	.21	.11
Other symptoms	.14	.13	.17	.22	.22	.15	.18	18.9	15320	S=D>G=A>all oth.	.08	.14
NONVERBAL REACTIONS												
Laughing	.85	.04	.03	.04	.05	.12	.04	3308.6	15320	J>SH>all others	.75	.05

(Continued)

TABLE 2.4
(Continued)

Variable	Joy	Fear	Anger	Sad-ness	Disgust	Shame	Guilt	F	df (X/6)	Newman-Keuls post hoc	eta EMOT.	eta COUN.
Crying	.08	.14	.15	.52	.07	.10	.13	488.1	15320	S>A=F=G>SH>J=D	.40	.10
Facial expres.	.16	.32	.41	.31	.40	.31	.26	79.7	15320	A=D>all oth.>G>J	.17	.19
Screaming	.08	.13	.23	.06	.08	.03	.04	131.0	15320	A>F>J=D>S>G=SH	.22	.09
Voice change	.15	.19	.33	.23	.18	.19	.18	49.7	15320	A>S>all oth.>J	.14	.17
Gesture change	.18	.16	.25	.14	.16	.18	.15	21.9	15320	A>J=SH>all others	.09	.14
Abrupt movement	.11	.21	.24	.06	.14	.09	.08	92.5	15320	A>F>D>J>SH=G>S	.18	.10
Moving toward	.41	.15	.09	.12	.06	.06	.08	340.2	15320	J>F>S>A=G>D=SH	.34	.13
Withdrawing	.02	.18	.18	.31	.24	.29	.25	143.7	15320	S=SH>G=D>A=F>J	.23	.12
Moving against	.00	.06	.29	.07	.12	.05	.07	269.1	15320	A>D>S=G>F=SH>J	.30	.15
Other reactions	.13	.20	.16	.18	.19	.17	.18	8.5	15320	—	.06	.14
VERBAL BEHAVIOR												
Silence	.13	.50	.24	.60	.41	.48	.48	278.3	15320	S>F=SH=G>D>A>J	.31	.10
Short utterance	.16	.21	.18	.19	.22	.19	.17	6.9	15320	D=F>all others	.05	.13
One/two sentenc.	.13	.11	.14	.12	.12	.14	.13	2.4	15320	—	.03	.10

(Continued)

TABLE 2.4
(Continued)

Variable	Joy	Fear	Anger	Sad-ness	Disgust	Shame	Guilt	F	df (X/6)	Newman-Keuls post hoc	eta EMOT.	eta COUN.
Lengthy utteran.	.34	.08	.29	.09	.15	.08	.11	217.1	15320	J>A>D>G>all oth.	.27	.16
Speech melody	.31	.11	.27	.14	.12	.11	.12	118.5	15320	J>A>all others	.20	.19
Speech disturb.	.06	.15	.15	.12	.07	.15	.12	30.2	15320	F=A=SH>G=S>D=J	.11	.16
Speech tempo	.22	.12	.28	.10	.11	.10	.10	101.3	15320	A>J>all others	.19	.13
Other verbal	.15	.08	.12	.08	.12	.07	.10	20.3	15320	J>A=D>all others	.09	.12
No. symptoms	2.2	3.2	2.5	2.3	1.8	2.1	1.8	187.7	15320	F>A>S>J=SH>G=D	.25	.20
No. reactions	2.2	1.8	2.4	2.0	1.7	1.6	1.5	135.1	15320	A>J>S>D=F>SH>G	.22	.24
React./Sympt.	1.06	.59	1.02	.93	.92	.75	.74	143.7	15320	J>A>S=D>SH=G>F	.24	.12

All comparisons between emotions significant below the .001-level, except 'One/two sentences'': p = .025.

seem to be changes in breathing and changes in heart rate. Both were mentioned for all emotions by a considerable number of respondents (see Table 2.4). Unexpectedly, another general symptom was "a lump in throat," which was mentioned by more than 20% of respondents for all emotions, except for the positive emotion joy. Tense muscles also seemed to accompany all negative emotions (though to the highest degree in the cases of fear and anger), while relaxed muscles were a typical symptom of joy.

The most interesting differences between emotions could be found in the *temperature symptoms*; these differences were in line with the hypotheses. The only emotion experienced as being "warm" was joy; "cold" emotions were fear and, to a lesser degree, sadness, while anger and especially shame could be characterized as "hot" emotions. As blood flow changes partly account for subjective temperature sensations, these results confirm common notions of a "glowing" face during joy, "turning pale" during fear, "red, hot" anger, and "blushing" when experiencing shame. As can be seen when comparing these results with the hypotheses in Table 2.1, the patterns are nearly identical. Interestingly enough, the pattern of physiological symptoms found for fear was exactly identical to Darwin's description (1872, p. 290): "The heart beats quickly and violently . . . the skin instantly becomes pale, . . . perspiration immediately exudes from it . . . the surface is then cold . . . breathing is hurried . . . one of the best-marked symptoms is the trembling of all muscles of the body."

The differences between emotions detected were also pronounced for most of the *nonverbal reactions*. Facial reactions included laughing/smiling, crying, and other changes in facial expression. As predicted, laughing indicated joy (and, but to a much lesser degree, shame), whereas crying accompanied sadness. However, crying was also mentioned by about 10% of respondents for all other emotions. Other changes in facial expression were found for all negative emotions, especially often accompanying anger and disgust. (These changes obviously included different types of facial expressions that had not been listed as response alternatives in the questionnaire, given the large number of different facial expressions and the difficulties in describing these verbally.)

Voice changes accompanied all emotions (again these were likely to consist of many different types of changes for different emotions), though they were significantly more often mentioned as signs of anger and sadness. The same was true for the one specific voice reaction we asked for, namely screaming, which was also mentioned mostly for anger. Gestural changes and abrupt bodily movements were generally not very frequent. Most often gestural changes were described for anger, joy, and shame, and abrupt movements for anger and fear.

Finally, three possible tendencies to act (Horney, 1937, p. 96–98) — moving toward other people, moving away from other people, and moving against other people (aggression)—were distinguished. Whereas "moving toward" was typical of joy, "moving against" was a differentiating characteristic of anger, and withdrawal was described for all negative emotions (though to a somewhat lesser degree for fear and anger). "Other reactions" (a residual category, like "other symptoms") did not distinguish between various emotions to a large degree.

The most predominant *verbal reaction* when experiencing an emotion was silence, except for the "active" (see p. 35) emotions anger and joy. These two emotions in turn were verbally accompanied by lengthy utterances (short utterances and sentences did not differentiate emotions much). Thus, people either talk a lot or they do not talk at all when emotionally aroused. This result, which seems to be a rather universal phenomenon, since the etas for emotion were much larger than the respective etas for country, again confirms that joy and anger may be seen as active, "social" emotions (see Babad & Wallbott, 1986) compared to the others studied here. Further evidence for this notion were the significantly more frequent speech melody and tempo changes for joy and anger, though for speech melody changes cross-cultural differences were nearly as important as differences between emotions. Finally, speech disturbances and "other speech reactions" were rarely mentioned for any emotion. Thus, verbal reactions do not result in distinctive patterns of reactions typical of specific emotions (as is the case for nonverbal reactions and especially the physiological symptoms) but only differentiate the two active, "social" emotions joy and anger (characterized by more speech activity and more speech changes) from the other five, more passive, "nonsocial" emotions.

Regulation and Control

For the amount of control of emotional reactions and symptoms, we had expected joy as a positive emotion to be controlled to a much lesser degree than the negative emotions (for which no specific predictions about differences had been made). The data (Table 2.3) fully supported the predicted difference between joy and all the other emotions. However, we also found differences between the negative emotions. Shame and guilt reactions were controlled most of all, followed by fear and sadness. Relatively little control was reported for disgust and anger. It is interesting that anger was controlled least of all the negative emotions. This does not replicate our earlier findings in the European countries, where anger was controlled to a much higher degree. In general, then, there seems to be little pressure to hide angry experiences. This may be a relatively universal phenomenon inasmuch as, for control, the amount of variance due to emotion is far larger than that due to country (which is very small for this variable). The fact that shame and guilt are controlled most is plau-

TABLE 2.5
Differences in Situation Evaluation Aspects Between Emotions

Variable	Joy	Fear	Anger	Sad-ness	Disgust	Shame	Guilt	F	df (X/6)	Newman-Keuls post hoc	eta EMOT.	eta COUN.
Expectancy	2.1	1.5	1.5	1.6	1.5	1.5	1.6	198.4	14353	J>S=G>F>all oth.	.27	.15
Unpleasantness	1.0	2.9	2.9	2.9	2.9	2.8	2.8	6507.8	14514	A=D>F=S>SH>G>J	.85	.05
Plan hindered	1.1	2.3	2.5	2.5	2.3	2.3	2.3	1120.2	11349	A=S>all others>J	.60	.10
Unfairness	1.1	2.0	2.5	2.1	2.3	1.8	1.8	650.4	10618	A>D>S>F>SH=G>J	.50	.18
Responsibility (answer alternatives treated as different variables)												
Yourself	.39	.30	.11	.18	.10	.59	.69	668.3	14710	G>SH>J>F>S>A=D	.45	.13
Relatives	.08	.04	.16	.08	.08	.06	.05	46.1	14710	A>J=D=S>all oth.	.13	.11
Friends	.13	.04	.17	.08	.10	.07	.06	53.0	14710	A>J>D>all oth.>F	.14	.11
Colleagues	.03	.03	.15	.03	.13	.05	.02	110.8	14710	A>D>SH>all oth.	.21	.07
Strangers	.01	.13	.12	.04	.19	.04	.01	154.9	14710	D>F=A>S=SH>J=G	.24	.11
Authorities	.04	.06	.13	.05	.11	.05	.02	59.7	14710	A>D>all oth. >G	.15	.12
Natural forces	.04	.07	.01	.12	.03	.02	.02	82.5	14710	S>F>J>D>all oth.	.18	.10
Supernatural	.03	.03	.00	.04	.01	.00	.01	26.6	14710	S=J=F>all others	.10	.09
Fate	.04	.06	.03	.18	.02	.02	.03	137.7	14710	S>all others	.23	.10
Chance	.07	.09	.03	.05	.07	.05	.04	17.1	14710	F>D=J>S>all oth.	.08	.09
"Others"	.30	.31	.73	.28	.62	.25	.17	490.1	14710	A>D>F>J>S>SH>G	.40	.15
(= Relat. or Friends or Coll. or Strang. or Author.)												
"Fate"	.11	.17	.05	.33	.07	.05	.06	260.9	14710	S>F>J>all others	.30	.14
(= Natural or Supernat. or Fate)												

(Continued)

TABLE 2.5
(Continued)

Variable	Joy	Fear	Anger	Sad-ness	Disgust	Shame	Guilt	F	df (X/6)	Newman-Keuls post hoc	eta EMOT.	eta COUN.
Coping (answer alternatives treated as different variables)												
No action neces.	.61	.12	.14	.19	.28	.17	.13	419.8	14791	J>D>S=SH>all oth.	.38	.09
Posit.influence	.22	.20	.36	.17	.19	.25	.33	62.0	14791	A=G>SH>J>all oth.	.15	.07
Escape	.01	.18	.09	.05	.13	.15	.17	90.4	14791	F=G>SH=D>A>S>J	.19	.09
Pretend	.04	.12	.13	.11	.17	.21	.17	54.9	14791	SH>G=D>all oth.>J	.15	.06
Powerless	.12	.37	.28	.49	.23	.21	.21	175.1	14791	S>F>A>D>SH=G>J	.25	.09
Immorality	1.1	1.9	2.3	1.9	2.4	2.0	2.2	491.2	10365	D>A>G>SH>F=S>J	.45	.22
Self positive	2.9	1.8	1.7	1.6	1.8	1.4	1.4	1253.4	12207	J>D>F=A>S>G=SH	.61	.12
Relations pos.	2.8	1.9	1.5	1.9	1.5	1.7	1.8	828.0	11447	J>S=F>G>SH>A=D	.54	.08

All comparisons between emotions significant below the .001-level; for Expectancy (questionnaire item 7), Pleasantness (item 8), Plan hindered (item 9), Unfairness (item 10), Immorality (item 13), Positive influence on Self (item 14) and on relationships (item 15) answer alternative "0 = not applicable" excluded from analyses.

sible when one considers the phenomenology of these emotions (Izard, 1977).

The Subjective Evaluation of Emotion-Eliciting Events

The results concerning the dimensions of evaluation of antecedent events and behaviors are shown in Table 2.5. Joy situations were reported to have been significantly more expected than sadness and guilt situations, which in turn were more expected than situations eliciting the other four emotions. Or to put it another way: sadness, guilt, and especially joy situations were more expected than other emotional situations. This result was similar across cultures.

The pleasantness dimension differentiates, as might be expected, between joy as a positive emotion, on the one hand, and all six negative emotions, on the other hand, with no large significant differences within the negative emotions and with nearly no effect from cross-cultural differences.

Plans were hindered least by joy situations and most by anger and sadness situations. The difference between joy and the other emotions was in line with the expectations related to the difference between positive and negative emotions. It is interesting to note that events were reported as being most obstructive to plans when anger and sadness were experienced. Again, country differences were not at all important for this variable.

Concerning the perceived unfairness of the emotion-eliciting event or behavior we found a clear rank ordering of the emotions. Anger-producing events were perceived as being the most unfair, followed by disgust-eliciting situations, sadness- and fear-eliciting situations, shame- and guilt-eliciting situations, and finally joy-eliciting situations, which were perceived as being the most fair.

The attribution of an agent or cause of the emotional experience is an important prerequisite for the evaluation of coping potential and action alternatives. Here again the effects due to emotion were much larger than the effects due to country, which implies relatively stable effects largely independent of cultural differences. Most of the answer alternatives provided in the questionnaire, like "relatives," "colleagues," "natural forces," or "the supernatural" were used quite infrequently by respondents. Thus, we report here only on four large classes of potential agents: the person him/herself, other people (e.g., relatives, friends, colleagues, strangers, or authorities), chance, and "fate" (combining the alternatives "fate," "supernatural," and "natural forces"). Thus we distinguish between four general attribution tendencies, "internal attributions" (self) versus "external attributions," which again are subdivided into attributions to other people, to chance, and to fate (compare literature on theories of attribution: Heider, 1958; Weiner, 1982).

The self was seen as the major cause of emotional experiences primarily in guilt and shame experiences, followed by joy, fear, and sadness, while disgust and anger were rarely caused by the experiencing persons themselves. Quite the contrary is found for "other people" as a cause of emotion. Other people particularly caused anger and disgust experiences, followed by all other emotions, while sadness, shame, and guilt were rarely attributed to others. Major differences thus existed between shame and guilt as internally attributed emotions, caused by the actor himself or herself, on the one hand, and anger and disgust as externally attributed emotions, caused by other persons. Looking at the single categories of "other people" we find an interesting additional difference between anger and disgust: anger was reported to be caused especially by relatives, friends, colleagues, and authorities, disgust more by strangers.

The other two attribution directions are less important in general. Fear was caused most often by chance, as also were disgust, joy, and sadness to some degree. "Fate" was a major reason for sadness, followed by fear and joy, but was of no major importance for all other emotions. Thus, we could distinguish at least five emotions with respect to the agent: the self as a major cause for shame and guilt, others for anger and disgust, and fate (but also others and self to some degree) for sadness. Joy and fear could not be related to one specific agent but had multiple causes.

To assess subjectively perceived coping potential we provided five possible answer alternatives in the questionnaire concerning ability to act. These are treated as separate variables in this analysis. For all five items the amount of variance explained by the emotion factor was much larger than the amount due to the country factor, suggesting again a high degree of similarity between countries, or universality.

Subjects reported that they thought no action was necessary to cope with the situation especially when experiencing joy, followed by disgust encounters, shame and guilt situations and then all other negative emotions. This may reflect the perceived urgency of action, though the rather low urgency to do something during disgust experiences was somewhat surprising. Subjects reported that they thought they could positively influence the situation mostly when dealing with anger- and guilt-eliciting events, followed by shame, joy, and the other emotions. High subjective coping potential tended to lead to the experience of anger.

The feeling of powerlessness was predominantly experienced when encountering sadness-inducing situations, followed by fear situations and to some degree anger situations (which in these cases may be caused more by "irritation" than by "hot anger"). Feeling powerless was rarely mentioned in joy situations.

Attempts to escape from a situation or pretending that nothing important had happened were generally reported less frequently than other coping attempts. Subjects attempted to escape from the situation especially when experiencing fear and guilt, and to some degree also when experiencing disgust and shame, but rarely during anger, sadness, and, above all, joy experiences. Pretending that nothing had happened was quite a common strategy for coping with shame, followed by disgust and guilt (the other negative emotions) and joy.

A statistically significant rank order of emotions was found for the question of morality or propriety of emotion-eliciting behavior. Disgust- and anger-eliciting situations were considered as being the most immoral, followed by guilt, shame, fear, and sadness situations, with joy situations again considered more moral than other emotions. The eta for "country" was small compared to the eta for "emotion" for this variable, indicating a high cross-cultural stability of these differential effects of the evaluation of the emotion-producing event.

The questions as to whether the subject's self-image and relationships to others were positively influenced by the emotional experience resulted in similar differences between emotions, with one important difference. The self was influenced least positively in situations where guilt or shame were experienced, while relationships to others were influenced least positively by anger and disgust experiences. This is in line with a finding on the causal agent of emotional situations reported earlier, namely that shame and guilt are usually seen as caused by the person him/herself, whereas anger and disgust experiences are generally seen as being caused by other people. The differences between the other emotions were not very pronounced (all other negative emotions affect self *and* relationships slightly negatively), with the exception of joy. Joy generally resulted in more positive self-esteem and more positive relationships to others than all negative emotions, which was to be expected. The etas here also show that for the results on both variables emotion differences were more important than country differences.

These data on the dimensions of subjective evaluation of emotion-eliciting events are generally in line with the predictions made by Scherer (1984a, 1986a) on the basis of the sequential "stimulus evaluation check" model as well as with similar theoretical approaches suggested by Frijda (1986), Smith and Ellsworth (1985), and Weiner (1982). Although the questions used in this study are too unspecific to consider these findings as "evidence" for the theoretical predictions, they would seem to lend at least some plausibility to the models proposed.

CONCLUSIONS

This progress report of the results of a large-scale cross-cultural study on emotional experience (which is continuing) seems to show rather convincingly that emotional experience is both quite specific for a number of individual emotions and more or less universal, that is, highly similar for people all over the world. It seems to us that the preliminary statistical analysis of the mass of data from this study shows two major patterns:

1. The differences between the specific emotions are significant, often strongly significant, for most of the aspects of the emotional experience studied. In many cases, the seven emotions studied were clearly differentiated in terms of a particular aspect of the emotion process, and these differences often corresponded to the pattern or rank ordering we had predicted on the basis of our earlier results.

2. Although there were significant effects due to "country" on some of the variables representing specific aspects of the emotional experience, the amount of variance in the data due to country differences was almost always lower, often much lower, than the differences between the seven emotions studied. An investigation of these cross-cultural differences showed that the general pattern was rarely reversed. When there were differences between countries, they were often differences of degree or emphasis. Thus the extreme view that emotional expression and emotional experience are primarily determined by social and cultural factors would seem difficult to maintain in the face of these data, unless one wanted to argue that modern development has reduced important cultural differences that existed earlier.

On the other hand, an extremely biological view, arguing for innate emotion programs unaffected by cultural factors, would be equally untenable. Although the cross-cultural differences are smaller than differences between emotions, they nevertheless exist (average eta across all variables = .27 for "emotion" and .12 for "country"; range = .85 to .03 for "emotion", .24 to .05 for "country"). They are particularly pronounced for variables such as intensity and duration of emotion. One of the important tasks in the future will be to disentangle these effects and to find reasonable explanations for the differences found. Given the lack of pertinent theoretical work concerning cultural factors in emotion elicitation and emotional experience this will not be an easy task. We feel, however, that recent progress in our understanding of the mechanisms in emotion elicitation, emotion expression, and emotional control may help to pinpoint the structures and processes that are likely to be affected by a variety of cultural factors. Further work of our group will be directed toward an investigation of these processes.

ACKNOWLEDGMENTS

The data reported in this paper are the result of a large-scale, collaborative, cross-cultural study. Therefore, the authors of this paper consider themselves primarily as reporters of the data collected by researchers in 27 countries. We wish to express our thanks to the large group of collaborators, without whom this project, the "International Survey on Emotion Antecedents and Reactions," would have been impossible, and who must be considered as coauthors, namely (in alphabetical order): Elisha Babad, Hebrew University of Jerusalem, Israel; Cleve Barlow, University of Auckland, New Zealand; Marek Cielecki, University of Warsaw, Poland; Cindy Gallois, University of Queensland, Australia; Jo Kleiven, Oppland Regional College, Norway; Jacques Cosnier, Université II de Lyon, and Monique Allés-Jardel, Université de Provence, Aix-en-Provence, France; Britt-Marie Drottz, University of Göteburg, Sweden; Heiner Ellgring, Max-Planck-Institute for Psychiatry, Munich, West Germany; Alfonso Jimenez Fernandez and José Miguel Fernandez-Dols, University of Madrid, Spain; Tsutomu Kudoh, University of Osaka, Japan; Hing-Keung Ma. Chinese University of Hong Kong, Hong Kong; David Matsumoto, Wright Institute, Berkeley, U.S.A.; Silvia Maurer-Lane and Silvia Friedman, Catholic University Sao Paulo, Brazil; Gerold Mikula, University of Graz, Austria; Alastair Mundy-Castle, University of Lagos, Nigeria; Rauni Myllyniemi, University of Helsinki, Finland; Usha S. Naidu, Tata Institute of Social Sciences, Bombay, India; S. Nyandia-Bundy and R. P. Bundy, University of Zimbabwe, Zimbabwe; Robert F. Norton, American University of Beirut, Lebanon; Dimitra Papadopoulou and D. Markoulis, University of Thessaloniki, Greece; Karl Peltzer, University of Malawi, Malawi; Pio Ricci-Bitti and Dino Giovannini, University of Bologna, Italy; Luis Soczka and Constanza Paul, University of Porto, Portugal; Velina Topalova, Bulgarian Academy of Sciences, Bulgaria; Ad Vingerhoets and J. Hendriksen, Catholic University of Nijmegen, Netherlands; C. Westenholz-Bless, University of Zambia, Zambia. We also thank Eva-Maria Kühn and Elke Schiller for their untiring help in data processing (done centrally in Giessen).

11 COGNITIVE DIMENSIONS OF EMOTION APPRAISAL

One of the most dramatic developments in the recent up-surge of interest in emotion has been the role of cognitive psychology. It may not be exaggerated to claim that the renewed interest in emotion, at least in psychology, is due largely to the massive investment of cognitivists in this area. It has become increasingly clear that cognitive factors involved in situation evaluation and causal attribution are strongly implicated in the differentiation of emotion. In addition, researchers in cognitive psychology have rediscovered the important impact of emotional factors on cognitive processes. In any case, the strong cognitive element in recent theorizing and research has led to a rapprochement of the two areas, both in terms of methods and theories. The positive consequence of this is that many theorists no longer see emotion and cognition as two extreme and incompatible poles. Increasingly, there is a realization that both aspects of human functioning are intricately related to each other (see Leventhal & Scherer, 1987).

One of the important issues for research in this area is the question of which criteria or dimensions are involved in the appraisal or evaluation processes that many theorists see as determining the differentiation of various emotions. I have suggested a component process model of emotion (Scherer, 1981b, 1984a, 1986a) in which I argue for a sequence theory of emotion evaluation involving five stimulus evaluation checks. These checks are listed in Table II.1. Interestingly, quite a large number of psychologists have independently postulated dimensions that are highly comparable to this set of stimulus evaluation checks (see review in Scherer, in press).

In order to evaluate these models, attempts at empirical verification are urgently needed. Unfortunately, the cognitive processes underlying emotion differentiation are very difficult to study objectively. One has to rely on introspection and on self-report. Studies in this direction have been reported by Smith and Ellsworth (1985) and Roseman (1984). We have attempted to use the ISEAR study to investigate the usefulness of the criteria suggested in the component process theory. The questionnaire that was administered in more than 30 countries on five continents (see Part I) included a set of rather simple questions trying to get subjects to report on some of the criteria they used in evaluating the emotion-eliciting event. These questions had been formulated according to the specification of the stimulus evaluation check model. In Chapter 3 (Gehm & Scherer) we use nonmetric analyses of these cross-cultural questionnaire data to obtain a first approximation on the cognitive evaluation patterns involved in emotion elicitation. While we acknowledge the serious limitations of this data set and the rather simpleminded way of assessing evaluation criteria, we can nevertheless attempt to get a first idea of the logical consistency of the prediction model proposed (see Scherer, 1984a, 1986a). The data reported in this chapter not only provide a fair degree of sup-

TABLE II.1
Description of Stimulus Evaluation Checks (SECs)

---

1. *Novelty check.* Evaluating whether there is a change in the pattern of external or internal stimulation, particularly whether a novel event occurred or is to be expected.

2. *Intrinsic pleasantness check.* Evaluating whether a stimulus event is pleasant, inducing approach tendencies, or unpleasant, inducing avoidance tendencies; based on innate feature detectors or on learned associations.

3. *Goal/need significance check.* Evaluating whether a stimulus event is relevant to important goals or needs of the organism (relevance subcheck), whether the outcome is consistent with or discrepant from the state expected for this point in the goal/plan sequence (expectation subcheck), whether it is conducive or obstructive to reaching the respective goals or satisfying the relevant needs (conduciveness check), and how urgently some kind of behavioral response is required (urgency subcheck).

4. *Coping potential check.* Evaluating the causation of a stimulus event (causation subcheck) and the coping potential available to the organism, particularly the degree of control over the event or its consequences (control subcheck), the relative power of the organism to change or avoid the outcome through fight or flight (power subcheck), and the potential for adjustment to the final outcome via internal restructuring (adjustment subcheck).

5. *Norm/self compatibility check.* Evaluating whether the event, particularly an action, conforms to social norms, cultural conventions, or expectations of significant others (external standards subcheck), and whether it is consistent with internalized norms or standards as part of the self-concept or ideal self (internal standards subcheck).

Note. Reproduced from Scherer, 1986a, p. 147. By permission of the American Psychological Association.

port for the theoretical predictions but also raise a number of intriguing questions concerning differences between emotions and between different cultures. We hope that this pilot study can stimulate further attempts at systematic measurement of the cognitive processes underlying the evaluation of emotion-eliciting events.

Obviously, one of the limitations of the questionnaire approach, asking about emotional experiences, is that one depends on the type of situations that happened to be reported. Clearly, this method is unlikely to yield a comprehensive model of the cognitive and symbolic bases of situation evaluation, given that it is improbable that all possible combinations of the underlying criteria will be present in the data.

If one does have a theory or model of the essential variables determining a phenomenon, facet theory is useful to provide a comprehensive empirical description of the domain to be studied. In Chapter 4 (Borg, Staufenbiel, & Scherer), two pilot studies on using facet theory to study the symbolic basis of shame are reported. Briefly, a "mapping sentence" containing all of the factors considered to participate in producing changes in a dependent variable is proposed to structure the empirically observable domain. In line with this mapping sentence situations are created in which the different levels of the major factors are systematically varied. Subjects are requested to imagine experiencing these situations and to indicate the degree of their emotional response. In this way, it becomes possible to study the respective importance of emotion-eliciting cognitive evaluation criteria in a highly systematic fashion. The results of these preliminary studies provide a large number of interesting suggestions for further research.

Studies of the dimensions of the semantic space for emotion-describing verbal labels have a long history. Unfortunately, the dimensions found in these studies are not always comparable, and one can identify a number of serious methodological flaws in the literature to date. One of the most serious problems, as with factor analyses and other scaling procedures generally, is that one is likely to get out what one puts in. In other words, the factors or dimensions found reflect the prior selection by the researcher of linguistic terms used in the similarity analyses. In Chapter 5 (Gehm & Scherer) we are reporting a study in which we attempted to avoid this drawback by selecting a very large number of adjectives. Even more importantly, we attempted to check the possibility of linking the dimensions and clusters found in the similarity analyses of emotion-describing terms to the cognitive criteria likely to be used in the evaluation of emotion-eliciting events. Again, we do not claim for the data reported here to settle the long-standing issue of the dimensions of emotional feeling. However, we do feel that the approach suggested, that is, a more comprehensive selection of emotion-describing terms as well as the attempt to provide a theoretical underpinning for the interpretation of the dimensions found, might be useful for future studies.

3 RELATING SITUATION EVALUATION TO EMOTION DIFFERENTIATION: NONMETRIC ANALYSIS OF CROSS-CULTURAL QUESTIONNAIRE DATA

Theodor L. Gehm
University of Giessen

Klaus R. Scherer
University of Geneva and University of Giessen

In recent years, a large number of cognitive models of emotion have been proposed, mostly by social psychologists, which highlight the importance of particular appraisal dimensions or criteria in the process of antecedent situation evaluation for the differentiation of emotional experience (see, e.g., Frijda, 1986, review in Scherer, in press; Lazarus, Averill, & Opton, 1970; Roseman, 1984; Smith & Ellsworth, 1985). On the whole, there is a remarkable degree of convergence of theorizing in this tradition, lending a high degree of face validity to the claims made. However, so far very few empirical studies have been conducted to test the hypotheses. In several statements of his component process model of emotion, Scherer (1984a, b) has proposed a set of preductions concerning the verbal labels that are likely to be used to describe emotional experiences following particular patterns of stimulus evaluation check outcomes. An example for such a prediction table (taken from Scherer, 1984a) is reproduced in Table 3.1.

While these predictions are fairly specific, there is a serious problem in testing them empirically. The hypothesized evaluation process consists of cognitive or even subcognitive operations in the cortex and in lower brain areas and is thus not directly observable. In addition, these evaluation processes are likely to operate at an extremely high speed and, at least in many cases, in a highly automatic manner. Furthermore, the assumption is that there is not just one pass through the evaluation checks but that, like a radar antenna, there is a continuous process of passes through the evaluation checks with the possibility of constantly changing outcomes.

TABLE 3.1
Hypothetical Information System States Required as Antecedents for Selected Emotions

Stimulus evaluation checks (SEC)	Joy	Fear	Anger	Sadness	Disgust	Shame
I Novelty	expected	unexpected	open	open	open	open
II Intrinsic Pleasantness	pleasant	open	open	unpleasant	very unpleasant	open
III Goal/Need Conduciveness	conducive	obstructive	obstructive	obstructive	irrelevant	open
IV Coping Potential	high	low	high	low	low	low
Va Norm-Compatibility	high	open	low	irrelevant	low	low
Vb Self-Compatibility	high	open	open	irrelevant	irrelevant	highly inconsistent

Source: Scherer, 1984a

62

Because EEG measurements are unlikely to provide information specific to the checks postulated, at least in the near future, verbal report seems to be the only methodological option to assess such stimulus evaluation check outcomes. Obviously this approach is highly limited. One limitation is that only those processes and their outcomes that are accessible to awareness or consciousness can be studied. This excludes the study of unconscious lower-level evaluation, e.g., schematic pattern matching or sensory motor checks in the limbic system or brain stem (see Leventhal & Scherer, 1987). Furthermore, probably only the end result of repeated passing through the evaluation check sequence is accessible to conscious retrieval and thus available for verbal report, given that the intermediate outcomes probably change too rapidly to be accessible.

One possibility of gathering verbal report of cognitive processes that has been used with much success in cognitive psychology consists of asking subjects to "think aloud." This method has been successful because it can be easily elicited by posing specific problems to be solved to subjects in laboratory situations. Unfortunately, this is rarely possible in the study of emotion. Emotions occur spontaneously and unpredictably in real life, and even if a researcher were present under such circumstances, the high degree of self-involvement and the speed with which the emotion process is unfolding would make it rather difficult to get the subject to "evaluate aloud." Because of the many difficulties, including ethical constraints, of producing powerful emotional states in the laboratory, it seems that this interesting method is of little use for the study of emotional experience.

Because the study of the ongoing evaluation process is rendered impossible by its speed, this implies that an assessment of the stimulus evaluation checks *independent* of the resulting emotional response is equally impossible. The emotional state as a result of the pattern of outcomes of evaluation checks has already occurred when we have opportunity to ask the experiencing subject about what is retrievable in awareness concerning the nature of the evaluation process. Obviously, this means that a direct prediction from independently assessed evaluation outcomes to resulting emotional experience is not feasible. Furthermore, because we can rarely study the emotional experience in situ and have to rely on recall of past emotional experiences, we obviously encounter the problem of confounding subjective feeling state characteristics with the post hoc interpretations and rationalizations if we attempt to question a person about the nature of the antecedent evaluation process in addition to the type of emotional experience.

In spite of these dangers, it would seem that this is the only approach open to us in trying to obtain further information on the relationships between antecedent situation evaluation and consequent subjective feeling state. Obviously, asking a person to report the subjective feeling experienced in a particular emotion-eliciting situation *as well as* to report on the various dimensions used in evaluating the situation does not provide an empirical *test* of the predictions made in Table 3.1. However, this procedure does seem to provide at least a possibility to postdict the use of certain emotion labels as a result of prior evaluation outcomes and to check, at a minimum, the logical consistency of the predictions. We can attempt to study whether the way in which the respondents link the state descriptions to particular outcomes of evaluation processes conforms to what the component patterning theory predicts *ought* to have preceded the emotional state. We can use deviations from the predicted patterns to further develop the theory as well as to attempt to establish the generality and universality of the checks postulated in the theory.

As described in Chapter 2, a part of the ISEAR questionnaire study was designed to obtain information relevant to this aim. In addition to asking respondents to report situations in which they had experienced one of seven emotional states described by verbal labels and to indicate the nature of their emotional responses in a number of modalities, we asked about the way in which they had evaluated the emotion antecedent event. In this chapter we attempt to investigate the extent to which the relationships found between the reported evaluation outcomes and the verbal label that had elicited the particular emotion report correspond to the predictions ventured in Table 3.1. As mentioned, we obviously do not consider this procedure as an empirical test of the hypotheses in a strong sense, given the limitations to the independence of the data. However, we believe that this approach may help to strengthen the plausibility of the predictions and to help refine the model.

METHOD

Formulation of Questions

As shown in Chapter 2, one question each was used for the five stimulus evaluation checks proposed by Scherer (1984a, b), with the exception of check five, for which two questions were used. For ease of reference we reproduce those questions from the ISEAR questionnaire (see Appendix C) in Table 3.2.

Obviously, these questions are by far too simplistic to render justice to the complexity of the stimulus evaluation checks proposed, including the various subchecks. However, given that the ISEAR questionnaire was designed to be administered to a very large number of respondents of different educational background in many different cultures across the

TABLE 3.2
Items of the ISEAR-questionnaire formulated as rudimentary
representations of the stimulus evaluation checks in Scherer's
component-process-model of emotion differentiation

Check I: Novelty-Check
Now please think back to the situation or event that caused your emotion. Did you *expect* this situation to occur?
1.) not at all   2.) a little   3.) very much   0.) not applicable

---

Check II: Intrinsic Pleasantness-Check
Did you find the event itself *pleasant or unpleasant*?
1.) pleasant   2.) neutral   3.) unpleasant   0.) not applicable

---

Check III: Goal/Need-Significance-Check
How important was the event for your *goals, needs or desires at the time it happened*. Did it *help* or *hinder* you to follow your plans or to achieve your aims?
1.) it helped   2.) it didn't matter   3.) it hindered   0.) not applicable

---

Check IV: Coping Potential Check
How did you evaluate your *ability to act on or to cope with the event and its consequences* when you were first confronted with this situation? Check one, the most appropriate, of the following:
1. _____ I did not think that any action was necessary
2. _____ I believed that I could positively influence the event and change the consequences
3. _____ I believed that I could escape from the situation or avoid negative consequences
4. _____ I pretended that nothing important had happened and tried to think of something else
5. _____ I saw myself as powerless and dominated by the event and its consequences

---

Check V: Norm/Self Compatibility Check
Subcheck a: Compatibility with external standards
If the event was caused by your own or someone else's behavior, would this behavior itself be judged as *improper* or *immoral* by your acquaintances?
1.) not at all   2.) a little   3.) very much   0.) not applicable

Subcheck b: Compatibility with internal standards
How did this event affect your *feelings about yourself*, such as your *self-esteem* or your *self-confidence*?
1.) negatively   2.) not at all   3.) positively   0.) not applicable

---

world, both the number and the complexity of questions had to be extremely limited. In a number of pretests and pilot studies, which included various back translation checks (see, e.g., Scherer, Summerfield, & Wallbott, 1983; Scherer, Wallbott, & Summerfield, 1986), the questions evolved into their final form.

Procedure

Details of the research procedure are described in Chapter 2. For the purpose of this analysis we used data from the following countries (the respective N is given in parentheses after each country): India (68), Zambia (119), Malawi (75), Zimbabwe (99), Nigeria (77), Botswana (82), Brazil (59), Lebanon (68), Portugal (88), Poland (87), Greece (71), Bulgaria (73), Spain (78), Israel (49), Hong Kong (83), Italy (98), New Zealand (61), Austria (69), Netherlands (71), Japan (199), Switzerland (113), France (72), Finland (76), Australia (95), West Germany (117), Sweden (84), Norway (36), United States (81).

The analysis of the cross-cultural differences in this data set is ongoing. However, the preliminary analyses showed an interesting relationship between various features of the emotional reaction, such as duration and intensity of the emotional experience, and the gross national product of the country concerned (according to which the countries are ordered in the preceding list). This suggested possible differences in the nature of the emotional process and the emotional experience between highly industrialized, "rich" countries and rural, "poor" countries (mostly developing countries). Therefore, we decided to run the analyses subsequently described for two independent samples of the overall study by dividing the set of countries studied at the median of the gross national product into rich and poor countries. So the sample of respondents from "poor" countries came from India, Zambia, Malawi, Zimbabwe, Nigeria, Botswana, Brazil, Lebanon, Portugal, Poland, Greece, Bulgaria, Spain, and Israel and the other samples from the "rich" countries—Hong Kong, Italy, New Zealand, Austria, Netherlands, Japan, Switzerland, France, Finland, Australia, West Germany, Sweden, Norway, and the United States.

As mentioned in Chapter 2, data were obtained for joy, fear, anger, sadness, disgust, shame, and guilt, and there were elaborate predictions for the first six of these (see Table 3.1).

As the questionnaire responses referring to situational antecedents of the emotions are qualitative and distinct, and the data available are not metric, we chose nonmetrical analyses to determine the emotion-specific patterns of situational antecedents. Using these methods one can quantify how far the outcome of one or several nonmetric variable(s) has an influence on the outcome of one (or several) predicted variable(s) and describe the relative importance of each predictor variable in a comprehensive model. Statistically speaking, the evaluation of situation antecedents are looked upon as (independent) variables "predicting" a particular emotion, and typical combinations of the values of these predicting variables discriminate each emotion from the others.

A number of approaches to the causal analysis of nonmetric data were proposed during the last decade, particularly in the field of social sciences (e.g., Goodman & Magidson, 1978). Virtually all of these techniques can be treated as modifications of ordinary least square regression analysis.

They divide the sample of data into subpopulations that are homogeneous in respect to the value of the independent variables and then examine the distribution of the dependent variable within each subpopulation.

For the present data set we chose the GSK-method proposed by Grizzle, Starmer, & Koch (1969) because it offers a rather general approach. There are several advantages to using this method with our data: Firstly, this (linear) approach leads to relatively stable results even if the data are not distributed equally for different outcomes of the variables (which is likely to be the case for our data). Secondly, using this approach one can examine hierarchical as well as nonhierarchical models. (In a hierarchical model a higher-order effect cannot be present unless all lower-order effects are also included in the model). Thus the influence of a special constellation of situational components for the elicitation of an emotion can be quantified.

The data were analyzed using the NONMET statistical package (Kritzer, 1982). In contrast to most other programs used for analyzing frequency tables, not only can relations between dependent and independent variables (symmetrical approach) be revealed, but one can also determine the effect of each outcome of a predictor variable for the outcome of each predicted variable. Thus one can easily describe which particular outcome of a situational check leads to a specific emotional experience.

In running these analyses we faced a number of minor problems. First, it was evident that our frequency tables often contain zeros or very low numbers (because certain outcomes of checks are rather unlikely for some emotions). As the NONMET algorithm requires about 20 to 30 cases in each cell and low numbers or zeros are tolerable only to a very limited extent, we had to exclude some categories that were used very infrequently. Nonetheless, a bias of the significance value could not be excluded completely in every case. Second, all seven emotions were judged by the same persons, and thus the data analyzed for different emotions cannot be considered as statistically independent. This problem was solved by replicating the analyses yielding significant models, using a reduced set of data and testing the models derived in a second run in which the information of only one emotion (determined by chance selection) was evaluated for each subject.

As the component process model of emotion differentiation takes into account many variables simultaneously, several analysis steps had to be performed. We chose the following strategy: in a first run it was separately determined for every predictor variable (every check) which combination of the four or (in the case of the coping check) five possible outcomes was most useful to distinguish each emotion from the others. In our case "most typical" did not necessarily mean "most frequent": For example, all situations except the ones eliciting joy were most frequently judged as being unpleasant. Nonetheless, the number of persons who judged the situations evoking shame or guilt as not describable in terms of pleasantness at all was relatively large. Thus, in spite of the general tendency to experience these emotions as unpleasant, for statistical and theoretical considerations we chose the alternative "not applicable" for the further analyses.

This step of determining emotion-specific outcomes of each check first led to an enormous reduction of the models to be tested in the second run (in which we simultaneously considered the outcomes of all the checks). But taking into account that such multiple predicting models may include not only the effect of each predicting variable but also effects of interactions between these predictors, many different models may be used to predict an emotion. Therefore—according to the strategy proposed by Kuechler (1979)—we determined the most appropriate multiple predicting model in the following manner: First we tested models containing *all* the combinations and interactions between the predicting variables (so-called saturated models). Then we tried to achieve greater economy by eliminating as many interactions as possible (while maintaining overall significance). If this proved to be impossible, we dropped one of the predictors, that is, the outcomes of one check, and tried the same procedure again. This procedure resulted in the most economic (in terms of a minimal number of interactions between predictors) but still comprehensive (in terms of many predictors taken into account) prediction model for each emotion. The significance of such a model is ascertained by testing the hypothesis that the pattern of data contains a significant error. Thus in contrast to most other statistical procedures, a model is considered to fit the empirical data if the significance level of the Chi^2 due to error is *greater than* the usual .05. (For further details of the procedure see Kritzer, 1982.) A comprehensive example including the main features of this technique is presented in Kuechler & Wides (1981).

RESULTS

The results of the nonmetrical analyses are shown in Table 3.3.

It should be recalled that we attempted to identify the constellation of answer alternatives that significantly differentiates a particular emotion from all other emotions. Consequently, Table 3.3 lists those answer alternatives by number (please refer to Table 3.2 for the text of the questions and the answer alternatives) which, as a complete pattern, differ from the typical answer alternative constellations for the other emotions. It should be noted that we report only the most economical model even though other models or constellations were also significant. Below the

TABLE 3.3

Patterns of typical situational antecedents of seven emotions. Numbers of typical response alternatives refer to answer alternatives in Table 3.2. Interactions in the prediction model are indicated as combination of the Roman numbers of the respective checks.

check	Joy poor	Joy rich	Fear poor	Fear rich	Anger poor	Anger rich	Sadness poor	Sadness rich	Disgust poor	Disgust rich	Shame poor	Shame rich	Guilt poor	Guilt rich
I		1		1	1	1								
II	1							3,2			2,0	2,0		
III			2,0	2,0	3	3	3	3	2,0	2,0	2,0	2,0	2,0	2,0
IV			5,3	5,3	2	2	5	5	1,3,4,5	1,3,4,5	3,4	3,4	2,3	2,3
Va			1,0	1,0	3,2	3,2	0	0	3	3	2	2	2	2
Vb					2	2	0	0	2,0	2,0	1	1	1	1
Sign. Inter-actions			III,Va	III,Va / IV,Va / Va,Vb / I,Vb		I,III / III,IV / III,Vb / Va,Vb	IV,Va / Va,Vb / III,Va	IV,Va / Va,Vb	III,IV / III,Vb / IV,Va / IV,Vb / Va,Vb	III,Va / III,Vb / IV,Vb / Va,Vb			III,Vb / IV,Vb	III,Vb
Chi² due to error			.4732	.0802	.2606	.1509	.6412	.2323	.1362	.2077	.8144	.2281	.5340	.0838

69

list of main effects in Table 3.3 (with the numbers of the typical answer alternatives), we list significant interaction, that is, cases in which the joint occurrence of particular types of alternatives in many questionnaires contributed significantly to the power of a model. The last row of Table 3.3 contains the Chi² values indicating the overall goodness of fit of the model. It should be kept in mind, that, as noted previously, a higher value indicates greater significance.

We will first turn to a review of the results for the individual emotions.

Joy

As one might expect, joy as the only positive emotion in the list of seven differs most notably from the other six emotions in the response to the question concerning the pleasantness of the event. The contribution of this variable to the significant differentiation of joy from the other emotions is so strong that little is added when other variables are introduced into the model. It is generally the case that situations eliciting joy were also described as helpful for one's plans, as being subject to positive influence by oneself, and as being in agreement with one's external and internal standards. Yet, a model containing all of these checks could be considered as overdetermined; a combination of several predictors could not explain more of the variance than the single variable of pleasantness.

Unfortunately, it is highly likely that respondents mainly used the pleasantness description to refer to their *response* rather than reporting on the *intrinsic* pleasantness of the event itself (as required by the theoretical notion contained in the intrinsic pleasantness check). Although the question on this check did ask respondents to indicate whether they found the "event *itself*" pleasant or unpleasant, it is highly likely that most respondents did not make this fine distinction between the stimulus-bound, intrinsic pleasantness and the overall pleasantness of the response or reaction. Thus, this result for joy has to be interpreted with great caution. It is unlikely that in the actual evaluation process the intrinsic pleasantness aspect has as powerful a role as is suggested by these data. In this case, we have a very powerful demonstration of the difficulty of getting respondents to discriminate between specific aspects of their cognitive evaluation on the one hand, and their responses or reactions in various domains, including subjective feeling, on the other hand. We feel that the very rudimentary nature of the questions used in this study could not do justice to this problem, particularly in the case of intrinsic pleasantness. Thus, we do not discuss the relationship of these results to the predictions listed in Table 3.1.

Fear

Before looking at the results in detail, it should be noted that because of the different connotations of fear-related terms in various languages, we cannot distinguish very clearly between anxiety/worry and fear/terror. Both varieties of this class of emotions are likely to be represented in the situations we collected. We had predicted that fear would occur when highly relevant events that are unexpected and that obstruct plans occur in situations where the person has a very low coping potential, in particular, low power. There are some interesting deviations from these expectations in the pattern of data for fear. Although, as predicted, respondents report that they had little power and the escape was often the only response alternative, quite frequently (in comparison to other emotions) respondents reported that the event did not hinder their plans. Rather, they thought that the event did not matter or that this criterion was not applicable. This raises an interesting issue. Apparently, fear-producing events take such significance for a person that any concern with ongoing goals or plans is suspended. The event and its consequences are not evaluated in terms of those concerns. The fear-producing event seems to raise a more central concern, that of survival or bodily integrity. It is possible, then, that there is a dramatic switch in terms of the priority of concerns whenever very basic "goals" such as survival or bodily integrity are endangered. Apparently, we do not consciously conceive of these very basic concerns as goals or plans. In the biological sense of survival as one of the "goals" of an organism, a fear-producing event thus would seem to be obstructive. However, in terms of conscious representation of the evaluation process, such events do not seem to be considered as relevant to ongoing plans or goals.

As expected, neither external, social norms, nor internal standards, such as self-esteem, are involved in fear-producing situation evaluations. Fear-producing events are apparently unrelated to this dimension of moral evaluation.

Interestingly, we do find a difference for our two samples for fear. For the rich countries, fear-evoking events are usually described as occurring unexpectedly, and there are a large number of interactions, which is not true for the poor countries. We can only speculate on the reasons for this difference. It might be possible that fear-producing situations, or at least anxiety- or worry-inducing situations, occur more frequently in poor countries, which would account for the fact that respondents in those countries might be more prepared for such events to happen. Many of the interactions in the case of the rich countries concern the fact that the events do not seem to be related to ongoing plans or to external or internal standards. Possibly, this might indicate that fear-producing events are seen as more arbitrary, imposed from the outside, unrelated to any predictable agent in the case of industrialized, rich countries. It may be that there is generally a higher need for control and predictability of events in these countries, explaining the explicit reference to the fact that fear-producing events cannot be evaluated on the basis of personal or social responsibility or other sources of predictability.

Anger

For both samples anger is caused by unexpected, hindering, and improper or immoral events. Yet, these events do not seem to be too overpowering: Among the various coping alternatives mentioned, the alternative of positively influencing or changing the situation is the most frequent one. As the events that caused the emotion are usually judged as immoral but not afflicting one's self-esteem, one might say that the anger-producing events are typically caused by factors completely beyond the individual's sphere of influence. As for fear and sadness (see the following section), the constellation of situational antecedents of anger turned out to be more complex for participants from rich countries. Thus, to evoke anger certain conditions are usually fulfilled at the same time: The emotion-eliciting event has to be unexpected *and* hindering, improper *and* still not affecting one's self-esteem, hindering but still changeable. Summing up these conditions and taking into account the relatively small differences between the characteristic patterns of both samples, one might say that anger is generally elicited by unexpected, yet surmountable external interruptions.

Sadness

The pattern found for sadness was again very similar for both samples. Sadness is determined by some hindering event that makes one feel powerless and dominated. This external strain is so powerful that significantly more often than for other emotions, moral standards or internal self-ideal standards are considered inapplicable. Only if these antecedents are present in this specific constellation is sadness likely to occur. As for fear, the outcome of the novelty check is important only for participants from the rich countries. They usually judge sadness as being evoked by some expected but nonetheless uncontrollable event. Again, this might be interpreted as a greater need for controlling the situation in this population. Sadness, then, can be seen as the emotion of being overwhelmed by some completely uncontrollable event.

Disgust

For disgust we had expected an evaluation of very low intrinsic pleasantness, discrepant from expectation, and low conduciveness to plans. In addition, the expectation was for low external norm compatibility, that is,

a type of behavior that is considered to be improper. The results generally support these predictions, except for the fact that the pleasantness check,
which was expected to be very important, did not turn out to be significant. This may well be due to the fact that the intrinsic pleasantness was
not very well captured by our question (see previous discussion) as well
as by the low discriminability between the negative emotions, which were
all judged as involving highly unpleasant events. Thus, this result does
not seem to be a disconfirmation of our hypotheses. It is interesting that
disgust events are seen as quite external, with little reference to the self,
even though the behavior or the event is considered to be very improper.
In general, like fear events, disgust events seem to be imposed by the environment, and they are rarely evaluated in terms of conscious plans and
cannot be influenced in a positive way. It would seem that one important
implication of this is that disgust experiences are fairly transitory: One
encounters a disgusting event, but there do not seem to be long-term consequences. We think the extraordinarily high number of interactions that
are necessary to predict disgust are worth mentioning: Obviously, disgust
is evoked only as the result of the evaluation of a relatively complex pattern of situational characteristics.

Shame and Guilt

Predictions are difficult for shame and guilt. The assumption was that
for both of these emotions the eliciting event would consist of one's own
behavior, which would be seen as highly relevant and discrepant as well
as abstractive in terms of one's own goals or needs. The decisive criterion,
however, is the evaluation of the behavior as highly incompatible with
both internal and external norms (with the implicit assumption that guilt
might apply more directly to external, shame to internal norms). The
results of the present study underline the importance of the norm compatibility check. Both shame and guilt are seen as being elicited by improper or immoral behaviors that are also in violation of one's internal
standards of behavior. In this respect there is no clear difference between
shame and guilt. In both cases the events are seen as being unrelated to
ongoing plans, just as for fear and disgust — they just seem to happen to
the person. However, in contrast to fear-inducing events, these lead not
to a suspension of ongoing events but to a parallel existence of ongoing
plan-related activity and shame or guilt feelings. Interestingly, neither
shame- nor guilt-inducing events are seen as involving the evaluation of
pleasantness. Even though they are clearly negative emotions, according
to our data they are not necessarily subsumed with these in terms of an
unpleasantness judgment.

The most obvious difference between shame and guilt in our data, in addition to the fact that there are more interactions in the case of guilt (which is difficult to interpret) is that of the coping mechanism judged as appropriate or possible: Whereas denying seems to be the typical solution for shame-inducing experiences, guilt-eliciting events are considered to be amenable to positive influence or at least to allow escape. It is possible that the possibility of positive influence implies the notion of "making good" ("repairing the damage done"). For shame, this is not the case to such an extent. One might argue that this is due to the fact that the self is "tarnished" once shame has occurred, something that cannot be easily rectified. This may also involve the fact that shame is usually dependent on the public exposure of one's frailty or failing, whereas guilt may be something that remains a secret with us, no one else knowing of our breach of social norms or of our responsibility for an immoral act. In terms of the difficult problem of differentiating between shame and guilt, these results may point to the major importance of public exposure for differentiating the two self-related emotions.

Summaries of the Individual Checks

Before turning to a more general evaluation of the significance of the present results, it may be useful to look at the role that the various checks have played in differentiating the emotions in this study. As we mentioned previously, the questions used to infer the outcomes of the different checks were highly simplified and did not allow us to obtain very differentiated information concerning the functioning of the respective check. In some cases, the formulation of the question may have even been ambiguous and may not have yielded the required information. Yet, on the whole, we feel that the set of data reported previously represents a useful first approach toward the empirical study of a theoretically postulated model of evaluation checks. Obviously, the present data do not lend themselves to drawing conclusions concerning the postulated sequence of these checks. It is possible, however, to make some general remarks concerning the particular checks. As a criterion, we use the importance of the respective check for the differentiation of the emotions studied.

The novelty check is particularly important for the emotions fear and anger. Here, the eliciting event is most often described as highly unexpected. In a way, the novelty check could be described as an initializing procedure, inasmuch as the assumption is that some type of new event needs to happen in order to elicit an emotion. By definition, this should produce a positive outcome of the novelty check. Thus, even for emotions like sadness, where unexpectedness does not seem to matter, there must have been a novel event at some point (e.g., the information that a relative died). What seems to be tapped by the question we used is the abruptness of onset and the degree of probability with which such an event could be reasonably expected. These, rather than the sheer detection of change in the environment, may well be the major criteria of the novelty check. In other words, what may differentiate emotions characterized by a novelty outcome of the first check might be the effect of the suddenness of onset and the degree of preparation for adjustment (linked to the degree of probability or expectation) to such an event. It might be interesting to speculate why the novelty check seemed to be somewhat more important for the rich compared to the poor countries. One possibility is that the need to control and predict events strongly results in more noticeable negative emotional effects of abruptly encountered unexpected events.

Our question concerning the second check did not allow us to obtain information relevant to intrinsic pleasantness. All evidence points to the fact that this question was answered in a very general way by subjects, referring to the overall positive or negative feeling tone of the experience. Consequently, very little can be said about the results, given that the distinction between positive and negative emotions in such general terms is rather trivial. It would be very important for further work to disentangle the evaluations of intrinsic pleasantness residing in the stimulus or event itself, and the overall response characteristics of feeling good or "positive" as a result of the complete evaluation sequence.

Compared to the first two checks, the remaining three checks were relatively much more important in terms of differentiating the seven emotions studied. The question as to whether the event helped or hindered reaching one's goals, related to the goal conduciveness subcheck, showed, as expected, that this check seems to differentiate between positive and negative emotions. Some kind of hindrance and frustration seems to be the basis of most negative emotions. The pervasiveness and strength of this effect renders understandable and justifiable the insistence on the role of interruption of ongoing plans found in the literature (e.g., Mandler, 1984; Simon, 1967). Interestingly enough, disgust-, shame-, and guilt-inducing events were perceived differently by our subjects. In these cases, they very often indicated that the dimension of helping or hindering ongoing plans was not relevant for their evaluation. We argued above that, at least in the case of guilt and shame, the eliciting factors are related to overarching and enduring norms and values as well as to self-concept and are thus not directly linked to momentarily changing plans. For disgust, on the other hand, one might assume that disgusting events are often seen as external intrusions, which are disagreeable but which do not really affect the ongoing course of action. While they may distract from pursuing goal-directed action, they do not seem to directly impinge on the latter.

Our results point to the central role for the coping potential check in differentiating the emotions. In most cases we found a rather specific constellation of coping alternatives for the emotions studied. We feel justified, therefore, in assuming that the evaluation of the response alternatives available to the individual are as important, if not more important, than the nature of the event eliciting the emotional reaction. This finding also highlights the adaptive significance of emotion, suggested repeatedly in this volume. As expected, the norm/self compatibility check was particularly important for shame and guilt. However, events and behaviors were frequently considered to be "improper" for other emotions as well, pointing toward a more general role for this check.

CONCLUSION

These results would seem to encourage further work along the lines indicated in this study. Clearly, the use of a highly streamlined questionnaire to be used with very large numbers of subjects across many cultures does not seem to be particularly suitable to get at the fine details of the cognitive evaluation process, and the particular checks and subchecks postulated in the component process model. The present results show that for many of the checks, we need to develop much more refined questioning procedures in order to get at important details of the evaluation process. It seems possible to use structured interviews, allowing a detailed discussion of particular points with the respondent, as the next step. Expert-system-based computer interviewing procedures could be used as a controlled form of questioning subjects about their cognitive evaluation processes. On the basis of the results of such studies one might eventually be able to construct a more detailed questionnaire to be used with a large number of subjects, possibly in different cultures.

We believe that it is vital to take into account individual differences and cultural differences in emotion-producing cognitive evaluation processes. While emotion is clearly in many respects a universal phenomenon with strong biological roots as well as with a fairly high degree of sociocultural patterning, it is one of the major hypotheses of the sequence model of emotion differentiation presented here that the criteria used in the evaluation tend to be highly specific for individuals and social groups. Consequently, it would seem difficult to understand emotion differentiation on an aggregate level. Thus, in future work we need not only to demonstrate individual and cultural differences but also to try to determine the sources of these differences (in terms of the underlying criteria used in the evaluation). Unfortunately, we have very little to go on so far, given that both in terms of conceptualization and measurement instruments we find very little in the literature that would seem relevant to issues such as differential control and power attributions, or their underlying motivations (e.g., specific need for control and/or power in different individuals and cultures). The task of developing the concepts and instruments that are necessary to better understand the process of emotion-eliciting event evaluation requires an interdisciplinary approach. Leads from the psychology of cognition and motivation as well as from social and personality psychology need to be integrated with approaches that are proper to the psychology of emotion. Similarly, work that is currently being done in sociology and anthropology (Collins, 1984; Gordon, 1984; Heelas, 1984; Levy, 1984; Lutz, 1986) will need to be integrated much more thoroughly than has been the case to date.

4 ON THE SYMBOLIC BASIS OF SHAME

Ingwer Borg
University of Giessen

Thomas Staufenbiel
University of Giessen

Klaus R. Scherer
University of Geneva and University of Giessen

INTRODUCTION

One of the most intriguing questions in the psychology of emotion concerns the process of emotion differentiation. Which are the factors that determine whether a particular event will produce anger, joy, shame, fear, or sadness? Many of the classic theories of emotion do not address this issue directly. The importance of evaluation or appraisal processes was first underlined by Arnold (1960a,b) and Lazarus (1966). In recent years, theorists interested in the differentiation of emotion have turned their attention increasingly to the study of the cognitive (and subcognitive) processes that are involved in event evaluation, trying to determine the dimensions or criteria that are responsible for eliciting differential emotional responses.

While some of these approaches have been mostly theoretical (Abelson, 1983; Dahl & Stengel, 1978; De Rivera, 1977), others have tried to make use of empirical research procedures to test theoretical assumptions or to inductively discover dimensions or criteria underlying emotion-eliciting evaluation processes. Because the object of study concerns cognitive, that is, internal processes, the main access for research consists in asking subjects to report their experience and to reflect upon the cognitive processes that have brought about the feeling state. While self-report measures are often beset by serious methodological problems, the nature of the processes to be studied render this procedure obligatory, given that so far we do have a methodology to assess cognitive processes independent of verbal report (Scherer, 1986b; Wallbott & Scherer, 1985a; see Overview of Part I in this volume). Two major approaches have been used in the research literature concerned with the study of cognitive dimensions of emotion elicitation: (1) asking subjects about emotion-eliciting events that really happened to them and attempting to obtain as much information as possible about the nature of the evaluation process (Averill, 1982; Scherer, Wallbott, & Summerfield, 1986; Smith & Ellsworth, 1985) (this approach is illustrated in further detail in Chapter 3 in this volume); (2) presenting subjects with stories or vignettes and asking them to indicate what a person to whom the described event would happen would feel, that is, which type of emotion is most likely to be evoked by the type of situation described (Roseman, 1984; Schwartz & Weinberger, 1980; Weiner, 1985).

In this chapter we are primarily concerned with the second approach. The advantage of using a vignette method consists in the fact that the emotion-eliciting situations are standardized, that is, all subjects are exposed to exactly the same situation, which is, of course, not the case when actual events experienced by different individuals are studied. Furthermore, the vignette approach allows us to systematically vary different factors of the situations and thereby the likely cognitive dimensions or criteria that will be involved in evaluating the described events. For example, in the studies by Weiner and his group (Weiner, 1985), variables such as ability and effort or controllability are systematically varied in order to study the effect of different causal attributions on the emotions elicited. In this way, an experimental approach to what is otherwise a highly individualistic phenomenon becomes possible.

One critique that is often leveled against the vignette method is that subjects are asked to put themselves into a situation and to imagine how they themselves or another person would feel. The argument is that this procedure is likely to result in stereotypical responses at the very best and pure artifact at the worst. Furthermore, it is argued that the imaginary responses described by the subjects are unlikely to have any relation to the responses subjects would show if they actually found themselves in the situation. This point of view seems to imply that spontaneous evaluations of emotion-eliciting events are somehow microgenetically pure and unique, affected only by the impressions of the moment. It can be shown for many domains of psychology, however, that perception, cognition, and behavior are to a large extent affected by stored symbolic representations of knowledge, prior experiences, social norms, and other schemata of this sort. For example, even something as fleeting as the experience of time seems to be affected by some sort of symbolic representation of experienced time (Fraisse, 1981; Galinat & Borg, 1987). A distinction between the spontaneously perceived or cognized information and a symbolic representation of information pertaining to the object cognized seems to be useful (Galinat & Borg, 1987). Equally, in social psychology there has been increasing interest in "social representation," a notion that goes back to Dürkheim, since it can be easily shown that social behavior is strongly influenced by shared, symbolically represented social knowledge (Moscovici & Farr, 1986).

We argue that emotional experience is similarly affected by symbolic representation of emotion-producing events and the dimensions or criteria used in evaluation. As in other domains, it is highly likely that these symbolic representations will influence the evaluation process in an actual emotion-eliciting situation. It would seem that this assumption can be particularly well defended in the case of emotion-producing cognitive appraisals, inasmuch as the values or criteria against which events are judged, such as the relationship of an event to an important goal or social value of the person, self-images, etc., are at least in part stable reference points and must therefore be stored in different parts of the central nervous system (see Leventhal & Scherer, 1987, for a discussion of the different levels that are likely to be involved). At least those emotion representations that are stored on the conceptual or symbolic level should be amenable to verbal report. Given the involvement of emotion representation in the actual emotion-producing process, it would seem reasonable to assume that judgments based on the symbolic representation bear a rather strong resemblance to actual evaluation judgments that would be occurring in natural situations. It is of course possible that these judgments are somewhat "stereotypical" in nature, due to the fact that it is indeed *shared* knowledge that operates in a culture which influences all our behavior, including emotion (see Gordon, 1981, 1984; Levy, 1984, on social and cultural effects on emotion).

While the method of obtaining judgments on imagined situations with systematically varied features seems highly promising, then, one of the shortcomings in the literature is that the complete domain of potential criteria or dimensions is rarely studied in a systematic and principled manner. We have suggested using facet theory (Borg, 1979; Guttman, 1959) as the basis for a more complete theoretical model of emotion-eliciting variables (Borg, Scherer, & Staufenbiel, 1986; Scherer, 1983). This approach is not only useful for a systematic description of the potentially emotion-inducing events, it also provides the basis for the development of a theory about the empirical structure of observations in the framework of the definitional system. In this chapter we use the emotions of embarrassment and shame as an example to demonstrate the use of facet theory in the study of cognitive processes underlying emotional experience. Before turning to the descriptions of the major assumptions of this approach, we briefly survey some of the factors that have been proposed in the literature as being responsible for shame induction.

Antecedent Conditions for Embarrassment and Shame

Shame is generally considered to be one of the most important "social" emotions because it tends to assure the adherence to social norms without requiring the use of external sanctions. This seems to be achieved by an internalization of the social norms and values that are linked to self-esteem. Because self-esteem depends to a large degree on the evaluation by reference groups (see the important contributions of symbolic interactionist theories, (Cooley, 1922; Mead, 1934), shame seems to imply a danger to our self-esteem based on a feared negative evaluation by others because of one's own shortcomings relative to important social values and norms. This essential core of the shame concept, of which embarrassment seems to be a mild form, has been expressed very cogently in Aristotle's Rhetoric (Aristoteles, 1935, p. 138). Much of what has been written about shame seems to confirm this core statement. Most often the discrepancy between a certain type of individual and the demands of the ideal self, resulting in a lowering of self-esteem, are underlined (Gaylin, 1981; Izard, 1977; Lynd, 1961; Piers & Singer, 1971; Solomon, 1976; Wicker, Payne, & Morgan, 1983). In terms of the symbolic representation mentioned previously, we can assume the self ideal to be represented by conceptual cognitive elements, and the presumed evaluation by a reference group as the representation of the meaning of one's own behavior for reference group members in relation to a set of shared social values. A comparison between the conceptual elements of the self ideal and the other-evaluation representation would yield slight embarrassment or shame, depending on the degree of discrepancy, the strength of the ego ideal, the importance of the values affected, and the importance of the reference group.

Self-esteem depends on the degree to which these values are realized in the behavior of a person, and one can argue that pride will result if the degree of realization exceeds some means, shame when it falls short of what can be expected minimally of a member of the reference group. As mentioned, it would seem that values can differ in importance and that the degree to which self-esteem is affected would depend on the relative importance of the respective value.

Reviews of shame-inducing experiences (see for example Izard, 1977, p. 397–399) show that many different types of shortcomings can produce the experience of shame, for example, clumsy behavior, moral failure, failure at tasks. Presumably, these different types of inadequate behavior are linked to different types of values toward which a member of a reference group would need to strive in order to be accepted and esteemed. Obviously, these values can vary greatly between different reference groups (see following). In our culture, there seems to be a standard set of values such as intellectual achievement, moral rectitude, social skills, and dominance.

Whereas the major determinants of shame discussed so far seem consensual for most theorists, there is less agreement concerning the responsibility for the shame-inducing behavior. Whereas Gaylin (1981, p. 76) and Solomon (1976, p. 306) argue that the person must feel himself or herself responsible for the behavior in order to feel shame, one could counter that everyday experience would argue against this assumption. People seem to feel shame even when their own behavior has been very normal, for example, in situations where external events intervene (as in the case of a toilet door suddenly opening to a crowded hallway because of a mechanical failure). Studies reviewed by Weiner (1985) support the notion that controllability of an event does not seem to be a necessary prerequisite to feeling shame (contrary to guilt). These researchers found that shame is often expected to result from lack of ability, which is in itself obviously not controllable by the individual. However, what does seem to be important is the personal locus of the attribution by the reference group; that is, the shame-experiencing person must be convinced that the behavior or event is indeed attributed to him or her by the others. To use the example mentioned before, failure at a task must be seen to be attributed to lack of ability rather than bad luck in order to induce shame.

Related to the problem of responsibility is the question of whether one can feel shame for behavior of others. It seems not infrequent that one feels shame because of the behavior of someone else, usually someone close. The very existence of the verbal formula "to be ashamed of someone" seems to point toward the existence of shame induced by the behavior of others. Again, it is obviously not because of a personal responsibility for the behavior itself that shame is felt in these cases. Somehow, the degree of affiliation to the other person, the impression of being perceived as being in a unit relationship with this other person must be at the root of this variant of shame. Although this is a fascinating issue, the factors involved seem to be extraordinarily complex (see Borg, Scherer & Staufenbiel, 1986). We do not pursue this issue in the present chapter.

Purpose of the Study

In a series of studies that we conducted at Giessen University we attempted to use facet theory to systematically investigate some of the features, dimensions, or criteria, which we will call *facets* in the following, that distinguish different types of shame behavior.

Mapping Sentence and Items

In this section, we discuss the facets that determine beliefs on the elicitation of embarrassment and shame. That is, given a set of different situations as described in the form of written vignettes, is it possible to predict how embarrassed or ashamed subjects believe they would feel in these situations?

In order to study this question systematically, one first needs a definition that specifies the bounds of the universe of situations to be studied. This definition reads: "A situation in which a person p is involved belongs to the universe of embarrassment/shame-inducing situations of p if and only if a system of values of some reference group is violated and the violation is or can be perceived by at least one member of this reference group."

The logical next step is to structure this universe by defining facets that conceptually distinguish different types of situations. Many such facets are possible if one is interested only in systematic classification. However, in the context of facet theory, any such facet not only introduces conceptual categories, it is also an empirical hypothesis. That is, of all possible facets that could be selected we choose only those where we have reason to hypothesize that the conceptual structure they induce in the universe of situations is, in some way or another, mirrored in the empirical judgments of the subjects on how much embarrassment or shame these situations are likely to elicit.

A very simple correspondence between the definitional and the empirical structure of the situations would be, for example, if the situations defined to be of type X lead to less embarrassment than those in category Y. Many other possibilities exist, and some of them will become relevant later.

One possibility for structuring the universe of shame-eliciting situations is to simply list a number of facets as in Borg and colleagues (1986), where the facets "Who is the actor in the situation?", "content of the violated values," and "actor's responsibility for violation" were distinguished. Yet, although these facets proved useful, to some extent, in organizing the empirical observations in a nontrivial way, a simple listing of facets is suboptimal for design, hypothesis development, and empirical testing. A better way is to incorporate such facets into a mapping sentence, which makes it clearer how the facets are related to each other. The mapping sentence in Figure 4.1 builds on the findings by Borg and colleagues (1986).

The mapping sentence distinguishes the universes of persons, situations, and responses. The person universe is facetted only in a most primitive way (male–female) to illustrate the general principle to facetize this universe. The response universe is the range of the mapping sentence, that is, what follows after the mapping arrow.

The content universe comprises those 10 facets that we thought most

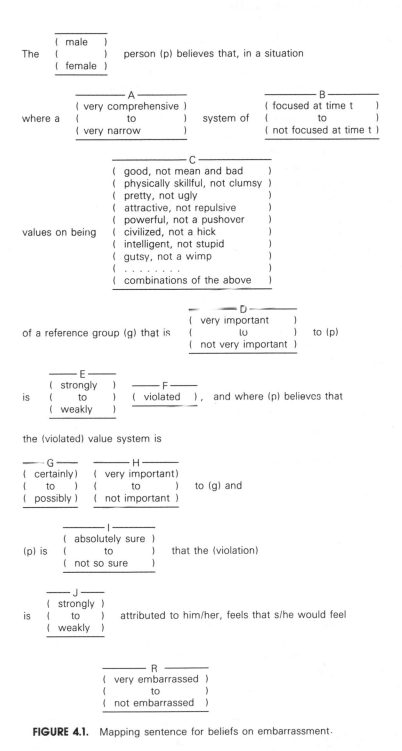

FIGURE 4.1. Mapping sentence for beliefs on embarrassment.

important. The core notion is that embarrassment is elicited because some values (suggested in facet C) of a reference group *g* are violated. The violation may concern few or many of these values (indicating the comprehensiveness or narrowness of the value system; facet A) that *g* focuses on at a particular time *t* (facet B). The subject *p* believes more or less strongly (facet I) that the violation is attributed to him/her by *g*. Attribution is to be understood in very general terms. It may range from intentional violation of values by *p* to cases where *p* is a mere bystander to a violation or belongs to the same social category as the violator.

Facet C represents a variant of the facet "content of the violated values" used in the Borg and colleagues (1986) study. It is expressed in such a way that the positively valued pole of each content scale is described. What is positive or negative was decided on the basis of what should be true for almost all reference groups *g* except some very special ones. (For example, among gangsters it might be considered embarrassing to be morally "good" rather than "bad.") The role of C in the mapping sentence is not to formulate a complete list of values for reference group *g* but simply to formally refer to a value system. Note also that the last element of C admits the possibility to form any subset of values from a universe relevant for the respective reference group *g*.

All situation facets, except facet C, are ordered in the same sense. That is, it is always possible to say which end of the facet should lead to the stronger response on *R*. In Figure 4.1, the strong response should always occur with the "upper" end of these facets.

Further facets, such as "controllability" or "responsibility," as discussed in the introduction, could be easily added, but even with what we have the number of situations formally described by this mapping sentence is enormous. If one limits the number of elements in the ordered facets to some finite number *n* and the number of subsets in C to *m*, we have $n^9 m$ different situations. Choosing a fairly small number for *n*, say 5 (for: very strong, strong, medium, weak, very weak), and an equally small number for *m*, say 15, this yields 30 million situations. Because none of them can be ruled out on logical or psychological grounds, we have to construct or select an appropriate sample.

Experience shows that constructing a sample of items from a very large universe (the typical case!) of items is not only easiest but also leads to the clearest empirical testing, if one tries to hold a number of facets constant (Canter, 1985). For example, one could decide that D should be limited to "very important reference groups" only. We decided to vary the facets A, E, and J, because we felt that the given items could be most reliably classified by these facets.

As a first test of the usefulness of our facets, no new set of items was constructed, however, but items were selected from Borg and colleagues

(1986) and from an unpublished data set collected by the authors as a follow-up to the former (1986) study. The item construction was done in the following way: For each structuple, a group of researchers thought of realistic situations that would satisfy the respective facet definition as clearly as possible. Because in this study the items were given, there was no possibility of systematically controlling all the facets. It was possible, however, to reliably classify most of the items with respect to those facets in which we are interested here. Table 4.1 lists these items for the Borg and colleagues (1986) study, together with their structuples. Each structuple shows the respective item's definition on facets A, E, and J, with 1 = strong and 0 = weak in the sense of the common order of the facets. For example, item 5 has structuple 010, because it was defined as weak on facet A (i.e., narrow value system), strong on J (i.e., strong attribution), and weak on E (i.e., weak violation of value system). In checking through the items, please note that what we present here are translations from German. Because of the different cultural context, the reader may feel that some of the structuples are odd definitions. Moreover, the structuples were assigned to the items according to what the investigators felt would be most appropriate for the subjects. These subjects were psychology undergraduates of the Jutus-Liebig-Universität in Giessen, Germany. For other subjects, such as psychology undergraduates at Michigan, other structuples might be in order. The assignment of structuples is always based on subjective judgment, which, however, can be checked by empirically studying interjudge agreement.

The items of the second study were similar in nature to those in Table 4.1. In this set of items a particular effort was made to specify the kind of observers or reference group (g) present.

Parenthetically, it may be noted that a slight modification of the domain part of this mapping sentence generates a definitional system for *both* shame *and* pride: All that needs to be done is to differentiate facet F into the elements "violation" and "realization" of relevant values and add a second range for pride responses.

Hypotheses

Because facets A, E, and J are ordered from 0 = weakly to 1 = strongly embarrassing, a partial-order hypothesis on the embarrassment scores follows automatically. That is, the situations with structuple 111 should be judged as most embarrassing, those with 000 as least embarrassing. All other items fall, by definition, in between these bounds and hence, if the definitions are indeed empirically useful, should be seen as intermediate in embarrassment. However, not all items are comparable. For example, nothing can be derived about the order of 101 and 010, even though the

TABLE 4.1
54 Items, with Means of Empirical Embarrassment Ratings and Structuples.

Item		struct.	mean
1	I am visiting acquaintances of mine. My dog does his business in the corner.	101	3.13
2	I am visiting friends. In a discussion, my mother rigidly insists she is right, even though she is wrong.	000	1.97
3	I am sitting on the toilet in the train. The door suddenly springs open to the corridor packed with people.	111	4.74
4	I am sitting with my sick grandmother in the doctor's office. Suddenly, she farts loudly. Everybody looks away.	000	2.29
5	While waiting at the bus stop, I am shadow-boxing, when I notice that some people are watching me from their windows and are laughing.	010	1.90
6	My brother insists in a discussion on something that is obviously absurd. Many people shake their heads.	000	1.29
7	I am attending a lecture of a colleague at a conference. He constantly mixes things up, because the slides are projected head down.	001	1.16
8	A neighbor tells me angrily that a member of my horseback rider's club tortured a horse while completely drunk.	101	2.16
9	My boss tells me to park the car in a place reserved for handicapped people. People who pass by point at the sign.	111	3.74
10	I am participating in a panel discussion together with another member of the Green Party, when he makes some blatantly anti-Semitic remarks.	111	4.71
11	I am making an official visit, together with an older female colleague of mine from the Union. She is made up to look 40 years younger than she is.	101	1.45
12	I lost my hair due to chemotherapy. On the bus, people turn around and look at me.	111	3.90
13	At an official occasion, I notice that my colleague right next to me is wearing a jacket soaked with sweat.	000	0.76
14	Our school class participates in a quiz on TV. A classmate of mine can barely answer a single question.	001	1.68
15	Concerning sex: I wanted to, but I was not able to . . .	011	2.75
16	I had promised to also boycott the exam. I asked secretly to get a take-home exam, because I needed the credit. Now my name appears on the notice board.	111	6.05
17	At a convention I notice that my colleague's paper is received with pitying smiles.	000	1.32
18	At the evening concert, the conductor of our orchestra slips on the polished floor and falls down.	000	1.29
19	In my office, a colleague repeatedly pays obnoxious compliments to our new female boss.	101	1.87
20	A member from my bowling club shows around sadomasochistic pictures in my presence.	101	3.50
21	A member of our travel group is stared at in the theater lobby because he is extremely short.	101	1.66

(Continued)

TABLE 4.1

(Continued)

Item		struct.	mean
22	When visiting my sister she tells me that I forgot the birthday of my little godchild.	111	3.66
23	On the street people look at my girlfriend, who wears super heavy makeup.	100	1.76
24	Accidently, I touch my female boss's bosom.	111	3.18
25	While in the cafeteria with a female colleague of mine, her dress zipper suddenly breaks open.	000	1.08
26	While in the cafe with a friend of mine, he accidently spills a cup of coffee over a lady's dress.	100	1.95
27	I greet somebody extremely cordially, and then I notice that he is a complete stranger that I had mistaken for a friend of mine.	111	2.66
28	At a party, I make a mean comment about a mutual acquaintance, when I notice that she is standing right behind me.	111	4.71
29	While struggling to get my suitcase on the upper rack in a full train compartment, the seam of my pants breaks open.	111	3.45
30	While walking down the street, I feel nauseated and have to throw up	011	2.71
31	I am at my relatives' New Year's party. When I bend down to pick something up, I fart rather loudly. Everybody laughs.	111	3.47
32	At a party, my girlfriend, who had too much to drink, makes a loud and very improper remark about the host. Uneasy silence follows.	101	3.29
33	My father is from Bavaria. The other day, he came to visit me in the dormitory wearing his leather shorts and Tyrolian hat.	100	1.29
34	I am pretty loaded and complain to the waiter that the bill is wrong. It turns out that he is right.	111	2.55
35	I am being introduced to my new boss. I am so nervous that I start stuttering.	111	2.81
36	I raise my hand in the classroom and state, just with other words, what was just pointed out to be wrong. The teacher gives it to me!	111	3.82
37	I am traveling to France with a student group. A participant constantly points out to the host how much cleaner it is in Germany.	111	4.16
38	While getting off the bus, the handle breaks off and I fall down. The people around me laugh.	110	2.16
39	My friend shows me a ballet piroutte. Some observers start grinning.	000	0.47
40	Our tennis club plays a tournament away from home. One of our player double-faults every serve. The people laugh.	000	0.74
41	I am in a sex shop, where I run into my boss.	111	2.68
42	In the youth hostel, a guy from our hiking group sits down right next to me in shredded jogging shorts. Some girls giggle.	000	0.79
43	While buying a ring with my fiancee, I notice that she has dirty fingernails.	000	1.58

(Continued)

TABLE 4.1

(Continued)

Item		struct.	mean
44	My fiancee and I are invited to visit distinguished acquain- tances. She shows up in tennis shoes.	000	0.82
45	I play tennis and I keep having problems hitting the ball prop- erly. A few observers watch with great amusement.	011	2.71
46	I come home unexpectedly and find my parents having sex.	011	2.92
47	In the bus, everybody stares at my Mongoloid brother.	101	1.68
48	In the train compartment, a kid is making fun of my ears that stick out.	110	2.26
49	A TV reporter interviews me on the street. My answers are rather stupid. In addition, I also stutter.	111	3.32
50	Due to a bet, I walk down the main shopping street in a night- gown.	011	2.21
51	I am sitting with my study group in a cafe. A rather proper lady looks disapprovingly at my buddy's long, greasy hair.	000	0.34
52	I am invited to a party given by my office superiors. I show up wearing much too casual and rundown clothing.	110	2.34
53	I brought a friend home. As we sit with my family at the din- ner table, he cracks a dirty joke.	111	2.34
54	I am at the swimming pool with an acquaintance from my fencing club. He practices sudden attacks without a sword. The people standing around laugh.	010	0.50

* Each structuple refers to facets A, J, and E from the mapping sentence in Figure 1.
A = comprehensive (1)/narrow (0) value system is violated. J = attribution of violation to
subject is strong (1)/weak (0). E = violation is strong (1)/weak (0).

former has two "strongs," the latter only one. The reason is that in 101 facets A and E are "strong," while in 010 it is facet J. Without any notions on the relative importance of the facets, these structuples are therefore incomparable. Formally, a structuple (aje) is stronger than (a'j'e') if and only if the former is stronger in at least one element and not weaker in any other; otherwise, the structuples are incomparable.

The partial-order hypothesis can be made for individual data or for data aggregated over subjects (such as means). Moreover, it can be hypothesized that it should hold for all items, or just for the averages of the items that fall into one structuple category.

Apart from such level or intensity hypotheses, one can also make predictions on the similarities of the items. A hypothesis that seems to suggest itself is to postulate that items that have similar structuples should correlate more strongly with each other than those with less similar structuples. Foa (1958) proposed the *contiguity principle*, which simply determines the similarity of structuples by counting their common elements. However, in such a general form, this principle makes little sense, because it assumes, among other things, that all facets have the same weight (see Borg, 1986, for a thorough discussion of the contiguity principle).

There is, however, another class of hypotheses, called *regional hypotheses* (Borg, 1979; Canter, 1985; Levy, 1981), that can be used to derive predictions on the similarity structure of the items. If the correlations are represented as distances in an SSA space (Borg, & Lingoes, 1987), then it should be possible to partition this space into regions such that all item-points representing category c of facet f fall into the same region (for all categories c and all facets f). This hypothesis is but a generalization of the usual discriminant analysis hypothesis, except that it does not impose restrictions such as linearity on the boundary lines, which do not follow from the substantive hypotheses.

The three facets A, E, and J are ordered in the same sense. Moreover, it is obvious that all three facets do, in principle, admit more than just two elements. For example, in facet A, one could distinguish situations into those that violate "very comprehensive," "comprehensive," "relatively narrow," and " very narrow" value subsets. But in order to be able to cut an SSA space into regions such that the points of every possible structuple form their own "cell" in the space, the partitioning lines of the three facets must be independent. Because the facets are ordered, the partitioning lines should also be ordered. This is the case if these lines form, for example, a primitive dimension system that splits the space into boxlike regions. This type of regionalization is known as a *multiplex* (Borg, & Lingoes, 1987). Because we consider three facets here, we predict a triplex, which requires at least a 3-dimensional SSA space.

Subjects and Procedure

In the following, we consider two studies on embarrassment and shame. Twenty male and 18 female beginning students of psychology at the Justus Liebig Universität Giessen participated in the first study, and 39 male and 52 female students in the second. The average age of the subjects in both studies was about 24 years. They were given a questionnaire listing 72 and 79 situations, respectively, and were asked to rate how embarrassed or ashamed they thought they would feel in each of these situations. All ratings were done in private with no experimenter present. The rating scale can be translated, roughly, as follows:

slightly uneasy		uneasy		embarrassed		somewhat ashamed		deeply ashamed	
0	1	2	3	4	5	6	7	8	9

Because the ratings in the first study turned out to be relatively low,

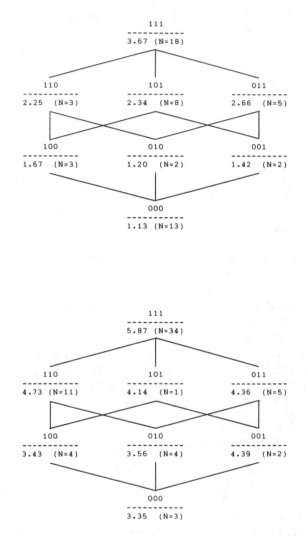

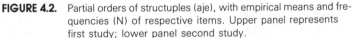

FIGURE 4.2.   Partial orders of structuples (aje), with empirical means and frequencies (N) of respective items. Upper panel represents
first study; lower panel second study.

we felt that subjects might have attempted to hide their feelings or give
socially desirable answers. Therefore, subjects in the second study were
explicitly asked to avoid social control strategies such as "playing it cool"
and, rather, to indicate how they thought they would *really* feel. This
resulted in much higher ratings.

Fifty-four of the items used in the first study are presented (translated
into English) in Table 4.1. They represent the set of items that was culled
for the analyses following. Of the items of the second study, 64 were culled

for data analyses. None of the items in the two studies were exactly identical, and only a few referred to similar situations. However, all items that were culled could be categorized consistently into the eight cells formed by the facets A, E, and J.

The culling of the items to be used in the data analyses was done on the basis of the definition of embarrassing situations and the mapping sentence in Figure 4.1. Situations that did not conform to these definitions, or that were too ambiguous for reliable structuple assignments, were eliminated.

Results

The partial-order hypotheses are most easily checked. We test them here for the average scores of structuple-equivalent items only. Figure 4.2 shows the results. Even though the culling led to a very uneven distribution of items over the eight structuple cells, and hence to parameter estimates that may not be too stable, it is obvious that the hypotheses are confirmed almost perfectly.

We now turn to our triplex hypotheses for the similarity of the items. Because they ask for at least 3-dimensional SSA representations, we test them first under this smallest space condition by mapping the μ_2 correlations (Guttman, 1981b) via the program SSA-I (Lingoes, 1972) into 3-dimensional ordinal SSA spaces. (Note that using montone correlation coefficients and an ordinal SSA approach is consistent with the regional hypotheses.) A 3-dimensional space is sufficiently large to represent the empirical correlations accurately: The alienation coefficient is K = .225, a low value for 54 points (see Borg, & Lingoes, 1987). Figures 4.3 and 4.4 show two projection planes of the SSA representation for the items from Table 4.1. These projection planes are the plane spanned by the principal components 1 and 2 (Figure 4.3), and the plane spanned by principal components 1 and 3 (Figure 4.4).

Looking at such SSA representations of the data, one is confronted with the question of whether it is possible to partition the point set such that the emerging regions comprise only points with common facet definitions. Figures 4.3 and 4.4 show partitioning lines induced by facets A, E, and J. It is obvious that the roughly vertical line in Figure 4.3 partitions the plane such that those points that represent situations where, by definition, a "comprehensive" value system is violated lie to the right of this line, and all points representing situations where only a "narrow" value system is violated lie to the left. At the same time, the more horizontal line induces an analogous partitioning with respect to facet J, with the weak-attribution items above this line, and the strong-attribution items below it. Finally, in Figure 4.4 (showing the plane orthogonal to that in Figure

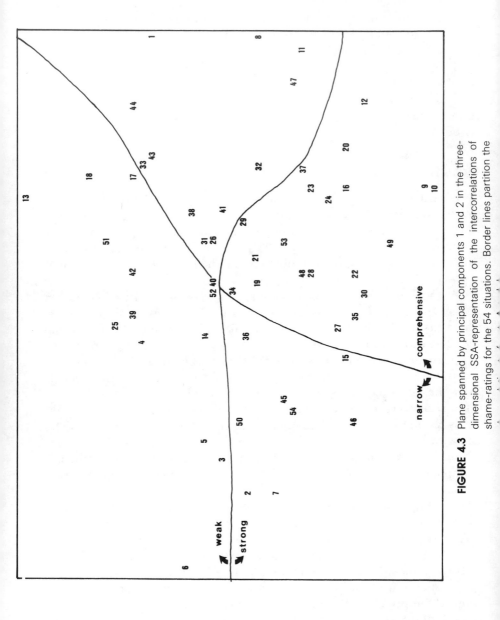

FIGURE 4.3 Plane spanned by principal components 1 and 2 in the three-dimensional SSA-representation of the intercorrelations of shame-ratings for the 54 situations. Border lines partition the

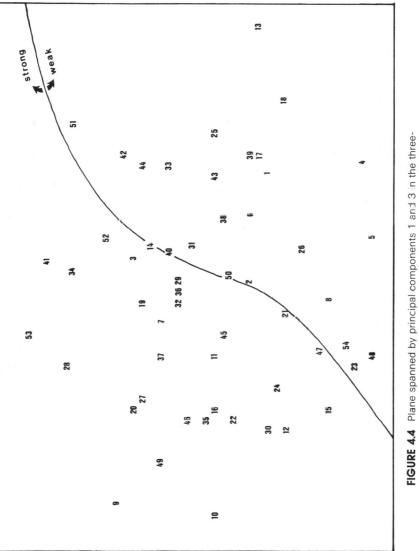

FIGURE 4.4 Plane spanned by principal components 1 and 3 in the three-dimensional SSA-representation of the intercorrelations of shame-ratings for the 54 situations. Border line partitions the plane relative to facet E.

4.3), facet F induces a partion line that separates strong-violation items from weak-violation items. The partition lines for A and E admit only one major error each (item 3 and 1, respectively). Otherwise, there are only a few quantitatively small errors.

Clearly, this outcome is exactly what the triplex hypothesis predicted. It is easy to see that by introducing further elements into facets A, E, and J, one should simply expect partitioning lines roughly parallel to those induced by the respective dichotomies. Thus, the structure hypothesized and supported by the findings renders further extensions of the definitional system feasible.

The usual question that emerges in this context is whether such partitionings can result by chance. It is easy to see that this is virtually impossible, even if we drop the triplex hypothesis in favor of the much simpler hypothesis that "some" partitioning into "relatively simple" regions should be possible. If one takes any 54 points and randomly assigns to them the structuples given in Table 4.1, and then mixes them thoroughly throughout this space, how likely is it that they can be partitioned into regions and, indeed, into a triplex? Obviously, this probability is extremely small.

However, we have an even better answer to this question, that is, we can look at a replication. The correlations of the 64 items of the second study can also be represented well in a 3-dimensional SSA space. The alienation coefficient is K = .247, which is low considering the large number of points (see Borg, & Lingoes, 1987). Most importantly, the structure of the point locations is such that the same type of partitioning is possible as before, that is, facets A and J induce a duplex in the plane of the first two principal components, and facet E splits the plane spanned by principal components 1 and 3, so that the same triplex results as above.

DISCUSSION

The findings reported concern only three of the ten facets of the mapping sentence in Figure 4.1. Indeed, as was mentioned, even more facets than just these ten may be studied. How many one selects is largely determined by practical concerns, but, in any case, it can be assumed that the situational determinants of embarrassment are quite complex or multifaceted. It is therefore remarkable that the three facets that were studied led to such clear-cut results. Apparently, they are major determinants of embarrassment.

Starting from these results, one can proceed by introducing more categories for facets A, E, and J, and/or by turning one's attention to further facets. Borg and colleagues (1986) studied the facet "Who is the actor?" with elements "subject him/herself," "member of a primary group," and "member of a secondary group." This facet also showed a systematic correspondence to the data, but it was dropped here in favor of the "attribution" facet, J, because this seems to capture a more fundamental psychological process. Although it should be most often true that the attribution is highest if the subject is the actor, this is by no means always the case. For example, consider item 10 in Table 4.1, where the subject is not the actor him- or herself, but attribution should still be very high by pronounced "contiguity" (see Introduction). On the other hand, attribution can be low even though the actor is the subject him- or herself. An example would be a situation where a brilliant student writes $2 + 2 = 3$ on the blackboard, and the reference group g attributes this violation more to a lack of concentration than ability.

Borg and colleagues (1986) studied another, Piaget-like facet that distinguishes value violations with respect to whether the violator is "responsible," whether he or she is "responsible, but acted not intentionally," or whether he or she is "responsible and acted fully intentionally." This facet proved empirically useless, however. This supports the suggestion made by Weiner (1985) according to which shame may be more closely related to ability, whereas guilt may depend more on effort or intention. From a methodological point of view, this shows that not every facet that leads to conceptually useful distinctions also corresponds to some regularity in the empirical observations. In other words, theoretical predictions based on facet theory can be falsified in this manner.

Borg and colleagues (1986) also computed, in addition to the methods previously shown, a conventional analysis of variance as a convenience for those who are unfamiliar with this type of data analysis methods. For the data considered above, such an ANOVA would treat the facet design AxExJ as a 2x2x2 factorial design. Even though ANOVA introduces extrinsic linearity constraints into the data analysis (Guttman, 1981a), the cell means of the factorial design may provide some insights into the structure of the data with respect to the facet design.

If there were more facets on the persons, an interesting question would be to ask whether they allow one to discriminate among the scores of the respective subjects. For example, it seems possible that female and males subjects have different belief systems on embarrassment. A very simple hypothesis might predict that the female scores are all higher, say, than the male scores. A more sophisticated hypothesis would predict where the scores are high, and where low, for each group. The best approach to study such questions for ordered facets would be to use partial order scalogram analysis (Shye, 1985).

Finally, from a wider perspective, a number of interesting questions could be asked on the relationship of the symbolic basis of embarrassment/shame to these emotions when generated in concrete situations. It may be assumed that the symbolic basis is but a generalization of such "experienced" emotions over a large number of situations. Thus, the beliefs about emotions should generally correlate positively with actually experienced emotions. In principle, it would be desirable to study each system by itself first, and then investigate how they are related. However, as soon as beliefs come into existence, this may prove a most difficult task, because it is not unlikely that they themselves play a role in how an emotion is experienced in a concrete situation, due to the norms and expectations they represent. Moreover, because even concrete experiences can only be reported using language, this in itself requires the use of symbolic representation.

5 FACTORS DETERMINING THE DIMENSIONS OF SUBJECTIVE EMOTIONAL SPACE

Theodor L. Gehm
University of Giessen

Klaus R. Scherer
University of Geneva and University of Giessen

THEORETICAL BACKGROUND

Concern with the nature of the subjective dimensions of emotions goes back to the beginning of experimental psychology. Wilhelm Wundt, the founder of experimental psychology, devoted a lengthy treatment to feelings in his textbook on physiological psychology (1905). He argued for three major dimensions of feeling states, *Lust/Unlust* (pleasantness/unpleasantness), *Erregung/Beruhigung* (activation/relaxation), and *Spannung/Lösung* (tension/relief). Many psychologists following Wundt have agreed that a dimensional system seems to be a useful tool in the attempt to provide a taxonomy of the emotions. In many cases researchers have used the lexicon of emotion labels in different languages to try to dimensionalize the semantic space formed by these labels (see summary reviews by Fillenbaum & Rapoport, 1971, p. 100ff.; Schmidt-Atzert, 1981, p. 37ff; Smith & Ellsworth, 1985; Traxel & Heide, 1961). All of the studies that have been done show that it is easily possible to construct a dimensional space to order the linguistic emotion terms, generally consisting of two to four dimensions. Furthermore, the nature of the dimensions has been similar across studies and bears a striking resemblance to the dimensions that keep appearing in studies using the semantic differential (Ertel, 1964; Osgood, Suci, & Tannenbaum, 1957). In general, one has little difficulty in identifying a hedonic valence and an activity factor. The third factor, while not always clearly potency, often can be interpreted in a similar way (see also Averill, 1975; Bottenberg, 1972; Bush, 1973).

One might wonder, therefore, to what extent a study of emotion labels reveals more information about the nature of words or semantic concepts in general than about the nature of emotion. Clearly, a taxonomy based on emotion terms is not necessarily relevant for a systematic ordering of naturally occurring emotional states. Yet it would seem that the importance of the verbal labeling of emotional states in social interaction and the important role of the cognitive representation of emotional states do warrant a close investigation of the semantic space formed by these labels. Furthermore, it does not seem impossible that the cognitive processes that seem to be involved in the elicitation and differentiation of emotional states (Lazarus, Averill, & Opton, 1970; Frijda, 1986; Mandler, 1984; Plutchick, 1980; Scherer, 1984a) might be somehow reflected in the dimensions of the cognitive representation of the emotion realm as mirrored in the emotion adjectives.

Thus, studies using modern multidimensional scaling methods to map the similarity relationships perceived by subjects as far as different emotion adjectives are concerned seem a useful activity within emotion research. However, much of the past work has suffered from methodological problems. It is well known, for example, that any kind of factor analytic or multidimensional scaling technique depends almost exclusively on the kind of material that is put into the analysis for its outcome. In other words, one is likely to strongly bias one's results by the selection of particular input materials. Therefore, either the use of these techniques has to be based on very clearly specified theoretical considerations concerning the nature of the stimuli (or in this case adjectives) to be investigated, or one has to strive for completeness in representation of the domain to be studied in order to avoid bias produced by selection.

To take an example of the latter case, Russell (1978, 1980) has proposed a two-dimensional theory of emotion differentiation, using multidimensional scaling studies of emotion adjectives to support this notion. Unfortunately, most of his studies have used fairly few and highly selected adjectives that make it possible that the type of representation he obtains in his analyses is biased by the nature of the adjectives selected for inclusion (see Scherer, 1984b). For example, by adding several adjectives related to an activity dimension and varying the intensity of these adjectives, one would tend to strengthen this dimension. Similarly, the exclusion of adjectives related to a potency of control dimension would tend to favor a two-dimensional solution, allowing one to neglect a possible third (potency) dimension. It would be useful, consequently, to attempt to replicate the results reported by Russell using a much larger and more representative number of emotion-related adjectives.

As far as the first point is concerned, that is, theoretical considerations of the origin of the dimensions, there have been only very few attempts made to address it (e.g., De Rivera, 1977). This lack of theoretical effort has been due, in part, to an absence of specific theoretical predictions concerning the nature of the cognitive processes involved in emotion differentiation. Given the recent increase in interest in trying to understand the factors or criteria that are involved in the cognitive appraisal preceding many emotional states (see Overview for Part II in this volume), it seems useful to investigate whether one could possibly use these theoretical notions to provide a theoretical underpinning for the dimensions found in similarity scaling studies.

In the present chapter we try to follow both leads. On the one hand, we have included in the study described a large number of emotion adjectives in an attempt to be complete in the coverage of emotion labels. Furthermore, we are trying to use the component process theory suggested by Scherer (1984a, b, 1986a), specifically the sequence theory of emotion differentiation, to point to a possible link between the cognitive processes involved in the elicitation of emotion and the dimensional structure of the semantic space of emotion terms.

Finally, it seems to us that another neglected question is that of interindividual differences in the nature of the semantic emotion space. Just as sizable differences in emotional reactivity have been found in studies of actual emotional states, and particularly in stress, it is possible that individuals differ in the way in which they cognitively represent emotion terms within a semantic space. Therefore, we have attempted to take a first look at the way in which such individual differences might be encountered in this area.

METHOD

Selection of Items

Trying to avoid any distortion resulting from a biased selection of the items investigated, we used a fairly comprehensive list of emotion-describing adjectives. This list was created by first drawing up a listing of as many terms as we could find in the literature on this topic and then eliminating synonyms as well as all terms that expressed only slight differences in the intensity of a particular emotional state. Thus, we finally obtained a list of 235 German terms (mostly adjectives but also including a few nouns such as "full of expectation") that we suppose to be not only comprehensive enough to cover the multitude of emotional states but also economical enough to do this without too much redundancy. (A slightly modified version of this list, containing also the English, French, Spanish, and Italian synonyms of each of the items investigated, is presented in Appendix F of this volume.)

Rating Procedure

The subjective semantic space of emotion-describing terms is usually in-vestigated by having subjects determine the degree of similarity of lex-ical terms designating emotions. In our study this task was performed by two groups of raters consisting of 10 subjects in the first study and 20 subjects in a second study (concerned with investigations of interindividual inconsistency). In this chapter we mainly present results from the first group. The second (a highly heterogeneous group of participants vary-ing greatly in age, from 18 to 78 years, and social status) was used only as a control group to determine the degree of reliability of our findings, and to provide information as to the possible discordance of individual decisions. Although the number of participants in our study is obviously too small to detect subgroups of participants with similar similarity struc-tures (a suggestion already made by Fillenbaum & Rapoport, 1971, p. 124), we nonetheless believe that this group is sufficiently heterogeneous to reveal interindividual inconsistencies in labeling or at least in grouping emotional states.

Taking into account the enormous number of comparisons to be made and considering that studies on limitations of different techniques have shown that different methods of rating similarities have led to only slight differences in the results of statistical analyses (see, e.g., Fillenbaum & Rapoport, 1971, p. 122), we chose an economical sorting procedure. As proposed by Russell (1980), we had our participants order the items in piles containing similar adjectives. In a first run there were 7, in the sec-ond run 10, and in the third run 15 different piles to be used. The three runs were performed independently, and no external criteria were im-posed for the sorting decisions.

Data Analysis

By counting the number of runs in which two adjectives were put into the same pile — according to a method described in further detail by Russell (1980) — we obtained a half-matrix of the rated similarities of each adjec-tive to the others. The values of this matrix were standardized to an inter-val of 0 to 1 and represented the average similarities of the adjectives. These data were analyzed by means of multidimensional scaling and cluster analyses.

Multidimensional scaling was performed to determine the underlying dimensions that were used to order this set. As the data available were only scaled in ranks, we chose the nonmetric technique proposed by Roskam (1975). Roskam describes the purpose and procedure of this method as follows: "Given the rank order or rating of the (dis)similarities among n objects (say: stimuli) the purpose of the algorithm is to find the coordinates of n points, representing the stimuli in a r dimensional space such that the distances among the points are in appropriately the same rank-order as the rank-order of the (dis)similarities" (p. 11).

Because of memory capacity limitations, it is impossible to process a 235 × 235 matrix in one run. Therefore, we first investigated the similarities of three subsamples of our complete data set: In a first sample of 40 items, we considered the 20 adjectives that occupied highly "central" positions in the cluster analyses reported in this section (which means in this case being "surrounded" by a satisfactory number of similar terms; for further details see the following), as well as 20 adjectives with average centrality. The second sample also consisted of 40 adjectives but, in order to determine the effects of the systematic selection of items in the first sample, this time determined on the basis of random selection. The third sample, again selected by chance, contained the biggest similarity matrix as could be processed by the computer (80 adjectives). In order to determine the number of dimensions, we constructed the configuration of the items in a 1- to 10-dimensional space and then compared the plot of stress values of this configuration to stress values obtained by Monte Carlo simulations. In brief, this procedure can be described as follows: The given data are scaled in several dimensionalities, and the stress is plotted as a function of dimensionality. This plot is then compared with similar plots derived from synthetic data in which the true dimensionality and the true error level are known. By finding the plot that best matches the actual plot, one can infer the dimensionality and error level of the actual data (for further detail see Kruskal & Wish, 1978, pp. 54 and 89–92).

Given the configuration of one of these samples one can (by minimizing a coefficient proposed by Guttman, 1968) adjust the position of other items within this configuration. Using this technique we were able to present a configuration including all of the 235 items investigated. In order to compare our findings to others, we have identified the respective positions of adjectives quoted in other studies to get an idea of the generalizability of our findings. We demonstrate this approach by using the list of adjectives investigated by Russell (1980).

Cluster techniques were also used, as in some cases there were characteristics of the material investigated that had an effect on the configuration of the items but still did not contribute strongly enough to become visible in a separate dimension (an assumption that was quite likely considering the number of data points analyzed in our study). As the results of cluster analyses vary to a great extent, depending on the algorithm which is used, we chose two very different procedures. First, we analyzed the data available with a hierarchical technique using the procedure DENSITY (see, e.g., Wishart, 1978, p. 55). The main advantage of this technique is that it needs no prior assumptions concerning the number of clusters into which items can be ordered, and thus—as already pointed out by Carmichael, George, & Juluis (1968)—this approach should form the basis for the definition of a natural cluster. The main idea of this procedure could be described as follows: "If entities are depicted as points in a metric space (. . .), a natural concept of clustering suggests that there should be parts of the space in which the points are very dense, separated by parts of low density" (Everitt, 1974, p. 30). Using this technique, first each items' density is determined by the average of the distances to a deliberately chosen number K of other items with small distance. Then the items are ordered according to their density value. This ordering determines whether an item is introduced to another cluster (in case there is an item with greater density within the item's neighborhood) or is the nucleus of another cluster. The resulting clusters are finally fused according to the nearest-neighbor criterion, so the resulting dendrogram can be interpreted as a depiction of the similarity of the clusters. To prove the stability of the DENSITY partition we reanalyzed our data with the nonhierarchic procedure CLUDIA (for further details of this method see Späth, 1975).

The degree of interindividual correspondence of the allocations investigated was determined by comparing DENSITY partitions of single subjects (taking the rather heterogeneous sample 2). These partitions were mutually compared by a coefficient proposed by Hubert & Arabie (1985). As this coefficient—which varies from 0 (chance agreement) to 1 (complete agreement)—is only rank-scaled, and as the statistical distribution of coefficients comparing partitions can be derived only by very complex statistical argumentation (see, e.g., Mielke, Berry, & Johnson, 1976), we tried to get a feeling for the absolute degree of correspondence by comparing the similarity of the partitions of the 20 raters to the similarity of Monte Carlo assignments. We therefore compared the real similarities of the 20 cluster solutions to those obtained by chance assignments of 235 objects. We assumed that the similarity of allocations for real ratings could only be higher than that for chance allocations. Thus, in a second run we compared real similarities to chance similarities that were generated with the underlying rule that 50 of the 235 items in each run were allocated to the same cluster. This rule represented th (very weak) substantive assumption that real similarity decisions were at most influenced by semantic networks between 50 pairs of adjectives simultaneously.

RESULTS

Interindividual Consistency of Subjective Emotional Space

As the degree of correspondence among different raters seems to be decisive for the question as to whether aggregate arrangements of emotion-describing terms can be interpreted, we begin with some details concerning the study of interindividual correspondence in the similarity judgments.

First, the number of clusters established by clustering ratings of different subjects separately varied to a great extent (20 to 48). Some authors (Carmichael et al., 1968) suggest interpreting this number as an indication for the number of natural clusters. In terms of individual differences in subjective emotional space one can interpret this finding as evidence for great interindividual inconsistencies in the semantic space formed by emotion-describing terms. This impression was confirmed by determining the degree of similarity among the different raters: The coefficient proposed by Hubert & Arabie (1985) varied between .026 and .220 among the different comparisons. These values were higher than the highest value of correspondence between pairs of chance assignments (which was .016). But contrasting this distribution to the distribution of correspondence among chance partitions (with the underlying hypothesis of close similarity of 50 items), the degree of correspondence established by our raters was rather low: For this sample of (slightly ordered chance assignments), the coefficient of correspondence varied from .034 to .088. A total of 64.2% of the agreement could be explained by the (rather weak) assumption that raters just knew that some adjectives to be ordered were synonyms or closely related, and even more impressive, the degree of correspondence between real judges was sometimes even lower than could be expected on the basis of this assumption.

Further results and details of the statistical methods used in this study are reported elsewhere (Gehm, 1987). It seems worth mentioning that a detailed analysis of the similarities of the ratings indicates that the degree of inconsistency increases with age and that subgroups of participants with similar education tend to judge similarly. These findings can be interpreted as arguments for developmental influences on the formation of a semantic space of emotion-describing terms within individuals. We want to point out that similarity rating data are affected by strong person-specific influences. On the other hand, it is well known that aggregating even fairly discordant ratings to average values representing a group mean results in rather stable estimates of general judgment tendencies in a population. Thus we feel justified to study the *average* similarity ratings across groups of subjects. We made the first group of 10 raters more homogeneous in age and social class for this purpose.

General Dimensions of the Semantic Space of Emotion-Describing Terms

The results of the multidimensional scaling procedures provide strong evidence for the assumption of two consistent dimensions underlying the similarity decisions investigated: Comparing the plot of the stress values for our data to the plot of chance data, we were able to show that the stress values of our data were considerably lower than the expected values of MDS-configurations for random rankings (as determined in a Monte Carlo simulation by Spence & Ogilvie, 1973), which indicates the existence of dimensional criteria during the process of ordering the data investigated. Second, we found that the shape and size of the plot of the empirical stress values was most similar to the stress values of random rankings with an underlying 2-dimensional structure (for further details see Spence & Graef, 1974).

This result was obtained for both item samples 1 and 2. (There are no Monte Carlo studies reported for samples as large as sample 3). Furthermore, as expected, the items chosen by chance selection (sample 2), although taken from the same data set of 235 items, always resulted in configurations with significantly higher stress values (which means lower dimensional discernibility); in addition, the plot of the stress values for this sample was similar to the plot of Monte Carlo data with a relatively high error level. We interpret this result as evidence for the assumption that the dimensionality of MDS-configurations depends to a large extent on the selection of items for investigation.

The assumption that strong interitem context effects determine the nature of the dimensional configuration was further supported by the results of systematic investigations of the arrangement of samples within the complete configuration. As an example, we want to illustrate the position of the items investigated by Russell (1978, 1980): Although Russell repeatedly found a rather systematic structure (a circumplex model) of the 28 items he investigated, we could in no case replicate his findings with our more comprehensive list of items: Neither the configuration of the total sample or the subsamples nor the adjectives used by Russell himself were ordered circularly in our study. This finding leads us to suspect that his selection of adjectives is not representative and that some aspects—especially the differences in activation implied by the adjectives he used—seem to be overrepresented.

As the stress plot cannot be looked upon as the only indication for the true underlying dimensionality (because other considerations such as interpretability, and stability enter into this decision; Kruskal & Wish, 1978, p. 48), we will now take a closer look at the configuration we finally settled on.

Figure 5.1 shows the 2-dimensional representation of sample 1.

Though labeling the dimension of an MDS-solution is obviously to some extent a matter of taste (and one should not deny that theoretical convictions contribute more to this designation than empirical evidence), we do not think that it is too farfetched if we label the horizontal axis with

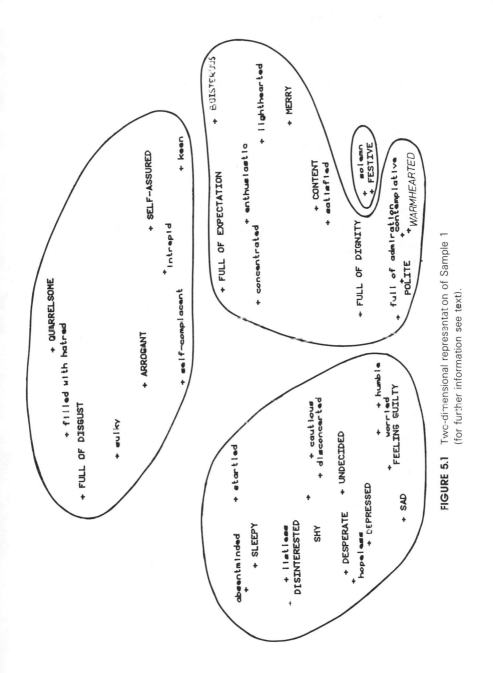

FIGURE 5.1 Two-dimensional representation of Sample 1 (for further information see text).

contrasts such as "pleasant" versus "unpleasant," "feeling fine" versus "feeling bad," or in more general terms, as a dimension of hedonic valence. The vertical axis seems to represent "power" versus "weakness," or "dominance" versus "submission," or a dimension of "power and control." These labels were confirmed by independent raters (colleagues of the authors — who, by the way, could not in accordance with our Monte Carlo results, give any meaningful interpretation to a 3-dimensional configuration.)

Both dimensions have been frequently suggested in the literature on this topic. Thus, the hedonic valence of an emotional state seems to be so decisive for the experience and comparison of emotional states that it has been regularly found even if only limited samples were investigated — see Block (1957), Bush (1973), Averill (1975), Russell & Mehrabian (1977), Russell (1978, 1980), Daly, Lancee, and Polivy (1983), or Smith and Ellsworth (1985). To a lesser extent this is also true for the dimension of control and power — see Bush (1973), Averill (1975), Russell and Mehrabian (1977), Russell (1978). The fact that we do not find an independent dimension of activation that has been generally proposed as one of the most important dimensions in the structure of the semantic space of emotion-describing terms — see Block (1957), Bush (1973), Averill (1975), Russell and Mehrabian (1977), (1978, 1980, 1983), Daly, Lancee, and Polivy, (1983), Smith and Ellsworth (1985) — is probably also due to an item selection criterion: As mentioned previously we excluded not only synonyms but also all those adjectives expressing slight differences in intensity. (Although activation could not be identified as an independent dimension in the MDS, the results of the cluster analyses strongly suggest that this criterion seems to have influenced the similarity judgments; see following.)

Trying to understand the mental processes leading to a judgment of similarity or dissimilarity of an emotion, we think it is interesting that our two major dimensions — hedonic valence and control/power — reveal considerable similarity to the parameters postulated by Scherer (1984a, 1984b, 1986a) for the process of emotion differentiation. According to the component process model, these aspects of the individual's evaluation of the actual situation are, among others, crucial for the elicitation of an emotion. It is true that there is a high degree of interpersonal variation in emotion similarity judgments and that the processes of comparing terms and eliciting emotions are likely to be organized in a completely different manner. Yet, we think that the correspondence between similarity judgments and theoretical postulates might, on the one hand, aid to infer the cognitive processes involved in comparing emotion terms, and on the other hand, yield information useful for the more detailed description of cognitive evaluation processes in emotion eliciting. Though we cannot suppose that people have insight into the cognitive processes that occur during the elicitation of an emotion, they nonetheless might be able to use the components of these processes as criteria for determining the similarity of different emotional states. This conjecture was also supported by the results of the cluster analyses, as we now describe.

Local Criteria for Determining Similarity of Emotion-Describing Terms

The DENSITY-algorithm led to a partition comprising 20 clusters, which was surprisingly well replicated by the (nonhierarchical) procedure CLUDIA. (In spite of the iterative algorithm of CLUDIA, this method did not produce a much better fit of the structure of clusters to the data analyzed [average distance of deviation for DENSITY partition: 66.05; for CLUDIA partition: 65.21]. A comparison of the standard deviation of the number of objects within one cluster [7.6 for the DENSITY solution versus 5.5 for the CLUDIA solution] indicates that the slight improvement of the squared distance of the CLUDIA solution is due to a more even distribution of items over the clusters rather than to basically different allocations.)

Of the 20 clusters produced by DENSITY, 16 were essentially maintained by CLUDIA, whereas the transformation of items (mostly among clusters in the nearest neighborhood) for four of them led to changes that we consider to be substantial enough to be excluded from further interpretation. Thus, trying to guard against overinterpretations, we suggest that at least 16 emotional states can be clearly distinguished for the adjectives investigated. The 20 clusters are portrayed in Table 5.1. Unstable clusters are indicated with "ns."

We named each cluster after its most central adjective (i.e., the one initiating the new cluster). To provide a rough impression of the contents of these clusters, a list of representative items for each cluster is presented in Table 5.1. The dendrogram for these 20 clusters is shown in Figure 5.2. (In this figure the 16 stable clusters are depicted in boxes).

Although the interpretation of a cluster solution is always fraught with the danger of overinterpretation, a number of points relevant to the structure found seem to be straightforward and worth mentioning.

First, the number of adjectives in the clusters varies to a great extent among the different clusters (even in the CLUDIA solution). Though all of them might be looked upon as clearly distinguishable emotional entities, the process of verbal labeling seems to produce different results. Thus, some emotional states seem to be only roughly differentiated by emotional terms, whereas others reveal a large number of similar verbal labels. This finding is in accordance with Levy's thesis of hypo- versus hypercognition of different emotions (1984).

TABLE 5.1
Short Listing of the 20 DENSITY-Clusters.

Number of Cluster		Central Element	Other Substantive Elements	Number of Objects
1		boisterous	adventurous, enthusiastic, full of life, lustful	14
2		depressed	discouraged, disappointed, scared, listless	8
3		disinterested	indifferent, bored, apathetic	8
4		full of expectation	tense, keen, anxious	10
5		festive	solemn	2
6		arrogant	self-complacent, contented	4
7	ns	polite	reflective, thoughtful, vigilant, serious	28
8		sleepy	apathetic, exhausted, absent-minded, sluggish	9
9	ns	shy	scared, intimidated, careful	9
10		feeling guilty	ashamed, humble, distressed, remorseful	8
11		self-assured	courageous, decided, undaunted	17
12	ns	quarrelsome	angry, malicious, furious	24
13	ns	sad	troubled, lonesome, concerned, bitter	28
14	ns	undecided	fearful, inhibited, disconcerted, puzzled	16
15		merry	pleased, cheerful, lighthearted	13
16		desperate	hopeless, inconsolable	5
17		full of disgust	nauseated, shocked	11
18		warmhearted	longing, tender, thoughtful	12
19		full of dignity	reverent, respectful, full of veneration	4
20		content	satisfied, relieved, confident	5

"ns" indicates that cluster is not stable. (Further information in the text.)

Second, the fundamental emotions, such as joy, fear, anger, sadness (Izard, 1977; Tomkins, 1962, 1963), were only rarely central for the clusters investigated. On the contrary, most often these clusters had a semantic flavor clearly divergent from these terms (see clusters 3, 5, 6, 8, 11, 18, 19, 20). Even though the so-called fundamental or basic emotions might be experienced as especially impressive or powerful, our results do not suggest that they must be considered as fundamental units for the process of comparing emotions.

Third, there was a great deal of evidence for some nondimensional criteria that (together with the 2-dimensional criteria) influence the process of comparing emotion-describing terms. A closer look at the dendrogram (Figure 5.2) reveals that the clusters can first be separated into two groups, one of which is further partitioned into three groups. These four groups of clusters, which we have designated A, B, C, D and labeled as "predominantly unpleasant," "well-being," "conflict," and "happy excitement," can also be distinguished within the 2-dimensional MDS represen-

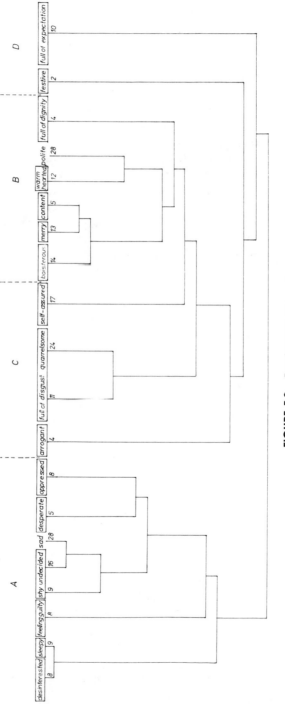

FIGURE 5.2. Dendrogram of emotion terms.

tation (the adjectives surrounded by circles in Figure 5.1). In this configuration, the clusters A, B, C are units, whereas group D is split up into two clusters divided by the items of group B. The cluster analyses solution and the MDS configuration can easily be brought into alignment by the supposition of a tetrahedral arrangement of these groups. Such a tetrahedron is presented in Figure 5.3.

In such a tetrahedron the groups of clusters A, B, and C might be located on or close to the base, whereas cluster group D might form the peak in the third dimension. In this structure the edge between cluster groups A and B is seen to represent the dimension of hedonic valence, and the edge between C and D, which is orthogonal to the former, the control/power dimension as revealed by the MDS analyses.

According to our interpretation, this configuration might provide a visual description of additional features of the subjective emotional space. First, it might account for the absence of a separate dimension of activation. A closer look at the clusters suggests that the connection between the two orthogonal edges described previously (representing the dimensions of hedonic valence and control/power) might be interpreted as the dimension of activation. The adjectives close to the hedonic valence edge might be interpreted as resembling a lower, and the adjectives close to the control/power edge a higher degree of activation. According to this

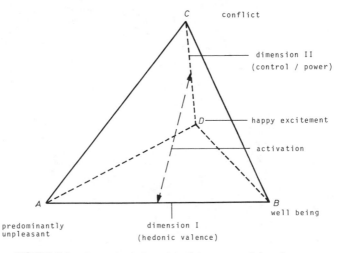

FIGURE 5.3. A tetrahedral model of the space of emotions (further information in text.)

model, emotional states with relatively low activation might be discriminated by their degree of hedonic valence, whereas emotional states involving relatively high activation might be distinguished by the respective degree of control or power. Thus, the ability of these dimensions to discriminate emotional states depends on the degree of activation.

DISCUSSION

We propose to interpret the results presented here in a general framework of theoretical considerations concerning a possible correspondence between the evaluation process involved in the differentiation of emotions and the processes of judging the similarity between emotion-describing terms. In spite of the rather different nature of the processes of comparing adjectives and experiencing emotions, the criteria elaborated here as determining the configuration of the semantic space of emotion-describing adjectives are very close to the nature of the evaluation checks we expect to be involved in the eliciting of emotional states. Criteria such as "hedonic valence," "control/power" and "activation" seem important for both the cognitive and subcognitive processes involved in the eliciting of emotions and the process of judging similarities within the semantic space of emotion-describing adjectives.

To pursue the possibility that the criteria used in the evaluation of emotion-eliciting situations are reflected in the dimensions of similarity judgments of emotion-describing terms, it seems necessary to further investigate both the process of adjective similarity rating in individuals and the evaluation or appraisal process underlying the elicitation of different emotional states. This will require detailed investigations of the elicitation of emotions (micro-measurement of the different stages of emotion arousal) and of the cognitive processes in judging the similarity of emotion-describing adjectives. We obviously know very little about these processes at present. Nonetheless, we hope that the apparent parallelism of criteria or dimensions suggested in this chapter will inspire future research in both areas.

III EMOTION SIGNALING IN PERSON PERCEPTION

There is little doubt that expression is one of the major response modalities in emotion. While this aspect of emotional responding is given a more central place in some theories, such as the "discrete emotion" theories proposed by Tomkins and Izard, there would be few theorists, if any, who would want to deny the importance of facial, vocal, and bodily motor responses in emotional arousal. This area is, historically speaking, one of the most traditional fields of research, given Charles Darwin's masterful discussion of emotional expression in his book "The expression of emotion in animals and men" (1872/1965). It might not be too farfetched, indeed, to argue that the most visible aspect of emotion, the facial expression of emotion, has also been responsible for keeping emotion research alive. The studies on the universality of facial expression of emotion (Ekman, 1973; Izard, 1977) have been widely cited and have constituted important examples for some of the central issues in emotion research. Unfortunately, given the long history of the interest in emotional expression in different bodily modalities, the empirical evidence is still scarce, particularly for response modalities other than facial.

Our research group has been working on the vocal expression of affective states during the last decade, trying to develop parameters and measurement methods that could be used to objectify patterns of vocal emotion expression. We have been attempting to study both the externalization of physiological changes during emotional arousal in objectively measurable acoustic parameters (the *expression*) and the use that naive listeners make of a variety of acoustic voice parameters in emotion attribution (studying the *inference* of emotion from vocal cues, the *impression*).

In Chapter 6, a series of studies in both domains is reviewed to provide an overview of our research in this area. There is now strong evidence that a number of acoustic parameters, particularly fundamental frequency and the energy distribution in the spectrum (particularly the formants) vary systematically with emotional state. In addition, there is strong evidence that listeners make use of this acoustic information to infer affective states. However, given the complexity of the phenomena in this area and the difficulty of systematically varying the essential parameters, combined with the problem of finding appropriate emotional stimuli, we will need much further research in order to better understand the phenomenon of vocal affect communication.

As mentioned previously, facial expression has been studied much more intensively. However, there are a number of features that have been neglected so far, in particular the role of context information in the judgment of emotion from facial information. Chapter 7 describes two empirical studies in which context information was systematically varied in order to study its effect on the evaluation of facial expression of emotion. Obviously, context and situation have been generally neglected in studying the effect of psychological variables, and we will be forced to increasingly consider these variables in trying to develop more ecologically valid models of the process of emotion signaling.

The large majority of studies on emotional expression has been directed toward a particular channel or modality of expression or communication. This is partly due to historical reasons, particularly to the specialization of researchers in relation to a particular set of variables or modalities. Although there have been a number of multichannel studies of emotion expression, they are often beset by methodological problems that render the interpretation of the results rather difficult. One of the major problems in this area has been the systematic manipulation of the stimulus material in such a way as to independently vary the cues in the different channels while maintaining naturalness of the stimulus patterns. Modern techniques of digital speech processing and video-technology are now providing the possibility of constructing stimulus material that is likely to be more adequate in relation to the demands of a properly constructed multichannel study.

In Chapter 8, we report a study in which digital resynthesis techniques have been used in combination with systematically produced dynamic facial expressions on videotape in order to systematically vary a number of cues in each modality (using different combinations). The results of this study point to a predominance of the visual stimuli in signaling emotion. It should be noted, however, that many features of the study may have biased the results in the direction of visual supremacy. More than the specific results found here, which may depend on the particular choice of the stimuli, we want to emphasize the use of modern audio- and video-manipulation procedures in the design of experimental studies that provide much better control of the variables under investigation than has been possible before. Given the increasing progress in the development of measurement systems and manipulation technology we are likely to witness, in the near future, a major increase in sophistication of the studies in this area.

6 EXPERIMENTAL STUDIES ON VOCAL AFFECT COMMUNICATION

Thomas Goldbeck
University of Giessen

Frank Tolkmitt
University of Giessen

Klaus R. Scherer
University of Geneva and University of Giessen

The voice is indubitably an important means of signaling emotion: As it transmits a verbal message, it also sends out information concerning the speaker's emotional state via acoustic cues such as fundamental frequency (pitch) and voice quality (see Scherer, 1979, 1986a, c). In this chapter we review several experimental approaches to studying the manner in which affective information is encoded into various acoustic parameters of the speech signal and how such parameters are used by the listener to attribute emotions. Our research has focused on two problems in particular:

- How do affective states modulate the acoustic parameters of speech?
- Do listeners reliably attribute different affect states on the basis of parametric variations of these parameters?

These questions can be illustrated using the modified Brunswikian lens model that Scherer (1978, 1982) has suggested for the study of vocal communication. Figure 6.1 shows a simplified model for the communication of emotion in the context of this model (obviously, a more realistic modeling of emotion signaling in social interaction requires a dynamic model with encoding and decoding working in both directions). Although it is obviously preferable to study vocal communication in an integrative fashion, measuring all parts of the model simultaneously in the same study (see Scherer, 1978), the complexity and practical difficulties of research in the area of vocal communication of emotion have not encouraged such

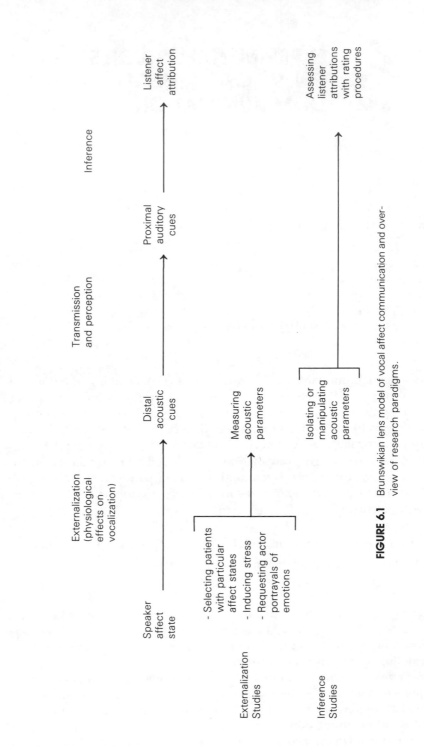

FIGURE 6.1 Brunswikian lens model of vocal affect communication and overview of research paradigms.

studies so far. Our own research has also dealt separately with the encoding and the decoding part of the model.

In this chapter, we review a number of studies conducted by our research group during the last decade that have attempted to throw light on these two aspects of the process of emotion signaling in the vocal channel of communication. Rather than providing empirical detail for the studies reviewed (most of which have been published independently), we try to review the major conclusions that can be drawn from these series of studies.

Externalization Studies

The purpose of externalization studies is to investigate the covariation between changes in affect state and changes in the resulting acoustic cues of vocalization during such states. The assumption made is that the physiological changes that accompany the affect state affect the vocalization patterns (particularly respiration, phonation, and articulation) and will thus result in noticeable variation in the acoustic cues of the speech signal. Externalization studies have been rendered highly impractical by the severe difficulty of experimentally manipulating emotional states because of both ethical and practical reasons (see Scherer, 1986a; overview for Part I of this volume). Similarly, given the private nature of emotional experience, it is rather difficult for researchers to have access to naturally occurring emotional states that could be used for externalization studies.

As is often the case in the process of scientific research, one can try to use naturally occurring pathology to study a specific process. Because the voices of mentally and emotionally disturbed clinical patients differ from those of healthy persons, and because such patients are often in a state of high affective arousal, we thought it would be interesting to determine whether successful therapeutic treatment, which should be accompanied by a decrease in arousal, is reflected in the acoustic speech patterns of such patients (Tolkmitt, Helfrich, Standke, & Scherer, 1982). The necessary speech material was obtained during interviews before and after treatment, in which depressive and schizophrenic patients had to utter standard sentences concerning their emotional states with as much emphasis as possible (e.g., "I feel angry," "I feed sad"). From these speech samples we extracted mean F0 values, spectral energy distributions, and formant frequencies of vowels that occurred in identical phonetical context. Both groups of patient showed a decrease in mean F0 after therapy (see Figure 6.2). For theoretical reasons (Scherer, 1979) we presume that this indicates a reduction in general arousal. Differential results with regard to spectral energy suggested that the voice of depressives also

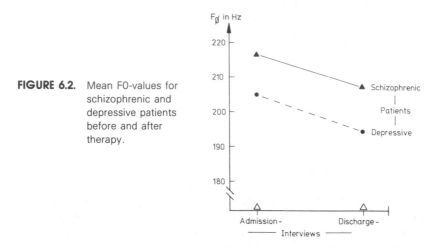

FIGURE 6.2. Mean F0-values for schizophrenic and depressive patients before and after therapy.

became more relaxed after therapy. Extraction of formant values showed significant before–after therapy differences that indicated a movement away from neutral frequencies that could be interpreted as an increase in the precision of articulation after therapy. In general, it could be said that significant changes in the acoustic parameters investigated suggest a decrease in arousal after therapy.

Although the induction of real emotions is beset by the difficulties described previously, there are many models for inducing stress-related arousal in the laboratory. While the type of affective arousal produced in such studies can vary remarkably across individuals, depending on the type of evaluation of the situation and the differences in the resulting emotion (see Scherer, 1986a; Scherer, Wallbott, Tolkmitt, & Bergmann, 1985), it seems useful to employ a stress-induction paradigm in an initial attempt to understand vocal reactions to change in arousal.

In a series of experiments, we used the standard laboratory stress-induction design with a variety of different stressors in order to study vocal changes following affect arousal. In addition, we wanted to get a clearer picture of the relationship between stress arousal and speaker-related variables on the one hand, and acoustic parameter variations on the other hand. To what extent, if at all, is the observed relationship between arousal and vocal expression affected by personality and situational factors? The three independent variables we used were coping-style (repressor vs. sensitizer), stress-type (cognitive vs. emotional), and stress-degree (low vs. high). To create cognitive stress, series of numbers with easy and difficult sequencing rules were used; the rules had to be discovered under time pressure. To induce emotional stress, two short movies were shown, one with a neutral theme and the other showing rather unpleasant surgery. After the applications of each stressor, text and spontaneous speech samples were obtained from each subject. These were used for formant- and F0-analyses, respectively. In addition, subjects had to give a subjective evaluation of each stressor at the end of the experimental session.

Subjects experienced the high-stress conditions as more stressful and described the cognitive stressors as more difficult to deal with and more strenuous than the emotional stressors. Therefore, on the subjective level we could be sure that the intended differential effect of the stressors had been successful.

Analyses of the free-speech samples did not yield the expected increase of mean F0 and F0 variability with increasing stress. For cognitive stress, there was a tendency in the opposite direction. Spectral analyses of the same speech material did not show any significant change in energy composition as a result of experimental treatment. This was contrary to our expectations. However, formant analyses of the standard speech samples produced some interesting results. For quite a number of vowel formants, significant interactions of similar structure for cognitive and emotional stress situations were obtained for the three experimental variables. The general tendency indicated that for repressors the formant frequencies increased under high cognitive stress and decreased under high emotional stress. The opposite seemed to be true for sensitizers. The study and the results are described in detail in Höfer, Wallbott, & Scherer (1985).

One reason that F0 and spectral analyses did not yield any appreciable changes as a result of the experimental manipulations may be due to the fact that the respective speech samples were always obtained after the application of the stressors. This could mean that the effect of the stressors had already faded by the time the speech samples were obtained. A clearer picture of the effect of stress on acoustic parameters might emerge if speech samples were obtained during stress application. Another factor that could have influenced the results is the fact that repressors, who score low on anxiety scales, are not a homogeneous group but can be further subdivided by the Social Desirability Scale (Crowne & Marlowe, 1964) into anxiety deniers (high SD scores) and low-anxiety subjects (low SD scores). It is likely that these two groups react differentially to stress (Asendorpf & Scherer, 1983).

To improve on the shortcomings of the earlier design, a further study (Scherer, Wallbott, Tolkmitt, & Bergmann, 1985; Tolkmitt & Scherer, 1986) was conducted in which the repressor category was divided into anxiety deniers and low-anxiety subjects; a third group, the high-anxiety subjects, was to represent the former sensitizers. In addition, we included both male and female subjects. This time, the cognitive stressors consisted of slides showing Raven Progressive Matrices test items of low and high difficulty and the emotional stressors were slides of harmless skin diseases (low stress) and very severe accident injuries (high stress). The subjects were exposed individually to the four stressors in random order; each stressor consisted of five slides that had been shown to have a high rating on stress potential in a prior pilot study. Each slide had a code consisting of two vowels and one digit that the subjects had to read out loud. These speech samples were taken to allow for spectral and formant analyses. In addition, the content of the slides had to be described in a semi-standardized sentence that on the one hand signaled the subjectively experienced cognitive difficulty or emotional impact of each slide and, on the other hand, could be used for F0 analyses. At the end of the session, the success of the experimental manipulation was verified by having the subject evaluate the stressors according to a scale that assessed the degree to which stress was differentially induced.

The manipulation check indicated that the two types of stress were subjectively experienced as qualitatively different, that is, emotional stress was judged to be more disagreeable and arousing. The degree of stress resulted in significant differences; for example, for high-level conditions, greater degree of difficulty in case of cognitive and a smaller chance of healing in case of emotional stress were reported. In addition, the stressors seemed to have affected females more strongly than males. Mean F0, F0 floor (the final F0-values of a declarative statement; see, e.g., Liberman & Pierrehumbert, 1984), formant locations, and spectral energy distributions were extracted from the relevant speech samples. While mean F0 did not covary with stress manipulation, F0 floor (as measured by the lowest 5% F0 values for each subject) of high anxiety and anxiety-denying subjects increased with stress, probably due to physiologically based changes in muscle tension.

For articulatory processes, as measured by formant locations and spectral energy composition, significant changes were found for females but not for males (see Figure 6.3).

For anxiety-denying females, precision of articulation (which was measured as the distance between actual and "ideal" formant values) increased under cognitive and decreased under emotional stress. These results were interpreted in terms of differential susceptibility to stress. As anxiety-denying females score high on the SD scale, their articulatory efforts were interpreted as compensatory attempts toward socially expected behavior. On the other hand, it can be assumed that low- and high-anxiety females do not hide their feelings (low SD scores), and one could argue (based on the articulatory results) that they were aroused by cognitive stress but not as strongly affected by emotional stress. As the

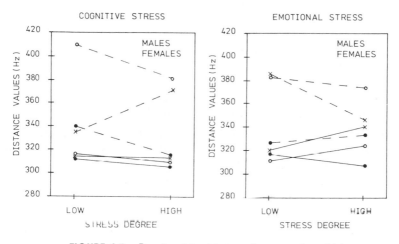

x- anxiety deniers (MAS low;SDS high)   x- anxiety deniers (MAS low;SDS high)
●- low anxious (MAS low;SDS low)   ●- low anxious (MAS low;SDS low)
o- high anxious (MAS high;SDS low)   o- high anxious (MAS high;SDS low)

FIGURE 6.3. Results of the formant distance values (Hz) (for details see text).

opposite reactions are probably considered to be the socially expected behavior, it was then argued that anxiety-denying females compensate for their natural reactions by hiding their cognitive arousal through precise articulation, and simulate (or at least do not mask) emotional arousal, resulting in inaccurate articulation.

In general, it was argued that stress seems to have a differential effect on phonation and articulation. Although phonation may covary at certain times with arousal itself, articulation seems to reflect the more cognitively controlled maneuvers of the subjects to cope with arousal. This may reflect important differences in the way in which affective and cognitive speaker states are encoded into the verbal messages.

The studies reported here indicate that the verbal message can and does serve as a medium for vocal affect expression. We have also shown in these experiments that situational factors such as the type and degree of stress, as well as personality factors such as copying style, influence the vocal correlates of the speaker's emotional state.

Inference Studies

The studies reported previously as well as a large number of studies in other laboratories show that changes in affect state do indeed lead to changes in a number of vocal parameters (see also Scherer, 1981; Scherer

& Scherer, 1981a; Scherer, 1986c). Consequently, one can assume that listeners are able to use this information to infer the emotional state of a speaker. A review of the literature shows that the accuracy of such affect attributions on the basis of vocal information alone is rather high (see Scherer, 1986a). Unfortunately, we know very little about the way in which the various acoustic parameters are used in the inference process that listeners use to arrive at attributions of speaker affect. In a series of studies we have tried to systematically study the role of different vocal parameters in this process. As described in Scherer and Scherer (1981b), the methods useful in this approach are masking or isolating particular vocal cues and systematically manipulating vocal cues.

In an early study, Scherer (1974, 1979; Scherer & Oshinsky, 1977) has used a Moog synthesizer to systematically manipulate a variety of acoustic cues in order to study emotional inference. Tone sequences modeled after the intonation contour of a short sentence, consisting of eight sine wave tones of differential pitch, duration, and contour were synthesized. The tape-recorded stimuli had to be rated as to whether they could express the following emotions: interest, sadness, fear, happiness, disgust, anger, surprise, elation, boredom. The parameters that seemed to have had the strongest influence on the judges' ratings were tempo and pitch variation. Moderate pitch variation led to an impression of sadness, fear, disgust, and boredom; extreme pitch variation and rising contour produced ratings of happiness, interest, and fear (see Table 6.1). The results therefore support the contention that attribution of specific emotions from auditory stimuli is based on characteristic patterns of acoustic cues. There was evidence that specific cues or cue combinations communicate the major dimensions of specific emotions.

Although this method allowed an elegant and very systematic manipulation of a variety of important acoustic parameters, the results are not directly comparable with studies on vocal signaling of emotion using speech material. Because nonlinguistic melodies were used, the attention of the listener was focused on the pure acoustic variations. Under normal circumstances, of course, emotion-induced vocal changes will occur over and above the linguistically determined vocal structure of an utterance. It is important to determine to what extent the nonverbal expression of speaker affect is independent of or interacts with the linguistically required changes in vocal parameters. For instance, a rising intonation contour is a linguistic feature to signal a question. To what extent does the vocal transmission of the speaker's state of emotion interact with such linguistic parameters as, for example, contour, form, and accent emphasis? Two models, the covariance and the configuration model, have been proposed (Ladd, Silverman, Tolkmitt, Bergmann, & Scherer, 1985; Scherer, Ladd, & Silverman, 1984). The covariance model states independence between

TABLE 6.1
Concomitants of Acoustical Dimensions

Amplitude	moderate	pleasantness, activity, happiness
Variation	extreme	fear
Pitch variation	moderate	anger, boredom, disgust, fear
	extreme	pleasantness, activity, happiness, surprise
Pitch contour	down	pleasantness, boredom, sadness
	up	potency, anger, fear, surprise
Pitch level	low	pleasantness, boredom, sadness
	high	activity, potency, anger, fear, surprise
Tempo	slow	boredom, disgust, sadness
	fast	pleasantness, activity, potency, anger, fear, happiness, surprise
Duration (shape)	round	potency, boredom, disgust, fear, sadness
	sharp	pleasantness, activity, happiness, surprise
Filtration (lack of	low	sadness
overtones)	moderate	pleasantness, boredom, happiness
	moderate	potency, activity
	extreme	anger, disgust, fear, surprise
Tonality	atonal	disgust
	tonal-minor	disgust, anger
	tonal-major	pleasantness, happiness
Rhythm	not rhythmic	boredom
	rhythmic	activity, fear, surprise

these two communicative systems, that is, speaker-state information and linguistic meaning are expected to be encoded independently of each other into quasi-parallel vocal channels. The assumption here is that relevant acoustic parameters covary with the strength of particular speaker states. The question remains as to how these two channels are kept separate during the transient acoustic production of speech. In the configuration model, the two channels (both the verbal and nonverbal cues) are supposed to exhibit categorical linguistic structures, and different speaker-state messages are expected to be conveyed by different configurations of categorical variables. For instance, a rising intonation contour, apart from its linguistic meaning, will interact with the transmission of speaker-state information.

We assume that vocal expression of affective speaker states can be better described by the covariance model, while the processes that control the vocal coding of more cognitive speaker states can better be understood in terms of the configuration model. These considerations could also bear on the conclusion reported concerning the differential coding function of phonation and articulation, the former seeming to covary with arousal, the latter seeming to be driven by cognitive coping strategies.

To throw light on these questions we performed a series of three experiments (Scherer, Ladd, & Silverman, 1984) using a corpus of civil servant–citizen interactions in which the verbally communicating participants were known to alternate between more or less emotional questions during the course of their interaction (Scherer, U. & Scherer, K.R., 1980; Scherer, Scherer, & Klink, 1979). In a first step we tried to objectify the impression of emotionality in the utterances by simply having vocal and written versions of all utterances be evaluated by two groups of raters according to their emotional content on five emotional scales (challenging, agreeable, polite, insecure, and aroused). Subsequent correlations of judgments within rater groups for each scale resulted in significant correlations for all scales in the audio condition but in rather small and inconsistent correlations for the transcript condition. The conclusion could therefore be drawn that, contrary to the transcript (that is, the content of the statements), the nonverbal aspects of the spoken statements carried clear emotional meaning, leading to high interrater correlations.

In the second phase of the study we tried to determine the extent to which individual acoustic parameters evoke affective judgments independently of or interactively with the content of the verbal message. Specific cues in the 24 utterances with the clearest emotional meaning were either degraded or emphasized by three masking techniques (see Scherer, 1982): (a) low-pass filtering was used to filter out the verbal content and the voice quality but leave the fundamental frequency (F0) contour; (b) the random splicing technique was used to remove the temporal organization and continuity of the F0 contour as well as the overall energy envelope, while the information about overall F0 level and range, and especially most of the spectral cues to voice quality, are retained; finally, (c) to control for the effects of temporal disruption, another masking condition that left voice quality intact was used—reversed speech. The 24 utterances of the four conditions (full audio, low-pass filtering, random splicing, and reversed speech) were presented to groups of subjects for evaluation on the same emotion scales as before. The analyses aimed at isolating the affective force that was retained after the various transformations. The results showed that all aspects of affect represented in the rating form were to a large extent directly communicated by voice quality cues, independent of the text and despite gross distortions of the F0 contours. This is strong evidence that much affective information is conveyed by voice quality, that is, spectral energy distribution independent of intonation and text. This tends to confirm the assumption of the covariance model that at least some of the affective force of an utterance can be seen as a parallel channel of nonverbal acoustic cues that convey affect in a direct and context-independent way.

Masking techniques, however, do not address one of the basic assumptions of the configuration model, namely that intonational cues signal affect in conjunction with the text. To investigate this assumption, the utterances were classified according to categorical and gradient features. The categorical features were contour type (rise vs. fall) and question type (why vs. yes/no); the gradient features were F0 range (low vs. high) and F0 standard deviation (low vs. high). Again all utterances were evaluated using the five affective scales, and ratings on each scale were then analyzed by means of multiple regression analyses. The results provided clear evidence of interactions between contour type and text in communicating aspects of speaker affect. The existence of such interactions points to the limitations of content-masking techniques as a method for investigating nonverbal affect cues.

The results of experiments that attempt to determine the affective force of isolated individual cues have to be carefully evaluated for potential interactions with verbal content. In general it was shown that the affective signaling functions of F0 depend in part on specific combinations of sentence type and contour type. This provides evidence for the existence of categorical linguistic organization of F0, and more generally, for the assumption that affective signaling may depend on configurations of category variables. However, it is also important to distinguish between linguistic and paralinguistic features of F0, inasmuch as overall F0 level and range, unlike contour type, do show covariance effects on affect judgments (see preceding).

By virtue of these studies, we expect that certain acoustic parameters function as transmitters of affective information from speaker to listener. Yet, one needs to be aware of the fact that both the verbal and nonverbal messages can interact with each other. This is an aspect we had to take into consideration in our further effort to get a clearer picture of the relationship between the various parameters.

The studies described confirm the hypothesis that vocal cues are powerful signals of emotional speaker state and suggest that the covariance model adequately describes the relations between the intensity of emotional state with graded features of acoustic cues. However, one of the limitations of the speech material used in the studies described so far concerns the fact that relevant acoustic parameters vary in an uncontrolled manner. Given that a corpus of natural utterances was used, we had no control over the nature and variability of the cues present in the material. Obviously, it is very desirable to use an experimental design in which a variety of acoustic cues can be orthogonally varied in a systematic fashion. The use of this experimental approach has become possible by development of modern methods of digital speech resynthesis using linear predictive coding (Markel & Gray, 1976). This method allows one to systematically vary a number of acoustic characteristics in digitized speech samples and to reconvert these manipulated speech samples into speech with help of digital-to-analog converters. With this method, one can take a natural speech sample and systematically vary isolated acoustic features, leaving all other cues unchanged. Although there is a loss of quality due to the digitalizing and the reconversion into an analog signal, the listener does not have the impression of artificiality as with synthetic, computer-produced speech.

The procedure used was as follows: First of all, the speech signals were digitalized with a sampling frequency of either 12 kHz or 16 kHz. For the purpose of manipulation of the speech samples, a number of acoustic parameters were computed and separately displayed on a terminal screen (cf. Figure 6.4).

Supported by an interactive computer graphics program, F0 contour, intensity, and duration of the signal could be varied continuously, independently, and in combination. We then modified the patterns of these parameters guided by several theoretical assumptions (see Bruce & Garding, 1978; Ladd, 1983; Liberman & Pierrehumbert, 1985); the new acoustical patterns were resynthesized and then made audible by using a digital-to-analog converter and an amplifier-loudspeaker system.

In the experiments described later we aimed at demonstrating that certain vocal cues systematically transmit affective information. On the basis of our earlier results we chose to test the hypothesis that intonation contour type, overall F0 range, and voice quality have independent effects on the attribution of affective states. Many linguistic descriptions of intonation also assume that these variables are independent, specifically Crystal, 1969, and Laver, 1980. According to this hypothesis, overall range

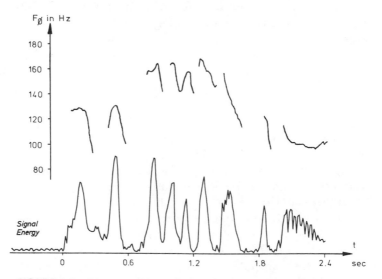

FIGURE 6.4. F0-contour (upper line) and energy contour (lower line).

and voice quality probably reflect states of arousal, whereas differences of contour types signal differences of cognitive attitude (see the results of a number of studies on vocal cues of emotional stress arousal, such as Hecker, Stevens, Bismarck, & Williams, 1968; Scherer, 1979, 1981a, 1981b; Williams & Stevens, 1981a; 1981b. See also the descriptions of contour meanings relative to attitudes by linguists such as Pike, 1945 and O'Connor & Arnold, 1961). We also decided to pursue the question as to whether there are parameters with continuous effects, that is, which are directly correlated to changes in the intensity of affective judgments.

In the light of the experimental evidence it must be noted that contours are not actually realized as up- or downdrifts but that, according to recent work on intonation (Bruce, 1982; Liberman & Pierrehumbert, 1984; Menn & Boyce, 1982), they represent types in a phonological system. A contour is formed by the F0-levels at the beginning and the end of a sentence as well as by those of the sentence-accent peaks (see Figure 6.5, points 1 to 6). The F0 range refers to the maximum and minimum values of the measured fundamental frequency. Voice quality refers to characteristics such as "hoarse," "sharp," or "resonant." Thus, it reflects properties not only of vocal fold action but also of the vocal tract characteristics generally.

In the first experiment we checked whether F0 contour, F0 range, and voice quality had independent effects on affective evaluations and verified their relationship to the degree of speaker arousal. We took into consideration the content of the text by choosing three different sentences. The parameters F0 range and F0 contour of the original speech signal were modified simultaneously; the bandwidth of intonational movements in

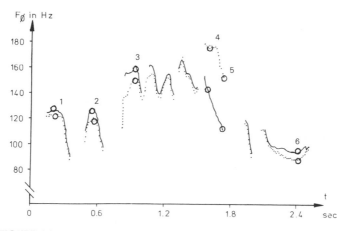

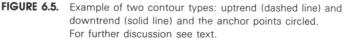

FIGURE 6.5. Example of two contour types: uptrend (dashed line) and downtrend (solid line) and the anchor points circled. For further discussion see text.

an F0 pattern was chosen as narrow and wide. The range was manipulated according to the assumption that F0 targets are scaled relative to minimum value of fundamental frequency (floor), which is seen as a speaker-dependent constant (see Ladd, Silverman, Tolkmitt, Bergmann, & Scherer, 1985).

Contours were manipulated with regard to the relative height of the accent peaks, described above as up-trend or down-trend (see Figure 6.5, dashed line and solid line respectively). These different acoustical patterns were then resynthesized on two selected voice quality types (normal and harsh), which were produced by two speakers under the instruction of pronouncing sentences in (a) a normal, relaxed, friendly, or (b) an annoyed, irritated, or angry fashion. The stimulus material (altogether 24 utterances) was judged in a rating session by listeners with respect to the speaker states and attitudes. The judges had to rate the emotional states using the scales aroused, annoyed, arrogant, and involved, and the cognitive attitudes on the scales emphatic, cooperative, contradicting, and reproachful. Analysis of variance procedures were used, given the factorial nature of the design. We found that F0 range and F0 contour, but less clearly voice quality, independently influenced the evaluation of the utterances. Variation of F0 range in particular led to significant effects on the emotional scales: It seemed that the relationship between speaker states and hearer attributions is indeed a continuous one (see Figure 6.6: The higher the F0 range of the utterance, the higher the degree of each speaker state is attributed by listeners). The predicted effect of the F0 contour could not be established in as clear a way; nevertheless, we found certain significant relations.

The (speaker-produced) voice quality showed only weak effects on attribution. Consequently, it is necessary to continue investigating the parameters involved by means of digital resynthesis. The reported findings

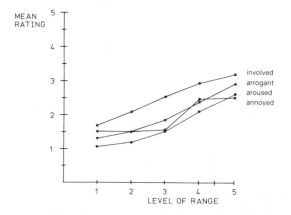

FIGURE 6.6 Ratings as a function of five F0-range levels.

were independent from the significant effects, which resulted from the evaluations of different sentences. This means that sentence-dependent effects on the one hand and acoustical patterns on the other influence the attribution of the listener in an additive fashion; a specific semantic content can enhance the emotional significance of a spoken word but cannot suppress the affective information inherent in the vocal expression. A detailed report of these studies can be found in Ladd, Silverman, Tolkmitt, Bergmann, and Scherer (1985).

The aim of the next experiment was to assess the generality of these results across different speakers. Therefore, we studied utterances of three speakers, maintaining the variations of the acoustical parameters mentioned previously. The same scales as in the former experiments were used by the listeners. Speaker-type clearly influenced the judgments of the judges: Every speaker seemed to convey specific emotional and attitudinal information in his vocal expression. However, because we found that only one of all possible interactions between speaker identity and the manipulated acoustic features was significant, it can be argued that both sets of variables affected the judges independently. This also applies to the semantic content of an utterance.

Having demonstrated clear evidence for the independent function of these acoustic variables, the question arose as to whether these vocal cues operate on the utterance as a whole or only on those elements of a sentence that coincide with syntactic or semantic structures. Furthermore, it was necessary to determine whether a finely graded variation of accent height is perceived continuously or categorically. From a set of utterances we chose two examples with sentence accents being judged as unstressed and as very highly stressed. The F0 peaks at these syllables were set to 120 Hz (unstressed) and 180 Hz (very highly stressed). This range is divided into five steps of accent height, and each was resynthesized with three additional F0 range patterns over the whole sentence.

The most general conclusion to be drawn from these experiments is the fact that features of cognitive attitude seem to be transmitted by linguistically coded aspects of sentence structure, whereas emotional information is conveyed via speech activity as a whole. Furthermore, the emotionally relevant cues seem to evoke continuous attributions while the cues signaling speaker attitude tend to be perceived categorically.

These findings are further supported by an experiment designed to prove this hypothesis (Tolkmitt, Bergmann, & Goldbeck, 1987). A two-part utterance containing a modal particle in the second part (*Wussten Sie schon, er ist* doch *gekommen* / Did you know he came after all?) was resynthesized with three different F0 ranges and three versions of durations on the focused word /doch/. We obtained 27 versions because these patterns were combined in a fully factorial design with three types of

F0-jitter. These rapid F0-perturbations are usually perceived as a trembling of the voice.

The analysis of variance of the ratings showed no significant interactions but strong main effects. This indicates that the experimental factors of F0 range, duration, and jitter influence listener attribution independently. We found that even small variations of the acoustic cues of F0 range and duration led to corresponding reactions of the judges. This corroborates the assumption that emotional information in vocal expression is perceived continuously. Despite the absence of significant interactions, we believe that systematic interaction between F0 range and duration cannot be excluded at the present state of this research. As it is shown in Figure 6.7, the low F0 range leads to the highest scores on the "grief" scale. If, however, the factor duration becomes shorter, the judges of "grief" decrease correspondingly; this also counts for the other experimental conditions, namely mean F0 range and high F0 range.

A low F0 range combined with long duration led to the highest ratings of grief; this attribution decreased continuously with mean F0 range/mean duration and high F0 range/short duration. We observed the inverse relationship for the emotion of joy.

The influence of the jitter was not very pronounced; this may be explained by the fact that the quality of resynthesis is still too poor to generate such subtle features with sufficient precision.

In a further series of experiments, with a design similar to that just described, we were able to confirm that the acoustical cues of F0 range, speech rate, and intensity are of major relevance in signaling emotion, with a slight predominance of speech rate and F0 range. It seemed to us

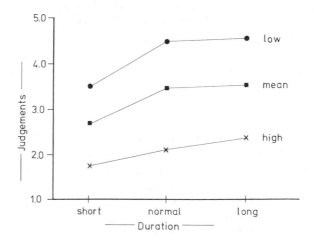

FIGURE 6.7.   The figure shows the factor F0-range as a function of duration for the rating label /grief/.

to be an interesting question as to whether it would be possible to neutralize a naturally spoken utterance with a strong emotional connotation by resynthesizing some of the acoustic cues described previously. Thus we varied the suprasegmental parameters (F0 range, speech rate, and intensity) with the intention of reducing their influence on the attribution of speaker states. If a high F0 range, for example, is usually judged as "joyful," we would reduce it, expecting that the number of "joyful" evaluations would decrease as range decreases. It is of particular interest to check whether the variations of the crucial parameters can sufficiently neutralize the signaling of a certain speaker state if the manipulation is restricted to sentence accents.

In a first attempt to answer these questions, an experiment was designed (Goldbeck, Bergmann, & Tolkmitt, 1986) in which it was possible to reduce the strength of the attribution of "anger." However, the basic impression of that speaker state could not be fully neutralized by only manipulating the suprasegmental patterns mentioned above. Apparently, voice quality (which was not changed) carries important information about the speaker state. In addition, the effects of the resynthesized acoustic patterns on attribution are stronger if the whole utterance is varied.

Combining Externalization and Inference

In a first attempt to combine externalization and inference, Wallbott and Scherer (1986b) used portrayals of different emotional expressions by professional actors. Two male and female actors from the Municipal Theatre of Giessen were asked to act out four emotional situations (joy, sadness, anger, and surprise) for which scenarios with a short vignette of the antecedent events and the nature of the situation were provided. In the course of the improvised dialogue the actors had to utter the statement "*Ich kann es nicht glauben* (I can't believe it)" at the apex of their emotional involvement. These target sentences were edited out of the dialogues and were presented under full-video, audio-only, video-only, and filtered-audio (lowpass filter at 400 Hz) conditions to four groups of judges for evaluation on the scales slow/fast, weak/intense, low pitched/high pitched, monotonous/melodious, and unpleasant/pleasant.

In terms of the accuracy of evaluations the group of judges in the full-video condition was most accurate. However, for the audio-only condition, clear attributional patterns also emerged for the four emotional portrayals. Figure 6.8 shows for the emotion /joy/ the correlations between the acoustic parameters "utterance length, F0 mean, F0 standard deviation" — in the sense of the lens model the distal cues (see introduction to this chapter) and the subjective ratings — percepts or proximal cues — and the accuracy of corresponding attributional evaluations. The high cor-

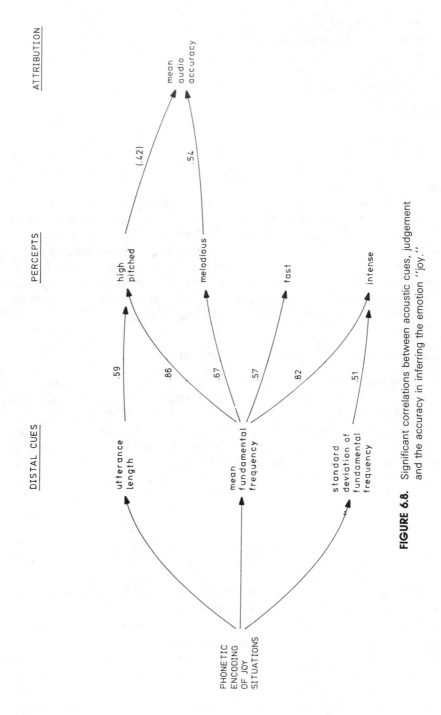

FIGURE 6.8. Significant correlations between acoustic cues, judgement and the accuracy in inferring the emotion "joy."

relations between F0 mean and the impression of high pitched and melodious indicates that nearly every variation of this acoustic cue affects both the subjective impression and the attribution (for details see Wallbott & Scherer, 1986b).

Conclusions

In this chapter, we reviewed a number of studies on the vocal expression of emotion that were conducted in our laboratory during the last decade. From these results, as well as from evidence found in the literature, there can be little doubt that vocal cues are very powerful signals of emotion. As one might expect on the basis of theoretical speculation, the physiological changes that accompany different emotional states strongly affect respiration, phonation, and articulation, and thus lead to rather pronounced changes in a large number of acoustical features of the speech signal. Listeners seem to be very sensitive to changes in these parameters, and they seem to very reliably infer specific emotional states from specific vocal cues. Unfortunately, the vocal communication of affect cannot yet be nicely modeled (e.g., using a modified Brunswikian approach) due to the lack of studies in which both externalization and inference have been assessed with the same speakers and speech materials as well as a focus on similar acoustic parameters. It is hoped that the increasing availability of modern speech-analysis hardware and software will make the task of comprehensively studying the complete process of vocal affect expression less onerous, leading to a multiplication of studies in this area.

One issue that has been repeatedly mentioned in this chapter is the important interaction of vocal cues to emotional state with paralinguistically used vocal parameter changes. Contrary to other domains of emotional expression, such as facial expression, vocal emotion signaling cannot be profitably studied independent of phonetic-linguistic concerns. Consequently, a close collaboration between psychology and the language sciences will be required to disentangle the complex web of factors that determine human vocal expression.

7 FACES IN CONTEXT: THE RELATIVE IMPORTANCE OF FACIAL EXPRESSION AND CONTEXT INFORMATION IN DETERMINING EMOTION ATTRIBUTIONS

Harald G. Wallbott
University of Giessen

> *Signals are us dependent on contextual sources of information as are words, and no point is more fundamental to understanding the behavior of communicating.*
>
> —(W.J. Smith, 1977, p. 224)

Context Effects in Emotion Recognition

In the 1920s Soviet film director Lew Kuleschov conducted an "experiment." He produced three short films consisting of two takes each. The first take was a picture of either a dead woman, a dish of soup, or a picture of a child playing. The second take was identical for each film: a close-up of an actor with a neutral facial expression. Viewers to whom these three films were shown stressed the actor's dramatic ability: his portrayal of thoughtfulness when looking at the soup, his deep grief when confronted with the dead woman, and his slight, happy smile when looking at the playing child (Gregor & Patalas, 1976).

In a series of studies, Warr and Knapper (1968) confronted subjects with photographs of persons taken from newspapers and short articles referring to these photographs. They found that judgments about the persons shown in photographs were to a large extent determined by the story and not by the photograph, and concluded that the verbal message results in a "frame of reference," which guides the interpretation of the photograph.

These studies illustrate the potential influence of "context information" on judgments of facial expression. The usual design for emotion recognition studies from facial expression is the following: Subjects or judges are confronted with close-up photographs of a sender, and their task is to judge these photographs by choosing the "correct" emotion from a number of given terms or to indicate the intensity of the recognized emotions on emotion scales. Thus, subjects are exposed to a static representation of the face (a photograph), free of context information. In real-life situations, on the other hand, an observer is rarely confronted with only a static face. The "real-life" observer receives not only information from facial expression but also information from other aspects, which include different behavioral modalities like gestures, voice, or body position, and from the situational context, in which a given facial expression occurs.

The relative influence of person information and context information on emotion attributions is still a matter of discussion. The only review so far, by Ekman, Friesen, and Ellsworth (1982a), concludes that, in fact, facial expression dominates emotion judgments, while context information becomes important only when facial expressions are ambiguous or the emotion portrayed is low in intensity. They arrived at that conclusion by reanalyzing some of the studies on the relative influence of both sources of information, such as, for instance, Goodenough and Tinker (1931) or Munn (1940). This general conclusion is confirmed by the results of studies conducted by Frijda (1969) and Watson (1972). Though this general conclusion may be correct in stressing the importance of facial expression information, the problem is that "context" is only vaguely defined and that, in fact, different studies conducted on the topic used different types of "contexts."

The two paradigms so far employed most often are the "person-scenario approach" and the "candid-picture approach." The person-scenario approach was originally introduced by Goodenough and Tinker (1931). Here, observers are confronted with photographs of facial expression and verbal descriptions of situations arousing emotion. The candid-picture approach was introduced by Munn (1940). Here, observers are shown actual photographs depicting a person in an emotional situation. Thus, in the first paradigm, context information is delivered verbally, whereas in the second paradigm, context is depicted visually. Given these different possibilities of confronting observers with "context," it seems important to be very precise about the meaning of "context" when comparing different studies.

A distinction of different types of contexts, with respect to the presentation mode, for instance, seems important, because it may be argued that the impact of context on an observer is different when context is presented verbally and when it is presented visually. Given verbal presentation, the observer has to infer the situation, which is usually described in rather abstract terms. Visual presentation, on the other hand, provides an observer with a larger quantity of information, which may also be more "vivid" and more "immediate" and thus more readily accessible than verbal description.

Such differences in the presentation of "context" may account for the fact that most studies using the person-scenario approach have found a dominance of person information (photograph) over contextual information (scenarios) (Frijda, 1969; Watson, 1972), while at least some studies with the candid-picture paradigm found context information to be very important (Spignesi & Shor, 1981; Turhan, 1960; Vinacke, 1949).

Emotion Recognition and Information Processing

Basically, research on emotion recognition has to be concerned with the integration of different cues within one judgment or attribution. These cues may be transmitted within the same nonverbal channel (if the time dimension is taken into account), in different nonverbal channels, or may be either person or context information cues. Thus, information integration models may be useful tools for studying such processes. Unfortunately, nonverbal communication research is rarely concerned with such models. But a lot of suggestions can be taken from "classical" social psychology research, where different information integration models have been proposed, such as the averaging model (Triandis & Fishbein, 1962) and the summation and multiplication models (Anderson, 1971, 1974). Apart from these "linear combination" models, the idea of "Gestalt" information integration models was originally proposed by Asch (1946). These models basically state that when new information is introduced, existing bits of information will be reinterpreted and thus will generally change in meaning, because impression formation is considered as a "Gestalt" process, which cannot be accounted for by relatively simple mathematical models.

When discussing information integration strategies in emotion recognition, it is important to note that different observers may use different strategies, as observed for instance by Frijda (1969). Frijda identified observers who readily discounted one piece of information when confronted with discrepant person and context information, each suggesting different emotions, while other subjects introduced new concepts to integrate discrepant information (like stating for instance that "in reality" a person shown on a photograph experiences quite a different emotion in the situation depicted). Similar strategies were discussed by Gollin (1956), who distinguished between "simplification" strategies—where part of the information is neglected; "relation" strategies—where an attempt is made to integrate information in a meaningful way; and "aggregation" strategies—in which all information presented is included but not integrated in the final judgment. Such different strategies of information integration are also discussed by Thayer and Schiff (1969), Knudsen and Muzekari (1983), and Asch and Zukier (1984).

A model describing the process of emotion attribution based on both person and context information can be formulated by using suggestions from social psychology and models from nonverbal behavior research (especially Frijda, 1969). The idea proposed by Frijda (1969) is that an observer will try to infer an emotion from person and context information separately. We propose that these two inference processes will result in two "lists of emotions" attributing different emotions with descending intensity/probability for person and context information separately. These lists of emotions may be described via linear regression with the succession of judged emotion intensities as a dummy variable:

	Most probable emotion	Second most probable emotion	Third most probable emotion	etc.
Dummy variable	1	2	3	etc.

The regression constant then indicates the intensity of the most probable emotion, while the regression coefficient may be considered as a measure for the unequivocalness of the cues presented. This allows an operationalization of both source intensity and source clarity, which are important factors in determining the relative importance of person and context information (Ekman, Friesen, & Ellsworth, 1982a).

Given two information sources and two resulting "lists of emotions," the observer then has the task of integrating both emotion inferences in order to arrive at a final judgment. To study these processes one could determine whether an observer would give different weights to the two sources of information (for instance via beta-weights for both person and context information in predicting judgments of combined stimuli). Furthermore, it may be predicted that an observer will use different strategies when confronted with concordant or consonant information cues and when exposed to discrepant or discordant information cues. Given concordant information (where the same emotion is depicted in person and context information), the integration of both sources should not be too difficult. The only point to study here is which information integration model (for instance averaging, summation, or regression) will depict the process most accurately. A more interesting point is to study information integration given discrepant cue combinations. We suggest that in such discrepant cases, where the major emotion inferred from person and context information is discrepant, the next most probable emotion from both emotion lists will be considered.

If this strategy does not result in concordant combinations, more complex mechanisms may be used. The observer may, for instance, try to integrate the discrepant information by restructuring the "lists of emotions."

He or she may try to separate the inferred emotion from the expression by stating that a person shown in a photograph does not express the experienced emotion freely but instead is using display rules (Ekman, 1972). Or the observer may separate the situational context from the expression by stating that the person depicted is experiencing not the emotion usually evoked by the situation but instead another emotion, which in fact is depicted in the photograph. In "Gestalt" terms this would imply that either person information is the "figure" seen against the "ground" of context information, or the other way around. If these strategies are still not successful, an observer may use the most "primitive" strategy and may totally discount either the person or the context information, thus arriving at an integrated judgment by using only part of the information given.

In terms of the "emotion list" model proposed above (to be described via linear regression), we may argue that for consonant combinations, the resulting list of emotions should be at least as intense and as unequivocal with respect to the main emotion inferred (or even more intense and more unequivocal if the two sources of information accentuate each other) as the "lists" for the judgments of person and context information presented separately. For discrepant combinations, on the other hand, the contrary may be expected. Given two interfering lists of emotion, the resulting list for combinations should be less intense and less unequivocal than lists based on separate judgments of person and context information, that is, the respective regression constants and coefficients for the combination judgments should be smaller than those for the person and the context judgments.

Thus, we propose to study information integration processes in emotion recognition in the following way: First of all, we need separate judgments of the different information cues in order to evaluate source intensity, clarity, and ambiguity for person and context information separately (compare Ekman, Friesen, & Ellsworth, 1982). Then we confront observers with combinations of person and context cues, using both discrepant and consonant cue combinations. The first question to ask, then, is whether person information or context information dominates combination judgments. The relevance of the different cues may be studied by using either correlation techniques, regression techniques, or relative shift measures as proposed, for instance, by Frijda (1969). The second question is, which models of information integration best describe judges' strategies? Given the literature in social psychology, averaging, summation, multiplication, or regression models can be studied. The third question, finally, should be concerned with judges' strategies of information integration, which seem to be especially interesting in the case of discrepant cue combinations. Such strategies may be studied by asking observers explicitly how they tried to integrate the different cues they were confronted with. Given the model proposed previously, such strategies might include aggregation, integration, reinterpretation, or discounting.

So far we have studied these processes in two studies that are basically replications of the classical Goodenough and Tinker (person-scenario) approach and the Munn (candid-picture) approach.

Study 1: The Person-Scenario Paradigm

In the first study we attempted to replicate the person-scenario paradigm, which was introduced by Goodenough and Tinker (1931). In this approach, person information is provided visually by photograph, and context information is provided verbally by description of situations to judges. In contrast to other studies (e.g., Watson, 1972), not only one sender but multiple senders should be used here. Furthermore, photographs and situation descriptions should be presented in different combinations in order to study not only consonant but also discrepant combinations of stimuli. Finally, the judges' task was not only to judge the emotions depicted but also to report which strategy of information integration they had used and which stimuli they payed the most attention to.

METHOD

Selection of Stimuli

The visual stimuli were selected from the series "Pictures of facial affect" (Ekman & Friesen, 1976). The photographs depicted one emotion with high intensity and other emotions with low intensity, that is, photographs selected were neither complex nor ambiguous with respect to the emotion depicted. Thirty judges (15 male, 15 female psychology students) watched the series of 65 photographs, which were presented as slides to groups of 5 persons each. They saw each slide for 25 seconds. Their task was to judge the emotions depicted on scales from 0 (= emotion not existing) to 8 (= emotion very intense) for the seven fundamental emotions: joy, sadness, fear, anger, surprise, disgust, and contempt. Based on these judgments, 11 photographs that were neither complex nor ambiguous were selected for the main study. The criterion was that only one emotion was judged as being very intense (mean across judges > 6.0), while the other emotions were judged as being of low intensity (second most intense emotion < 3.0).

In most studies so far, verbal situation descriptions were made up ad hoc by researchers (Frijda, 1969; Watson, 1972). To obtain higher ecological validity, in this study actual reports describing real situations were used, employing material from a large-scale questionnaire study (see

Scherer, Summerfield, & Wallbott, 1983; Scherer, Wallbott, & Summerfield, 1986). In these studies subjects had to describe situations in detail in which they had experienced the emotions joy, sadness, fear, and anger. Selection of situation descriptions thus is reduced to only these four emotions. From the material of these questionnaire studies, following a coding procedure described in Scherer, Wallbott, and Summerfield (1986), situations that typically elicited the respective emotion were selected.

The 24 situation descriptions thus selected were judged by a group of judges (16 female, 15 male psychology students). As in the selection of photographs, it was the judges' task to evaluate on scales from 0 to 8 the intensity of the emotions joy, fear, anger, surprise, sadness, disgust, and contempt, which a person in the situation described would experience. Given the fact that 11 photographs were selected, 11 situation descriptions were used that also were judged as being of low ambiguity and complexity (with the exception of situations judged as indicating high intensity of joy/happiness. These situations were usually ambiguous in that surprise judgments generally were also high. Thus, joy and surprise interfere in these descriptions).

This selection process resulted in three photographs depicting joy, three photographs depicting surprise, four photographs depicting sadness, and one photograph depicting contempt. Of the verbal situation descriptions selected, two were judged as conveying sadness, fear, and anger respectively, and five as conveying joy (and to some degree, surprise).

Combination Judgments

In the main study observers were confronted with combinations of person and context information. The 11 photographs were combined with the 11 situation descriptions three times, resulting in 33 combinations. In order to select such combinations, the pre-ratings for the photographs presented alone and the descriptions presented alone were used. "Consonant" combinations were defined as combinations where the dominating emotions inferred from photograph and description alone were the same (e.g., a photograph depicting sadness combined with a situation judged as eliciting sadness). "Discrepant" combinations included photographs judged as conveying a positive emotion (joy) and descriptions conveying a negative emotion (e.g., sadness). For "ambiguous" combinations, photographs and descriptions conveying two negative but different emotions were combined (e.g., fear and anger). The relative concordancy of combinations was operationalized by computing correlations between the intensity judgments for the seven emotions resulting from the photograph-only and the description-only pre-ratings (averaged across judges). For the 11 consonant combinations, the average r between photograph-only and description-only judgments was .86, the average r for the 11 discrepant combinations was $-.33$, and the average r for the remaining 11 ambiguous combinations reached .10. Combinations were arranged in three sets of stimuli, so that each judge could be confronted with 11 stimuli but saw each description and each photograph only once (that is, not in different combinations). Each set contained consonant, ambiguous, and discrepant combinations. Ten observers were confronted with each set of combinations.

Observers received a booklet depicting on the left side of each page a photograph (format 15×10 cm) and on the right side a situation description (on the average about four lines of text). Of the 30 judges, 16 were female and 14 male, and all were psychology students. Their task was to do the following: on seven scales (representing the seven fundamental emotions) from 0 to 8 they had to judge in which intensity which emotions were conveyed by the combination of photograph and description. After that, subjects had to answer two open-ended questions: They had to describe the conveyed emotion in their own terms, and they had to report on the strategies of information integration that they had used to judge the respective combination (question: "How did you arrive at your decision?").

Coding of Information Integration Strategies

The strategies of information integration were determined for each stimulus combination and each judge separately by coding the answers to the two open-ended questions. Taking proposals in the relevant literature (see earlier discussion) into account, the following coding system was used:

- "Only person or person dominating": In the free descriptions of the emotion, judges name only that emotion that is characteristic of the person information alone.
- "Only context or context dominating": Judges name only those emotion terms that are characteristic of the context information alone.
- "Aggregation": Judges name not only the emotion term relevant to context but also the emotion term relevant to person.
- "Reinterpretation of person information": The emotion depicted in the photograph is reinterpreted to fit the context information, for example, indicating that a sad facial expression in fact means that the person is crying "for joy."
- "Reinterpretation of context information": The situation description is reinterpreted to fit the photograph, for example, indicating that a

letter from a friend, which when judged alone, indicates joy, may contain "bad news."

- "Integration": Both sources of information are integrated by inferring additional information that is not originally included in the partial information. Sadness and anger, for example, may be integrated to resignation, joy and anger may be cynicism, or a happy facial expression in a situation provoking anger might result in "a person with a good sense of humor."

- "Incompatibility": Judges mention explicitly that the components do not fit together or provide a "meta comment" like "this combination doesn't make sense."

Using this coding system, the total material of 330 descriptions (30 judges with 11 judgments each) was coded by two independent coders. The percent agreement reached between the two coders was 84%. In the statistical comparisons to be reported, the number of judges with the respective information integration strategy were used as variables.

Statistical Analysis

Given the theoretical considerations, the following questions were to be asked of the data: To what extent are the combination judgments determined by the photographs and by the verbal descriptions? Which models of information integration (averaging, regression, or summation) are adequately able to depict the combination judgments? Which strategies of information integration (which was especially interesting when looking at discrepant combinations) are used by observers?

To determine the relative contribution of person information and context information to combination judgments, several parameters were computed. For each combination (N = 33), correlations between the intensities of the seven emotions (averaged across judges) for the person judgments and the combination judgments as well as between the context judgments and the combination judgments were determined. Higher correlations between person and combination compared to context and combination would indicate that person information determines combination judgments to a larger degree than context information. Furthermore, an index of "relative shift" between person and context information (Frijda, 1969; d = the sum of absolute differences between combination judgment and person judgment for the seven emotions/sum of absolute differences between combination judgment and context judgment for the seven emotions) was computed. If d is larger than 1.0, person information dominates. Furthermore, multiple regression analyses were computed to determine the beta weights to each combination for person and context information using the judgments for the seven emotions averaged across judges in each stimulus condition.

To study the most appropriate model of information integration, an (unweighted) averaging model, a summation model, and a weighted regression model with the average beta weights for the three combination groups was computed. Furthermore, for each "list of emotions" (i.e., the distribution of intensity judgments across the seven emotions averaged across judges in each condition), for each person judgment, context judgment, and combination judgment, a linear regression with the succession of intensities as a dummy variable was computed separately. It was hypothesized that especially in discrepant combinations, the resulting regression for the combination judgments should be less steep than those for consonant combinations, because in cases of discrepant combinations, two different main emotions for person and context have to be integrated in the judgments.

To compare discrepant, consonant, and ambiguous combinations, an analysis of variance approach was used in which the three groups of combinations (discrepant, consonant, neither discrepant nor consonant) were compared with respect to the different variables. To determine differences between groups, post hoc comparisons were computed (Newman-Keul's test).

Results

All ANOVA-results are depicted in Table 7.1. First of all, the a priori classification into discrepant, consonant, and ambiguous combinations is statistically significant when considering the correlation between person judgments and context judgments alone (thus justifying comparing these three groups of stimuli in the other parameters studied). The correlations between person judgments and combination judgments are rather high for all three groups of combinations (average r = .84), which implies that person information (facial expression) determines combination judgments to a large degree. A significant effect due to the relative consistency of combinations is found for the correlations between context judgments and combination judgments. Although for discrepant combinations the context information does not influence the combination judgments to a large degree, the correlation between context and combination judgments increases with increasing congruency of combinations. That means that context information becomes more important in determining consonant combinations compared to discrepant combinations. This result is replicated when looking at the relative shift index. The significant effect found is especially due to the difference between consonant combinations and all other combinations. In consonant combinations, context information is more important than person information, whereas in all other combinations, person information dominates context information.

TABLE 7.1
ANOVA Results for the Person-Scenario Study

| Variable | Combinations means | | | F | df | p | Newman-Keuls post-hoc-com-parisons |
	discrep-pant N=11	ambig-uous 11	conso-nant 11	mean			
Correlation photo/scenario judgment	−.33	.10	.86	.21	148.93	2/30	.000	CON>AMB>DIS
Correlation photo/comb.-judgment	.82	.77	.94	.84	3.10	2/30	.060	– –
Correlation scenario/comb.-judgment	−.05	.49	.91	.45	40.91	2/30	.000	CON>AMB>DIS
Relative shift index	.55	.59	1.05	.73	4.07	2/30	.027	CON>AMB=DIS
Averaging model	8.15	6.56	4.17	6.29	6.52	2/30	.005	CON<DIS=AMB
Summation model	10.39	11.01	10.08	10.49	<1	2/30	n.s.	– –
Regression model	5.32	5.29	4.05	4.89	2.32	2/30	.116	– –
beta-weight photo	.90	.78	.52	.73	3.63	2/30	.039	DIS>CON
beta-weight scenario	.26	.41	.48	.38	<1	2/30	n.s	– –

(Continued)

149

TABLE 7.1
(Continued)

Variable	Combinations means				F	df	p	Newman-Keuls post-hoc-comparisons
	discrepant N=11	ambiguous 11	consonant 11	mean				
Regression constant (Comb. judgment)	5.08	5.19	5.45	5.24	<1		n.s.	--
Regression coefficient (Comb. judgment)	−.73	−.77	−.90	−.80	3.88	2/30	.032	CON>AMB=DIS
Strategies of information integration (averaged N):								
Photo dominating	2.41	2.36	1.14	1.97	1.97		n.s.	--
Scenario dominating	.59	.82	.22	.54	1.10		n.s.	--
Aggregation	.46	2.09	7.14	3.23	28.86	2/30	.000	CON>AMB=DIS
Reinterpretation Photo	.73	1.12	.55	.80	2.05		n.s.	--
Reinterpretation scenario	.23	.23	.05	.17	1.01		n.s.	--
Integration	3.41	1.59	.73	1.91	9.82	2/30	.001	DIS>AMB=CON
Incompatibility	2.23	1.64	.18	1.35	7.56	2/30	.002	CON>DIS=AMB

Another indicator for the fact that context information becomes more important in the more concordant combinations is found when looking at the beta weights for personal information and context information in predicting the combination judgments. The beta weights for person information decrease significantly from discrepant to consonant combinations, whereas the beta weights for context increase (though not significantly so) from discrepant to consonant combinations.

Concerning the question as to which model of information integration best predicts combination judgments, the statistical results show that the summation model cannot be considered as an adequate description of the strategies of information integration used by judges. The averaging model proves to be far more effective. Furthermore, there is a significant effect for this model with respect to the discrepancy/consonancy distinction. An averaging model seems to be especially adequate for consonant combinations, though predictions of this model for discrepant combinations are significantly less accurate. Even better than the averaging model is the prediction capacity of the weighted regression model (using averaged beta weights across the 11 combinations for each group), though here we find no differences between discrepant and consonant combinations.

The results so far show that facial expression in general dominates context information, but that a more differentiated view, that is, comparing consonant and discrepant combinations, indicates that context information becomes more important when combinations are consonant. Furthermore, the more complex averaging model and especially the regression model seem to fit the strategies of information integration of judges far better than a simple summation model.

When looking at the linear regressions, we find some evidence for the proposed model (see previous discussion) depicting how judges use consonant and discrepant information combinations to infer emotions. It was hypothesized that combination judgments based on consonant information should be at least as unambiguous as judgments based on the bits of information presented separately, while combination judgments based on discrepant information should be *less* intense for the major emotion inferred and less unequivocal than judgments based on person and context information separately. On the average, the intensity of the main emotion of the lists of emotions (operationalized via the regression constant for intensity judgments of the seven emotions) lies between person and context judgments for the combination judgments. The same is true for the regression coefficients (whereby a larger negative value indicates a steeper decrease, that is more unambiguous judgments). Here also the data for the combination judgments lie between person and context judgments. Most importantly, we find differences between discrepant and consonant combinations (which reach significance for the regression coefficient of the combination judgments, though not for the regression constant). Whereas for consonant combinations the intensity of the main emotion in the combination judgments is larger than both the intensities for person and context alone, for discrepant combinations the intensity of the main emotion for the combination judgments lies between the intensities for person and context judgments alone. Conversely, for discrepant combinations, the regression coefficient for the combination judgments is smaller than the regression coefficients for both person and context, whereas for ambiguous combinations and especially for consonant combinations, the regression coefficient for the combination judgments lies between the regression coefficients for both singular judgments.

This implies that consonant combinations result in more unambiguous and more intense judgments than judgments of person and context alone, while discrepant combinations are less unambiguous and less intense than both singular judgments involved in the combination. We can conclude from this that single bits of information even in discrepant combinations are not "lost" (discounting strategy) but that they influence combination judgments, which results in greater ambiguity with respect to the dominating emotion.

The number of the different strategies of information integration coded from judges' reports show a number of significant effects that are in line with the theoretical predictions and the results reported so far. We do not find differences between consonant and discrepant combinations for "context dominating," "reinterpretation of person information," and "reinterpretation of context information," but the other strategies studied differ significantly between groups. For consonant combinations especially, more "aggregation" is found compared to ambiguous and discrepant combinations. For consonant combinations, the emotions inferred from person and context are rather similar, and judges obviously use the aggregation strategy demanding the least cognitive efforts to integrate the bits of information. For discrepant combinations, on the other hand, "integration" strategies are dominant. Via interpretation and extrapolation of the given bits of information, perhaps through using their own experiences as well, judges try to combine the discrepant information. For discrepant bits of information, the strategy of "incompatibility" is also mentioned more often. It seems that if integration is not possible because combinations are too discrepant, judges make this incompatibility explicit. The fact that "person information dominating" is mentioned by judges more for discrepant than for consonant combinations confirms the results that for consonant combinations context information is more important than for discrepant combinations.

We can conclude that judges do not use the same strategies of information integration independent of the material given to them but that different strategies of information integration are used depending on the consonancy or discrepancy of the given material. It is important that discounting strategies were rarely reported, whereas, on the contrary, we could show that both person and context information influence combination judgments, even for discrepant combinations. Judgments of emotion thus are not determined by person information, that is, facial expression, alone. Given these rather conclusive results, an attempt was made to replicate the results of this study in a second study, in which the candid-picture approach following Munn (1940) was used. The results of this second study are reported in the next section.

Study 2: The Candid-Picture Paradigm

In the candid-picture paradigm, photographs of real emotional situations as presented in newspapers and magazines are used. The research strategy is basically the same as the one reported in the last study. Judges are confronted either with person information only, context information only, or the total photograph.

The advantages of this approach include the fact that the stimuli used are more realistic, given that emotional situations that really happened are depicted. Furthermore, person and context information are provided in the same medium of presentation, that is, photograph (compared to photograph and verbal description in the previous study). Disadvantages result especially in problems of selection, because such photographs may not depict a representative sample of possible emotional expressions and situations, and the fact that there is no criterion for the emotion that the person depicted in such pictures really experienced in the given situation (Wallbott & Scherer, 1985a). The only criterion for the emotion experienced thus is the agreement between judges viewing such photographs. Furthermore, the type of shot and camera angle reduce and manipulate the information both for the person domain and the context domain. This means that we work with stimuli with more "ecological validity" but that these stimuli cannot be defined as precisely as in the person-scenario paradigm presented previously.

Selection of Stimuli

Only those photographs were selected in which a person with emotional facial expression was depicted in a situation. The facial expression of this person had to be clearly visible. Furthermore, the context, that is, characteristics of the emotion-eliciting situation, also had to be depicted in a way that when presented alone allowed inferences about possible emotional experiences. After an intense survey of newspapers, magazines, and press agents' archives, about 60 photographs were selected. This material was judged by two independent judges concerning the criteria just mentioned, and furthermore selected with respect to pictorial quality.

This second selection resulted in 24 photographs, which were reproduced three times each on black and white slide film using a repro-camera. In one series of these 24 photographs, context information was excluded by blackening everything in the photograph except the acting person. Person information in this study includes not only facial expression but also head and body orientation and posture, because in most photographs the persons are depicted not in close-up but, instead, showing at least head and upper body (finding photographs with a close-up of a facial expression as well as relevant context information turned out to be nearly impossible). In the second series, the acting person was blackened, resulting in a photograph with only the context.

Judgment Studies

Three groups of 10 judges each (in each group 5 male, 5 female subjects, all psychology students) watched either the series of 24 person slides, 24 context slides, or the 24 slides presenting all the information. Each stimulus was presented for 30 seconds. The judges' task was to indicate the emotion depicted on scales for the seven primary emotions from 0 to 8, whereby multiple choices of emotions were possible. No time limit was imposed for these judgments. Instructions for the group that saw only the person included the request "to judge the emotion(s) the person depicted is experiencing." The group watching only the context slide was instructed "to judge the emotion that the person (indicated by the blackened part of the picture) would experience in the given situation." The group watching the original complete photographs was instructed "to judge which emotion the target person (who was marked with a cross, because on some photographs more than one person was depicted) experienced in the given situation." Furthermore, in each group the subjects were asked to describe the recognized emotion(s) in their own words and to report what caused their judgments.

The judgments in the three groups were treated in exactly the same way as in the first study. Again, the 24 combinations were subdivided into three groups of stimuli (3 × 8 photographs) according to relative consonancy and discrepancy of partial information using the correlations between person judgments alone and situation judgments alone (criterion: "discrepant" = $r < -.15$; "consonant" = $r > .60$). An ANOVA approach was used to compare discrepant, consonant, and ambiguous combinations with respect to the different indicators.

RESULTS

All results are shown in Table 7.2. As in study 1, the separation between

TABLE 7.2
ANOVA Results for the Candid-Picture Study

Variable	Combinations means			mean	F	df	p	Newman-Keuls post-hoc-comparisons
	discrepant N=8	embiguous 8	consonant 8					
Correlation person/context judgment	-.28	.22	.96	.30	117.21	2/21	.000	CON>AMB>DIS
Correlation person/comb. judgment	.57	.55	.99	.70	3.89	2/21	.037	CON>AMB=DIS
Correlation context/comb. judgment	.26	.34	.97	.52	9.70	2/21	.001	CON>AMB=DIS
Relative shift index	.62	1.06	1.12	.94	<1		n.s.	--
Averaging model	2.39	3.53	1.29	2.40	10.94	2/21	.001	CON<DIS<AMB
Summation model	4.78	5.30	3.96	4.68	1.68		n.s.	--
Regression model	2.37	3.34	1.26	2.32	6.56	2/21	.006	CON<AMB
beta-weight person	.69	.53	.60	.51	<1		n.s.	--
beta-weight context	.45	.22	.40	.36	<1		n.s.	--
Regression constant (Comb. judgment)	1.98	2.65	3.41	2.68	4.25	2/21	.028	CON>DIS
Regression coefficient (Comb. judgment)	-.39	-.55	-.73	-.56	4.99	2/21	.017	CON>DIS
Reinterpretation	1.13	1.00	.38	.83	1.01		n.s.	

discrepant, consonant, and ambiguous stimulus combinations is also statistically confirmed. The average correlations between emotion judgments based on person and context information for the three groups are nearly identical to the ones in study 1. Also similar to study 1, the correlation between context judgments and combination judgments increases from discrepant to consonant information combinations. These results imply that in photographic depictions of real emotional situations, context information becomes more important when the context is consonant to the person information provided. Not confirming the results of study 1, we find here that the correlations between person judgments and combination judgments for the three groups of combination also increase with an increase in consonancy of informations. Thus, consonant combination judgments are determined to a large degree by both person information and context information, whereas discrepant combination judgments are influenced to a lesser degree by both sources of information. It may be argued that both sources of information interfere to a larger degree here than in the person-scenario study, where in discrepant combinations person information clearly dominated context information. These interferences may reduce the correlation between person judgments and combination judgments.

The beta weights for both person and context information do not differ depending on the relative congruency of combinations. In general, the beta weight for person information is larger than the weight given to context information, but the difference between both weights is smaller than in study 1, where person information got a higher weight. The relative shift index does not show any significant differences between the three groups of stimuli in this study, though the means (confirming the results of study 1) increase from discrepant to consonant information combinations. As in study 1, for consonant combinations, context is more important than person information. On the average the relative shift index is even higher than in study 1, which implies that for candid-picture stimuli context is in general more important than in the person-scenario approach, that is, the relative importance of person information and context information is to some degree determined by media factors. Greater "immediacy" of visual compared to verbal presentation may account for this finding.

The prediction accuracy of the models of information integration tested in this study largely replicates the results of study 1. The summation model is the worst in predicting combination judgments, whereas the averaging model and especially the regression model are more accurate. Averaging and regression models are (again replicating study 1) especially effective for consonant information combinations.

More pronounced than in study 1, the linear regressions provide evidence for the proposed model of information integration. The intensity of the dominating emotion, that is, the regression constant, increases from discrepant to consonant information combinations significantly, and the (negative) regression coefficient increases in the same way. Consonant information combinations thus result in more unambiguous judgments of the dominating emotion and in less pronounced intensities of the other possible emotions.

Furthermore, we again find significant differences between the combination groups when comparing the regression data for the combination judgments with the regression data for person judgments and context judgments alone. For combinations classified as ambiguous, both the regression constant and the regression coefficient of the combination judgments lie between the respective values for the singular judgments (regression constant: combination = 2.65, person = 2.72, context = 2.50; regression coefficient: combination = .55, person = .56, context = .50), that is, intensity and ambiguity of the combination judgments fall in between the respective values for person and context judgments. For discrepant combinations, both the intensity of the main emotion as well as the regression coefficient for the combination judgment are *smaller* than the respective values for the singular judgments (regression constant: combination = 1.98, person = 2.07, context = 2.39; regression coefficient: combination = .39, person = .43, context = .48). Discrepant information combinations thus result in more ambiguous and less intense judgments than judgments based on information from person or context alone. In contrast, for consonant combinations, the intensity of the main emotion as well as the regression coefficient is *larger* than the respective values for both singular judgments (regression constant: combination = 3.41, person = 3.08, context = 2.66; regression coefficient: combination = .73, person = .65, context = .56).

Thus, for consonant combinations, the combination judgment is more intense and more "secure" than the judgments for person and context formation alone. For discrepant combinations, on the contrary, the combination judgment is less intense and "less secure" than the judgments based on person and situation information alone, while for ambiguous combinations, the combination judgment lies in between the judgments for person and context information. These results are much more clear-cut than those found in study 1 and fully confirm our predictions.

The coding of the free responses concerning information integration strategies of judges (in this study just the category "reinterpretation" was used, because judges did not report as explicitly as in study 1) did not result in significant differences between discrepant and consonant combinations, though the respective means again indicate that "reinterpretation" is used more for discrepant combinations than for consonant combinations.

DISCUSSION

We may conclude from the results of both studies that there is no general dominance of person information or context information in emotion judgments. The relative importance of both sources of information is determined by the discrepancy or consonancy of both sources. If partial information is discrepant, the result show that person information (facial expression) dominates context information in determining total judgments; that is, when confronted with discrepant information, judges base their judgments more on facial expression than on situational context information. For concordant combinations, on the other hand, the reverse effect was found: If person information and context information are similar with respect to the emotion depicted, both are of nearly equal importance in determining combination judgments; in fact, the more consonant combinations are, the more context information may dominate person information in determining combination judgments.

This is especially demonstrated by the linear regression data. Whereas for discrepant combinations the resulting regression line for the combination judgment indicates that the judgments are less unambiguous and the dominating emotion less intense than for the partial judgments, for consonant combinations we find exactly the reverse effect. Here the combination judgments are more unambiguous and more intense than the partial judgments.

The models of information integration tested in both studies show that their accuracy of prediction for the combination judgments also depends to some degree on the consonancy or discrepancy of the single bits of information. The summation model in both studies was least accurate, which implies that such a simple strategy of information integration does not account for the behavior of the judges. Both regression and averaging models resulted in better predictions for consonant combinations than for discrepant combinations. The integration of information given consonant combinations thus can be explained with linear prediction models, whereas the predictions for discrepant combinations are significantly worse.

Discrepant combinations thus have to be explained by more complex strategies of judges, which cannot be readily described using simple linear mathematical models. In these cases, judges either use strategies of interpreting and interpolating information that are able to resolve the discrepancy, or they discount partial information. The results show that especially the strategy of information "aggregation" (i.e., a simple combination of both pieces of partial information, which in fact can be described with models like the averaging model) is used more when judges are confronted with concordant than with discrepant information combinations, while more complex strategies like "integration" or other strategies of reinterpretation are used significantly more often when judges are confronted with discrepant combinations.

Thus, the different processes involved in emotion judgments as well as the relative importance of person and context information cannot be studied independently of the partial information used. Therefore, general statements concerning the general dominance of one information source in determining judgments or general models of information integration seem to be too simplified. A mediating factor that influences all these processes is the relative concordancy or discrepancy of information. Without considering this factor, combination judgments and the strategies used by judges cannot be predicted accurately.

The second factor found to be of importance is the medium of presentation. Comparing the results of both studies it seems that in the candid-picture study, context was of larger importance than in the person-scenario study. We have argued that this may be due to the greater "immediacy" and "vividness" of visual presentation of information compared to verbal presentation. This difference implies that it is very important of specify the *type of context information* used in such studies very precisely. In the two studies presented here we used verbal and visual presentation of situational context information simultaneously with visual person information. Of course, other types of context are possible and should be studied. We thus present a framework as a guideline for further studies.

Such a framework, in which studies on emotion recognition can be placed, has to include two dimensions: One is the "type of context" dimension. We can consider the face alone as a cue to observers, but already on that level different bits of information are available to an observer, such as the upper face or the lower face. Thus, the *context within one nonverbal channel* has to be taken into account. Furthermore, other bodily and vocal cues may be available to an observer. This may be called the *context of other nonverbal channels*, within which facial cues are perceived. As indicated by our two studies, not only the person but also the situation in which a person is acting may be an important cue. This aspect will be called the *situational context*.

The second dimension is the "static-dynamic" dimension. Cues may be studied either in a *static* fashion (by using photographs and/or verbal descriptions, as in the studies presented here) or in a *dynamic* fashion, by using film or video. By combining these two dimensions, we can distinguish six basic approaches to the study of recognition of emotional expression within different contexts and either on the static or dynamic level (see Table 7.3). These different approaches differ with respect to the complexity of information provided and with respect to ecological validity, that is, dynamic presentation approaches "real-life" situations more closely than static presentation.

TABLE 7.3
Perception of Er ,otion Based on Facial
Expression Within Different Contexts

		Context within one channel	Context of other channels	Situational context
Static presentation		Intrachannel context information	Simultaneous behavioral context information	Simultaneous situational context information
	c.f.	different parts of the face involved in a facial expression.	other nonverbal information accessible at the same time as facial expression.	situational information accessible at the same time as facial expression.
Dynamic presentation		Contingent intrachannel context information	Contingent behavioral context information	Contingent situational context information
	c.f.	succession of different facial expressions.	succession of nonverbal behaviors surrounding a facial expression.	situational information surrounding a facial expression.

To sum up, when studying the relative influence of person and context information on emotion attributions, we think that it is important to keep in mind which operationalization of context has been used. With the two studies reported here we have filled only one cell of this matrix: the simultaneous situational context information. Work now is in progress in which dynamic presentation (video) and contingent situational context information will be used to test the suggestions presented here.

8 MULTICHANNEL COMMUNICATION OF EMOTION: SYNTHETIC SIGNAL PRODUCTION

Ursula Hess
Dartmouth College, N.H.

Arvid Kappas
Dartmouth College, N.H.

Klaus R. Scherer
University of Geneva
and University of Giessen

INTRODUCTION

In natural interactive settings people use a variety of different nonverbal cues to communicate, including voice intonation and quality, facial expression, proximity, and eye contact. Thus Birdwhistell (1961, p. 5) refers to the human as a "regulated multisensory station in a transmission system, a multichannel interactor." The experimental study of those clues, however, has encountered various methodological difficulties, due in part to the inherent problems of studying each communication channel and in part to the complications of multichannel research.

In the study described in this chapter we investigated the role of facial and vocal expression in the attribution of emotions and attitudes. The experimental design we chose was selected after a critical consideration of previous studies in the field and is presented as a new approach to exploring the relationship between facial and vocal expression. We first briefly summarize the research on facial and vocal expression respectively, defining some of the important parameters and methodological problems, and then discuss some of the difficulties encountered in multichannel studies.

The face is a very important source of information in social interaction. Ekman (1978) describes the face as a multimessage, multisignal semiotic system. Our present research, however, is limited to the role of facial expression in communicating emotion. Three important questions have been pursued in this field:

• Are emotions accompanied by distinctive facial muscle movements (expression)?
• Does facial expression convey relevant information about the underlying emotional state (impression)?
• What are the communicative functions of facial expression?

Research concerning the first question has yielded the tentative conclusion that even though many emotions do have certain elements of expression in common, such as brow knitting, different emotional states are accompanied by specific facial patterns (Davis, 1934; Ekman, Friesen, & Ancoli, 1980; Feleky, 1914; Frijda, 1953; Frois-Whittmann, 1930; Wiggers, 1982).

Concerning the second question, results have not always been unanimous. Darwin (1872), like others later on (e.g., Goodenough, 1931; Langfeld, 1918; Levitt, 1964; Munn, 1940; Woodworth, 1938), came to the conclusion that emotional facial expressions accompanying emotional states are an effective source of information concerning these emotional states. On the other hand, a number of researchers (Fernberger, 1927, 1928; Guilford, 1929; Landis, 1924, 1929; Sherman, 1927) were not able to confirm this claim. Ekman, Friesen, and Ellsworth (1982b) reanalyzed some of these studies and pointed out a number of methodological flaws that may account for the contradictory results. After reanalysis of nine studies (six using pictures of posed and three using pictures of naturally occurring emotional facial expression as stimulus material), Ekman, Friesen, and Ellsworth concluded that facial expression is a valid source of information about underlying emotional states. However, not all emotions can be recognized equally well from facial expression.

The third question has been considered mainly by ethologists and developmental psychologists. Darwin (1872) proposed that emotional facial expression plays a major role concerning cooperation among members of a society because it allows an exchange of information about affective reactions and behavioral tendencies. More recently, several ethologists have found proof for this claim (Bernstein, 1970; Hinde & Rowell, 1962; Sade, 1967; Van Hooff, 1962). In the field of human interaction, the importance of facial expression has also been asserted, especially concerning interaction between mothers and their infants (Darwin, 1872; Emde, 1984; Emde, Kligman, Reich, & Wade, 1978; Trevarthen, 1984). The evidence thus points to an affirmative response of the three questions mentioned above: Facial expression has a specific and functional role in communicating emotional states.

The study of vocal expression is relatively new although some early investigations were attempted. Darwin (1872), for instance, discussed the vocal expression of emotion in his work "The expression of emotion in man and animals." An important problem in the study of vocal expression lies in the very nature of speech. Although it has long been possible to depict facial expression easily, only the invention of records and magnetic tape as well as the development of electro-acoustic analysis facilities have made research on speech possible at all. In recent years computer technology has played an important part in the analysis of acoustic parameters of speech.

In the research on vocal expression, a number of parameters of speech have been analyzed (e.g., pitch, rhythm, spectral composition). In the following discussion only the two parameters used in our study—intonation and voice quality—are considered.

Intonation refers to the pitch contour of an utterance. The perceived pitch of a voice is dependent on the fundamental frequency and the spectral composition of the speech signal. Voice quality depends on the characteristics of vocal tract resonance and of phonation. The characteristics of vocal tract resonance are determined not only by physiological processes such as articulatory movements but also by facial expression, as Tartter (1980) has shown. In her experiment, stimulus persons spoke on the telephone in two situations—while smiling and not smiling. Judges listening to the respective utterances were able to determine whether the speaker was smiling or not—purely based on the characteristics of the voice as transmitted over the telephone. Thus, facial expression produced variations of voice quality that were judged to be friendly (smiling) or unfriendly (not smiling).

The importance of intonation and voice quality for emotional information is readily apparent in everyday speech as expressed by phrases such as "monotone voice" or "harsh voice," which may be used to indicate specific emotional states such as sadness or anger. Nevertheless, experimentation in this field has been problematic. Although Scherer (1981a) demonstrated in a review of 28 studies that vocal expression is judged more accurately than facial expression, vocal indicators of specific emotional states have not yet been found.

With regard to intonation, considering the whole intonation contour—as opposed to specific parameters of the same—may be a solution to this problem (Williams & Stevens, 1972, 1982; see also the following). Furthermore, intonation should not be regarded alone but in combination with other parameters of speech such as voice quality (see Chapter 6). With the selection of voice quality the problem arises that an acoustic classification of voice quality has not yet been successfully developed. Therefore, a phonetic approach (Laver, 1980) must be used.

Although there is evidence that facial and vocal expression are important and valid cues for the attribution of emotions and attitudes, the research so far does not sufficiently reflect the multichannel nature of emotional communication.

Since the 1960s there have been several attempts to look into the relationships between different means of expressing emotion and the joint effect of the information communicated through different channels. Three main groups of questions addressed in multichannel studies of emotional expression can be distinguished:

1. Questions concerning the use of channels
    *   the accuracy of attribution on the basis of information from different channels
    *   the relative importance of information from different channels
    *   the integration of information from different channels
2. Questions concerning a specific topic of interest, such as
    *   the attribution of emotions and attitudes
    *   deception
    *   the attribution of personality features
    *   clinical questions
3. Questions concerning differences between judges
    *   relationships between differences in personality variables
    *   sex-related differences in the ability to judge nonverbal information from different channels
    *   sex-related differences in the ability to judge nonverbal information from different channels
    *   differences in the ability to encode and decode nonverbal information in different channels

Table 8.1 lists a number of multichannel studies and the questions addressed.

In the following discussion only the three questions concerning the use of channels are addressed. We focus on the topic of attribution of emotions and attitudes communicated facially and vocally.

METHODOLOGICAL PROBLEMS
OF MULTICHANNEL STUDIES

The studies of Levitt (1964), Mehrabian & Ferris (1967), and Bugental, Kaswan, Love, & Fox (1970a) are described as good examples of the dominant approach to these questions. Later on particular problems arising from the experimental designs in the studies reviewed are discussed.

Levitt (1964) addressed the question as to whether information is con-

TABLE 8.1
Selected Multichannel Studies and Questions Addressed

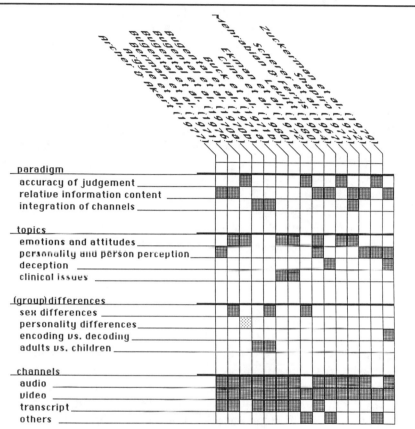

veyed by different channels with the same accuracy. As stimulus material she chose audio-video sequences of subjects uttering a short text (three sentences long) while at the same time portraying a certain emotion (joy, surprise, fear, disgust, anger, or contempt) vocally and facially. With respect to the channels the stimulus material was concordant (i.e., with the same emotional information encoded in the face and the voice).

Three groups of raters judged either the audio, the video or the full audio-video sequence. The results showed that:

- the emotions could be judged with greater accuracy using the video than the audio information
- the judgments on the basis of the full audio-video sequence were more accurate than the judgments using the audio information alone but not better than the judgments based on the video-only stimuli.

(Video-based judgments were thus more accurate than audio-based judgments in this study, as in most multichannel experiments. However, many of these studies do not evaluate the expression of pure emotion — when this is evaluated in voice-only or face-only experiments, video-based judgments are as accurate or more accurate than audio-based judgments.) The general finding that the facial information was a better basis than vocal information for judging the portrayed emotion has been confirmed in other studies (Berman, Shulman, & Marwitt, 1976; Ekman & Friesen, 1967; Graham, Ricci-Bitti, Argyle, 1975).

Mehrabian and Ferris (1967) investigated the relative importance of the information from different channels. They used discrepant stimuli, that is, stimuli simultaneously expressing different information in each of the two channels studied. The method of producing the stimuli was different from the one employed by Bugental and colleagues (1970a, see following), who also used discrepant stimuli. The stimulus material used by Mehrabian and Ferris consisted of slides and audio-tape. The slide showed the face of a woman portraying either "like," "dislike," or "neutrality" toward an imagined other person. The audio stimulus consisted of the word "maybe" (chosen because of its neutral semantic meaning) spoken as if to show "like," "dislike," or "neutrality" toward another person. These stimuli were combined into all possible combinations. The slide and the audio recording were presented simultaneously to raters who were asked to judge the attitude of the stimulus person toward the imagined other person on a "like/dislike" scale. In the analysis of variance, only one main effect for the face is significant. A regression analysis estimated the facial information as being 1 ½ times more important than the vocal information. The general tendencies of this study were confirmed by Zaidel and Mehrabian (1969) and Bugental and colleagues (1970a).

The latter (1970a), using discrepant stimuli, addressed the question as to how the information from different channels is integrated. The authors asked subjects to speak a sentence (which could be either positive or negative in content) with a "positive" voice while showing at the same time a "negative" facial expression, or vice versa. The stimuli were combined into all possible combinations according to the three channels: verbal content, vocal, and facial expression. Raters watched the videotapes and judged the sequences on a "friendly/unfriendly" scale. The authors found a strong effect for the facial expression and a strong interaction between verbal content and vocal expression that could be explained neither by a summation nor by an averaging model of integration. They proposed a discounting strategy as described by Anderson and Jacobson (1965) for the explanation of their data. The data concerning the integration of information expressed through different channels is not in accordance with the findings of Mehrabian and Ferris (1967).

The major problem with these studies is the failure to study the integration of the information from different channels. No generally agreed-upon procedure has been proposed as yet. This may be due to the methodological problems these studies share. In the following section these problems are discussed and a solution to them is proposed.

A NOVEL EXPERIMENTAL APPROACH

Production of Stimuli

An important point concerns the method of producing the stimuli. Researchers like Bugental and colleagues (1970a) have asked an actor to speak a sentence with a negative vocal expression while at the same time maintaining a positive facial expression or vice versa. The method is questionable for the following reasons: First, the actor is free to choose his/her own negative or positive expressions. This may lead to the actor's employing stereotyped expressions. On the one hand, one may argue that these are derived from observations the actor has made and are therefore valid as representations of negative or positive emotions. On the other hand, results concerning the interaction between channels may be biased because stereotyping may result in either overestimating or underestimating the homogeneity of judgments, as Wallbott and Scherer (1986b) have recently shown. This method of producing the stimuli also entails difficulties in encoding both vocal and facial stimuli with the same skill. Zuckerman, Larrance, Hall, De Frank and Rosenthal (1979) have found a correlation between the ability to encode information vocally and facially, but this correlation proved to be quite small even for extreme expressions. Furthermore, there are practical limitations to the simultaneous vocal and facial encoding of emotional information. For example, producing the relaxed smile typical of a positive face with the supralaryngeal tension necessary for an angry voice (Laver, 1980) is, for anatomical reasons, very difficult if not impossible.

Length of the Stimuli

The length of the stimuli is also of special relevance to an evaluation study of the kind described previously. It has been shown that facial expression can be judged quite well even with very short presentation times (Rosenthal, 1982). This is not, however, true for vocal stimuli. Some parameters like voice quality cannot be judged at all on the basis of one word. Laver (1980) and Rosenthal (1982) estimated that at least 2 seconds are needed for the judgment of auditory cues and an even longer period if more than one channel is presented for evaluation.

Presentation of the Stimuli

The way the stimuli are presented—which media and which modalities are used—also has a major impact on the results. Mehrabian and Ferris (1967) have presented the vocal stimuli via magnetic audio-tape and the visual stimuli by presenting a slide. In normal life this combination of stimuli is not found. Obviously, stimuli should be as free of media effects as possible if any deductions concerning the "normal" processing of information in different nonverbal channels are to be made. Four propositions evolve from this discussion:

1. The variation of the stimuli should not be conducted arbitrarily by an actor or subject but should be determined on a theoretical basis.
2. The stimuli should be produced and controlled separately for each channel.
3. The presentation of the stimuli should allow enough time for each channel to be adequately judged.
4. The presentation of the stimuli should be as natural as possible.

The question addressed in our study concerned the relative importance of the information expressed through different channels for the attribution of emotions and attitudes. To answer this question, stimuli with discrepant information in the audio and video channel were presented and judged by naive raters on several emotion/attitude scales. (For economy of style, "audio" and "video" channels will refer to vocal and facial channels respectively.) An analysis of variance was conducted. It was expected that, in keeping with the discussed findings, the facial information demonstrated by the video channel would be more important than the vocal information.

Method

First some general considerations concerning the production of the stimuli in view of the propositions just suggested are discussed. Then a more detailed description of the production of the stimuli will follow.

The stimuli consisted of three different short scenes (1 minute) showing a person speaking. The scenes were composed of five sequential utterances of a one-sided telephone call. That is, the scene consisted of one person talking on the telephone to an imagined interlocutor; subjects were told that these sequences were part of a (video-) telephone conversation. Ecological validity was assured because one often observes one person speaking on the telephone. The utterances were of the kind common in telephone calls and semantically coherent. It was ensured that the sequence would be long enough to provide adequate time for judgments. Video-

and audio-stimuli were produced independently. The stimuli were of the same length and could be combined as desired by dubbing the video recording synchronously with the audio recording. As a result, stimuli with completely synchronous audio/video channels were produced.

In the following section the general procedure of the stimulus production is described separately for the video and the audio stimuli. The video stimuli were produced using FACS (Ekman & Friesen, 1978; for details see following text) as a means of controlling facial expression. Specifically, a FACS-trained actor portrayed either a "positive" or "negative" facial expression. The AU-combinations used for this variation of the facial expression were selected on the basis of a study by Wiggers (1982). In his study, the facial expression predicted by Ekman and Friesen (1978) for eight emotions were judged. For the production of the stimuli we chose a "happy" and an "angry" facial expression on which at least 90% of Wiggers' subjects had agreed with respect to the emotion displayed.

The two emotions were chosen based on the argument that a person showing a happy or angry face will be perceived as being friendly or unfriendly toward another person. In a communicative process these emotional facial expressions could be interpreted as "positive" or "negative" cues for the attribution process with which this study is concerned.

The stimuli were produced in three intensities as Wiggers (1982) found that different intensities of facial expression were judged as different intensities of emotional state. Differently to Wiggers, we presented our stimuli using video-tape rather than still photos. Ekman (1978) has shown that the AU-combinations can be judged more precisely from moving pictures than from still photos because of the dynamic display of facial muscle movements in the former. During each utterance the appropriate facial expression occurred two times. The position of the expression in the utterance was selected according to semantic content because a facial expression can be considered as having a function for the linguistic segmentation of speech. In this way it was ensured that no idiosyncratic or extreme expressions were used.

For the audio stimuli, the production required two steps, as voice quality and intonation were varied independently. As it is not yet clear which parameters of F0 carry information about the emotional state of the speaker, a decision was made to transfer the intonation contour as a whole. Obviously, it is not possible on the basis of this design to decide whether specific F0-parameters or the "Gestalt" of the intonation contour is the carrier of emotional information. However, this question was not to be investigated in this study.

General Procedure

For this study three experiments were run:

1. Rating of the video-only stimuli.
2. Rating of the audio-only stimuli.
3. Rating of the combined audio-video stimuli.

Experiments 1 and 2 were conducted during the same session (with a break in between). The video stimuli were always presented first, as subjects were not supposed to know the verbal content of the scenes for this task.

Stimuli

In the following section the method of production of the stimuli for these experiments is described separately.

Video Stimuli.   It was ensured in a pretest that the three texts used were emotionally neutral in content. The actor was filmed separately for each of the five utterances he made. This was necessary as the video recording was to be dubbed with an audio track later on and mouth movements had to be synchronized. The facial expression was controlled using FACS (Ekman & Friesen, 1978), as explained above. The segments were then rated by naive subjects according to a "positive/negative" scale and three control scales (ironic, natural, appropriate), which were employed to ensure that only those stimuli that appeared to be quite natural were selected Those stimuli that failed to meet the requirements of the control scale were discarded. Segments that had been given a "medium" rating of intensity, on both the positive and negative scales, were then selected and combined to form three whole texts, each one with a positive and a negative version. The complete stimulus set consisted of six situations (3 texts × 2 variations).

Audio Stimuli.   The production of the audio stimuli required two steps as explained previously. The utterances were spoken synchronously to the mouth movements on the video recording. The use of FACS to produce the same movements seen in the film helped to control the synchronization. FACS was also used to produce the first variation — voice quality — because, as discussed, changes in facial expression create changes in voice quality (Tartter, 1980). To produce the second variation — intonation — the following pretest was run.

Segments were spoken with positive or negative intonation. (The intonation was varied intuitively by the speakers as there are no satisfactory theoretical concepts from which an appropriate intonation contour could be deduced.) The stimuli were then rated by naive subjects according to a positive/negative scale and the three control scales. The selection of the stimuli ensued in the same fashion as for the video stimuli.

The intonation contour of the stimuli thus selected was then transferred by means of digital resynthesis (see Chapter 6 of this volume) to the original sentences. The stimulus set consisted of 12 situations (3 texts × 2 voice qualities × 2 intonations).

Audio-video stimuli. For the production of the discrepant audio-video stimuli, SMPTE time-code was written onto the video tape. Using a custom-made triggering device, the audio recording was then transferred directly from the computer to the audio track of the tape with the SMPTE time-code specifying the exact location on the tape. As it was not possible to find a speaker who could control facial and vocal expression equally well, actor and speaker were not identical. A pretest was run that showed that this was not obtrusive or even noticeable. The stimuli set for this experiment consisted of 24 situations (3 texts × 2 facial expressions × 2 voice qualities × 2 intonations). The following table shows the variation in the modalities for one text. For the experiment described here only the results concerning concordant audio channels were used (i.e., no. 1/4/5/8) for each text. For the three experiments two sets of stimuli with different sequential order were produced.

Subjects

Experiment 1 and experiment 2: Subjects were 34 (17 male, 17 female) paid students (psychology students were excluded to reduce the chance of subjects knowing the stimulus persons, FACS-trained collaborators from the psychology department). Experiment 3: Subjects were 32 (16 male, 16 female) paid students (psychology students were excluded for the reason just cited).

Procedure

The three experiments were run following the same scheme. Subjects were

TABLE 8.2
All Possible Combinations for Facial Expression,
Intonation, and Voice Quality

	Facial Expression	Intonation	Voice Quality
1	positive	positive	positive
2	positive	positive	negative
3	positive	negative	positive
4	negative	positive	positive
5	positive	negative	negative
6	negative	positive	negative
7	negative	negative	positive
8	negative	negative	negative

told that they would hear/see part of a (video-) telephone conversation. They were to hear/see only one participant. They were then asked to judge the stimulus person according to the impression they had of him.

Scales

For all three experiments the same rating scales were applied. They consisted of three parts:

- 5 unipolar emotion scales: joy, anger, sadness, fear, surprise
- 6 bipolar attitude scales: positive/negative, excited/composed, arrogant/insecure, friendly/unfriendly, approving/disapproving, interested/bored
- 2 unipolar control scales: natural, ironic
- a free-answer opportunity

Two sets, A and B, were balanced over subjects to control for order effects.

RESULTS

The question we set out to investigate concerned the relative importance of information from two different nonverbal channels. In order to answer this question, the two channels under consideration — voice and face — were first investigated separately. The dependent variables were the five emotion scales and seven attitude scales. The mean values for these scales are shown in Table 8.2.

For the audio-only and video-only stimuli, two separate ANOVAs for repeated measures (BMDP2V) were computed; for audio-only stimuli a three-factor ANOVA with the factors Intonation, Voice quality, and Text; and for the video-only stimuli, a two-factor ANOVA with the factors Facial expression and Text. In order to estimate the percentage of explained variance for the variations of the independent variables $Omega^2$ was calculated. Table 8.3 shows F-values, p-values, and $Omega^2$ for the significant effects for the scales HAPPY, ANGRY, and NEGATIVE/POSITIVE, as these were considered central in view of the variations intended. The percentage of explained variance is displayed in Figure 8.1.

The results indicate that both vocal and facial expression affect the attribution of emotions and attitudes. If the audio stimuli are presented as the only source of information intonation contributes up to 17.6% (scale) and voice quality up to 1.7% (aroused) of the total variance. The video stimuli could explain up to 45% of the total variance if they were presented as the only source of information.

A closer view of the data with respect to the use of the stimuli in the

TABLE 8.3a
Facial Expression

Judgments	Positive	Negative	
Emotions*			
Happiness	2.9 (1.8)†	1.2 (.8)	t = 8.7; p < .001
Anger	2.0 (1.4)	4.7 (1.7)†	t = 12.3; p < .001
Sadness	2.1 (1.8)	1.8 (1.3)	n.s.
Fear	1.8 (1.5)	2.6 (1.9)†	t = 3.3; p < .001
Surprise	2.0 (1.5)	2.6 (1.9)†	t = 2.5; p < .05
Attitudes**			
Negative	3.4 (1.5)	5.8 (.9)†	t = 14.2; p < .001
Exited	3.2 (1.4)	5.4 (1.0)†	t = 12.9; p < .001
Insecure	4.0 (1.3)	3.6 (1.5)	n.s.
Unpolite	2.8 (1.2)†	5.2 (1.0)†	t = 15.4; p < .001
Unfriendly	3.0 (1.3)†	5.7 (.9)†	t = 17.1; p < .001
Disapproving	3.3 (1.5)	5.9 (.9)†	t = 14.9; p < .001
Bored	3.4 (1.5)	3.6 (1.3)	n.s.

† significantly different from neutral
* Unipolar 7-point scale
** Bipolar 7-point scale

TABLE 8.3b
Vocal Expression

Judgments	Positive	Negative
Emotions*		
Happiness	3.2 (1.6)†	2.0 (1.2)
Anger	1.5 (1.1)	2.2 (1.5)
Sadness	1.3 (.9)	1.5 (1.3)
Fear	1.3 (.8)	1.4 (1.1)
Surprise	2.3 (1.5)	1.9 (1.3)
Attitudes**		
Negative	2.9 (1.5)†	4.2 (1.3)†
Exited	3.3 (1.5)	3.9 (1.3)
Insecure	3.8 (1.0)	3.6 (1.3)
Unpolite	2.7 (1.1)†	3.7 (1.2)
Unfriendly	2.5 (1.2)†	4.0 (1.3)†
Disapproving	2.6 (1.1)†	3.9 (1.1)†
Bored	2.9 (1.4)†	3.9 (1.4)†

† significantly different from neutral
* Unipolar 7-point scale
** Bipolar 7-point scale

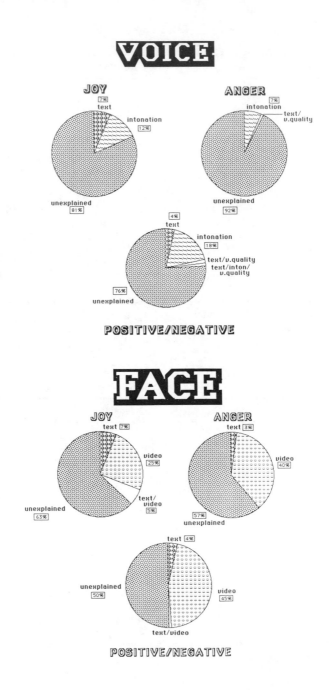

FIGURE 8.1. Explained variances for facial and vocal stimuli

multichannel experiment shows that the concordant audio stimuli with the POS Variation (POS intonation + POS voice quality vs. NEG intonation + NEG voice quality) were more positive/happy than the NEG stimuli were negative/angry, that is, the variation was more successful for the POS stimuli than for the NEG stimuli. The opposite is true for the video stimuli, that is, the variation was more successful for the NEG stimuli than for the POS stimuli.

Table 8.4 shows the ratings for the concordant POS (POS video + POS audio) and NEG (NEG video + NEG audio) stimuli and the judgments for the two discrepant combinations POS/NEG (POS video + NEG audio) and NEG/POS (NEG video + POS audio).

These results indicate a clear difference for the attribution of emotions and attitudes for the concordant POS and NEG stimuli. Thus the intended variations of the independent variables were effective. The POS/NEG and NEG/POS stimuli were also quite different from each other. In general the combination POS/NEG was judged as being more positive, less aroused and bored.

For further analysis of the interaction of the audio and video channels an ANOVA for repeated measures (BMDP2V) was calculated using the factors Facial expression, Vocal expression (concordant intonation + voice quality), and Text. In order to estimate the percentage of variance explained for the variations of the independent variables, Omega² was again computed. Table 8.5 shows F-values, p-values, and Omega² for the significant effects for the scales HAPPY, ANGRY, and POSITIVE/NEGATIVE. The percentage of explained variance is displayed in Figure 8.2.

DISCUSSION

The following section is divided into two main parts, the discussion of the results and an evaluation of the new methodological approach employed.

The discussion of the results consists of three sections:

* discussion of the ratings for the concordant and discrepant stimuli
* discussion of the analysis of variance conducted with the whole stimulus set
* proposal of a model to explain the somewhat discrepant results of the first two sections.

The addition of concordant information in the audio channel to information in the video channel has, as Figure 8.3 indicates, an impact on the attribution of emotions and attitudes. The direction of this impact,

TABLE 8.4

F- and p-values and explained variances for facial stimuli and vocal stimuli for the scales 'happiness,' 'anger', and 'negative/positive'

Face

	Happiness			Anger			Negative		
	F	p	Omega²	F	p	Omega²	F	p	Omega²
Text	36.0	.001	6.7	28.4	.001	3.0	25.7	.001	4.0
Facial Expr.	127.1	.001	24.7	349.5	.001	39.8	270.7	.001	45.0
Text/Face	28.1	.001	5.1				6.9	.05	.8
total									
expl. Variance:	36.5%			42.8%			49.8%		

Voice

	Happiness			Anger			Negative		
	F	p	Omega²	F	p	Omega²	F	p	Omega²
Text	20.3	.001	6.5	34.5	.001	6.8	14.4	.001	3.9
Intonation	73.6	.001	12.1	3.5	.05	.8	72.1	.001	17.6
Text/V.Q.							5.6	.01	1.4
T/In/V.Q.							5.4	.01	1.2
total									
expl. Variance:	18.6%			7.6%			24.1%		

TABLE 8.5a
Facial and Vocal Expression

Judgments	Positive	Negative	
Emotions*			
Happiness	3.5 (1.6)	1.3 (.8)	t = 12.0; p.<.001
Anger	1.3 (.7)	3.8 (1.9)	t = 12.3; p<.001
Sadness	1.4 (.9)	1.8 (1.4)	n.s.
Fear	1.3 (.7)	1.7 (1.3)	n.s.
Surprise	2.1 (1.4)	1.5 (1.0)	t = 3.5; p<.001
Attitudes**			
Negative	2.8 (1.3)	5.5 (1.2)	t = 15.3; p<.001
Exited	3.6 (1.3)	3.8 (1.4)	n.s.
Insecure	2.7 (1.3)	4.7 (1.5)	t = 10.1; p<.001
Unpolite	2.5 (1.1)	4.8 (1.4)	t = 13.5; p<.001
Unfriendly	2.3 (1.1)	5.2 (1.5)	t = 13.4; p<.001
Disapproving	2.6 (1.2)	4.9 (1.5)	t = 12.0; p<.001
Bored	4.4 (1.0)	3.3 (1.5)	t = 6.1; p<.001

  * Unipolar 7-point scale
 ** Bipolar 7-point scale

TABLE 8.5b
Facial and Vocal Expression

Judgments	Pos/Neg	Neg/Pos	
Emotions*			
Happiness	3.3 (1.5)	1.6 (.9)	t = 9.7; p<.001
Anger	1.5 (1.1)	2.8 (1.7)	t = 6.4; p<.001
Sadness	1.6 (1.3)	1.6 (1.2)	n.s.
Fear	1.5 (1.2)	1.6 (1.2)	n.s.
Surprise	2.0 (1.3)	1.8 (1.3)	n.s.
Attitudes**			
Negative	3.0 (1.1)	4.8 (1.3)	t = 10.6; p<.001
Exited	3.7 (1.1)	4.3 (1.1)	t = 3.5; p<.001
Insecure	4.2 (.9)	3.8 (1.3)	t = 7.9; p<.001
Unpolite	2.8 (1.2)	4.0 (1.3)	t = 6.8; p<.001
Unfriendly	2.5 (1.1)	4.1 (1.3)	t = 9.4; p<.001
Disapproving	2.9 (1.2)	4.3 (1.4)	t = 7.6; p<.001
Bored	2.7 (1.2)	4.1 (1.3)	t = 2.5; p<.01

  * Unipolar 7-point scale
 ** Bipolar 7-point scale

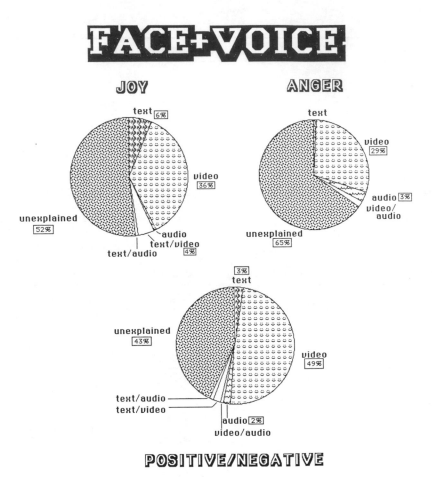

FIGURE 8.2. Explained variances for multichannel stimuli

however, was different for the concordant negative (NEG) and the concordant positive (POS) stimuli. Whereas the POS audio/video stimuli were rated as being more positive/happy and less negative/angry than in either video-only or audio-only conditions, the NEG audio/video stimuli were considered differently. In their case, the ratings vary somewhere between the rating for the video-only and the audio-only stimuli. That is to say, while the intensities for the combined POS audio/video stimuli are higher compared to either of the single channels, the intensity of the NEG audio/video stimuli is reduced with respect to the video-only stimuli and enhanced with respect to the audio-only stimuli.

An explanation of these findings may be found in the nature of the

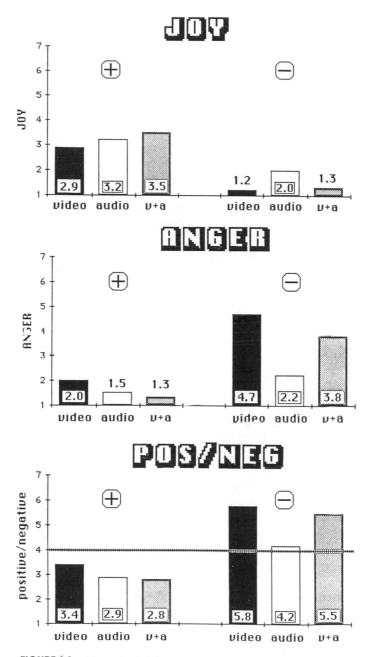

FIGURE 8.3. Means for facial, concordant vocal, and concordant facial/vocal stimuli for the scales 'happiness', 'anger', and 'negative/positive'

stimuli used. As explained, the variations of the different stimuli were not equally successful, that is, for the audio stimuli, the POS stimuli were more positive than the NEG stimuli were negative, whereas for the video stimuli the situation was reversed. Thus, in the case of POS audio/video stimuli the "stronger" audio stimuli were combined with the "weaker" video stimuli, while for the NEG audio/video stimuli the "weaker" audio stimuli were combined with the "stronger" video stimuli. But even though this may explain why the ratings for the NEG audio/video stimuli were somewhere in between the ratings for the audio and the video stimuli, this cannot explain why the POS audio/video stimuli were rated as even *more* positive than either of the two contributing channels. With regard to the discrepant audio/video stimuli, a similar problem arises.

Table 8.4 shows that the two combinations POS/NEG (i.e., positive facial expression + negative vocal expression) and NEG/POS (negative facial expression and positive vocal expression) were rated quite differently. The question as to which channels conveyed which information thus seemed to be of importance for the information integration process. In the following section these differences are inspected more closely, taking into account the differences in stimulus "strength" mentioned above.

The combination POS/NEG was generally judged to be more positive/happy and less negative/angry than the combination NEG/POS. If we group the attitude scales according to the three dimensions Osgood (1966) proposed ("pleasantness," "activity," and "control"), we can observe that the ratings for the POS/NEG stimuli for the dimension "pleasantness" were closer to those for the video stimuli, while for the dimension "activity," they were closer to the ratings for the audio stimuli. For the NEG/POS stimuli, on the other hand, the ratings for the dimension "pleasantness" were closer to those for the audio stimuli. With regard to the relevant emotion scales the combination POS/NEG was judged to be more happy and less angry than either single-channel stimulus. A comparable result for the combination NEG/POS was not found. These somewhat confusing results indicate different information integration strategies used for the two stimulus combinations. The reason for this may once more be found in the nature of the stimuli themselves. Before proceeding with an explanation of these findings, the result of the analysis of variance should be considered.

As Figure 8.2 clearly indicates, facial expression is the most important factor for the attribution of emotions and attitudes. Surprisingly, the percentage of variance explained by facial expression is even higher in the audio/video condition compared to the condition where facial expression is presented as the only source of information.

As mentioned before, facial expression is a very important source of information in a social context. Facial expression is also not only the most

TABLE 8.6
Explained Variance
(multichannel)

	Happiness			Anger			Negative		
	F	p	Omega^2	F	p	Omega^2	F	p	Omega^2
Text	63.3	.001	6.5	7.3	.01	1.2	31.5	.001	3.0
Facial Expr.	346.1	.001	36.1	297.0	.001	28.9	483.0	.001	48.5
Vocal Expr.	6.1	.01		33.0	.001	3.2	19.1	.001	1.9
Face/Voice				16.5	.01	1.5	11.1	.001	1.0
Text/Face	43.2	.001	4.4				20.3	.001	1.9
Text/Voice	10.5	.01	.9				10.4	.01	1.0
total									
expl. Variance:		48.4%			34.8%			57.1%	

181

influential source of nonverbal information but also the channel of non-verbal information that can best be controlled (Ekman & Friesen 1969, 1974; Ekman, Friesen, & Scherer 1976; Zuckerman, Spiegel, De Paulo, & Rosenthal, 1982; Zuckerman, Koestner, & Colella, 1985). However, it has been found that under certain conditions, especially if deceptive behavior of an interaction partner is expected, people rely more on the audio channel. Zuckerman and colleagues (1982) found that subjects who rated very discrepant stimuli suspected deceptive behavior of the stimulus person even though this was not mentioned in the instructions.

As the inspection of the audio/video stimuli shows, the combination POS/NEG—which consists of the weaker video and the weaker audio stimuli—is not very discrepant (so that subjects would not suspect deceptive behavior) while, on the other hand, the combination NEG/POS is very discrepant and may thus lead subjects to suspect deceptive behavior on the part of the stimulus person. In this case the judgments of the NEG/POS stimuli should be more influenced by the audio channel than the judgments of the POS/NEG stimuli, which is indeed the case, at least for the "pleasantness" dimension of scales. The other finding in need of explanation was the ratings combination POS/NEG, which was judged to be more positive/happy and less negative/angry than any of the stimuli it consisted of. These stimuli could be interpreted as a mildly positive/happy face with a neutral voice; bearing in mind the function of facial expression in social interaction this could be named a "normal" social combination. It may be that subjects interpreted it as such and therefore judged this *combination* as more positive/happy than its components. This would lead to the proposition of a weighted averaging model for the information integration process with the specific weights varying according to social context (deception, "normal" social interaction), which implies that different integration modi might be used for different social situations.

APPENDICES:
TOOLS FOR EMPIRICAL
RESEARCH ON EMOTION

These appendices contain the English and the Spanish version of the two questionnaires on physiological, situational, and social aspects of emotions as described in Chapters 1 and 2.

Both have been used for transcultural studies in countries all over the world. The German, Portuguese, Spanish, Italian, and French translations are available from the authors.

Furthermore, additional material for research on emotion, such as a list of terms describing emotional states in five major languages, and a "library" of descriptions of emotion-eliciting situations as reported by our subjects, is provided.

APPENDIX A: "EMOTION IN SOCIAL INTERACTION" QUESTIONNAIRE

Note: The questionnaire covered four emotions: "joy or happiness," "sadness or grief," "fear or fright," and "anger or rage." The questions reproduced here were identical for all four emotions.

Instructions to Subjects

The present study is concerned with the investigation of events and situations that provoke emotional reactions. We shall ask you to describe situations and events that have led to emotional reactions on your part. On the following pages you will find four emotions each illustrated with two different words. Please describe for each emotion one event or situation which, in the last few weeks, has resulted in your experiencing the respective emotion more or less intensely.

We should like you to give the following information for each event:

Where did it happen?	Please describe the place where the event occurred. Did it happen in your living room, in a restaurant, in a public place, etc.?
How long ago was it?	
Who was involved?	Please indicate who else was involved in the situation and your relationship to these people.
What happened?	Please describe the nature, cause, and development of the event.
How long did it last?	Did the feeling continue for some minutes, hours, or days?

We shall also be asking you some questions about what you said and how you otherwise reacted. Furthermore, we shall ask a series of questions about your feelings and your behavior during the event.

You should not try to specify only extreme situations, in which your emotional reactions were very strong and very obvious. It is equally important to recall those events in which you reacted emotionally without anybody noticing it.

Perhaps you will have difficulties in recalling one event for each emotion right away. Try, then, to recall the events that have happened during the last few weeks and try to think of an appropriate situation.

The Questionnaire

Think of a situation in which you experienced: _____
Description of the situation
    Where did the event occur? _____
    Who was involved? _____
    What exactly happened? _____
    _____
    _____
    How long did the feeling last? Was it some minutes, hours, days? _____
    In what way did the situation end? _____
    _____

Description of your emotional reaction

    In your opinion, what words would best describe your emotion? _____
    How strongly did you feel this emotion? (Please circle the appropriate number)
    not at all 0 1 2 3 4 5 6 7 8 9 very much
    What did you say? _____
    What were your bodily reactions (for example, trembling or a churning stomach) and your nonverbal reactions (for example, specific facial expressions, voice qualities, or gestures)?
    _____
    _____

Control of emotion

    How strongly did you try to control what you said?
    not at all 0 1 2 3 4 5 6 7 8 9 very much
    What did you do? _____
    How strongly did you try to control your nonverbal reactions?
    not at all 0 1 2 3 4 5 6 7 8 9 very much
    How did you do that? _____
    What would you do differently, if you found yourself again in such a situation?
    _____

Personal information

    Sex: male   female

    Age: _____ years

    Number of brothers and sisters: _____

    Marital status: _____

    Number of children: _____

    Nationality: _____

    Nationality of parents: _____

    Number of years spent at university: _____

    Where did you spend most of your life: _____

    In a country district   a town   a city

    In which country/nation: _____

    Where do you now live permanently (present place of residence):

    In a country district   a town   a city

    In which country/nation: _____

    Languages spoken:

    Mother language (specify): _____

    Other languages (specify): _____ _____

                  _____ ____ _____

    Occupation: _____ _____

    If you are a student, please indicate field of study:

    _____ _____

    Father's occupation: _____

    Mother's occupation: _____

APPENDIX B: ANTECEDENT AND REACTION CODES USED IN THE "EMOTION IN SOCIAL INTERACTION" STUDIES

In this appendix all codes that have been developed to code the free-response questionnaires are reported. As for some analyses antecedent categories and symptom/reaction categories can be combined into broader categories, the combination rules are also given.

1. **Codes for characteristics of the reported emotion**

Which emotion?

1 = joy
2 = sadness
3 = fear
4 = anger

How long ago was it?

1 = today
2 = yesterday
3 = up to a week ago
4 = up to a month ago
5 = several months ago
6 = several years ago

Where did the event happen?

(location)
1 = inside, familiar place
2 = inside, unfamiliar place
3 = outside
4 = transport

Who was involved?

1 = alone
2 = one other person known
3 = one other person unknown
4 = several persons known
5 = several persons unknown
6 = one person known & one unknown
7 = one person known & sev. unknown
8 = persons known & unknown

Time

  1 = past or present
       (still going on)
  2 = future

Reality

  1 = realistic, actually perceived
       or anticipated (cognitive)
  2 = imagined or dreamt, unreal-
       istic fantasies

Immediacy

  1 = own experience (event
       happened to subject)
  2 = empathic experience (event
       happened to other person,
       subject empathizes)

How long did it last?

  1 = under 5 minutes
  2 = 5 minutes to 1 hour
  3 = 1 to 24 hours
  4 = several days and longer

Description of situation (compare antecedent codes)

Intensity

  0 − 9

Handle the situation differently?

  1 = the same
  2 = something different

Control of verbal behavior

  0 − 9

Control of symptoms/reactions

  0 − 9

Verbal behavior

  1 = says nothing
  2 = "inner" talk
  3 = exclamation, affect word,
       humming
  4 = sentences, complete expres-
       sions, discussion

2. Antecedent codes

JOY = 1

  00 = uncodable
  01 = GOOD NEWS (immediate social context). *Example*: an unexpected job
       offer
  02 = GOOD NEWS (mass media). *Example*: cheering news in newspapers or
       on TV
  03 = CONTINUING RELATIONSHIPS WITH FRIENDS AND PERMANENT
       PARTNERS. *Example*: pleasure from contact with friends
  04 = CONTINUING RELATIONSHIPS WITH BLOOD RELATIVES AND IN-
       LAWS (see 03)
  05 = IDENTIFICATION WITH GROUPS (actual and reference). *Examples*:
       pleasure in belonging to a club; returning to your own country after a
       holiday

06 = MEETING FRIENDS, ANIMALS, PLANTS. *Examples*: seeing one's dog again; meeting one's friend for dinner

07 = MEETING BLOOD RELATIVES OR IN-LAWS (see 06)

10 = ACQUIRING NEW FRIENDS

11 = ACQUIRING NEW FAMILY MEMBERS. *Examples*: birth of a baby; marriage of one's brother

12 = PLEASURE IN MEETING STRANGERS (short-term chance encounters). *Example*: talking to a stranger on a train

13 = PLEASURE IN SOLITUDE. *Example*: being left alone with one's own thoughts

14 = NEW EXPERIENCES. *Examples*: adventures; planning a holiday

15 = SUCCESS EXPERIENCES IN ACHIEVEMENT SITUATIONS. *Example*: passing an examination

16 = ACQUIRING SOME MATERIAL FOR SELF OR OTHER (buying or receiving). *Examples*: presents from others; buying something nice for oneself or others

18 = RITUAL. *Examples*: religious, academic ceremonies, festivals, birthdays

19 = NATURAL, ALSO REFINED, NONCULTURAL PLEASURES. *Examples*: sex, food, nature, landscape

21 = CULTURAL PLEASURES. *Examples*: art, music, ballet, etc.

22 = ACQUIRING NONMATERIAL BENEFITS (emotional support, altruism). *Example*: helping an old lady cross the road

23 = HAPPINESS WITHOUT REASON.

31 = "SCHADENFREUDE." *Example*: malicious pleasure in another person's misfortune

SADNESS = 2

00 = uncodable

01 = BAD NEWS (immediate social context). *Example*: not selected for a job

02 = BAD NEWS (mass media). *Example*: bad news in newspapers or on TV

03 = PROBLEMS WITH FRIENDS, ANIMALS, PLANTS. *Examples*: quarrels, disappointments, estrangement, rejection

04 = PROBLEMS WITH BLOOD RELATIVES AND IN-LAWS (see 03)

05 = PROBLEMS WITH GROUPS (actual and reference). *Examples*: feeling rejected, an outsider, etc.

06 = TEMPORARY SEPARATION FROM LOVED FRIENDS, ANIMALS, PLANTS (indication that they will come back)

07 = TEMPORARY SEPARATION FROM LOVED BLOOD RELATIVES AND IN-LAWS (indication that the relative or in-law will come back)

08 = PERMANENT SEPARATION FROM LOVED FRIENDS, ANIMALS, PLANTS.

09 = PERMANENT SEPARATION FROM LOVED BLOOD RELATIVES AND IN-LAWS)

10 = DEATH OF FRIENDS, ANIMALS, PLANTS

11 = DEATH OF BLOOD RELATIVES AND IN-LAWS

12 = HARMING A STRANGER OR STRANGERS. *Example*: running over their dog with one's car

13 = UNEXPECTED OR UNWISHED-FOR SOLITUDE. *Examples*: having to spend a holiday on one's own; having little social contact; having not made new acquaintances yet when living a new place

14 = END OF PLEASURABLE EXPERIENCE. *Examples*: end of holiday; end of nice evening with friends

15 = FAILURE TO ACHIEVE WHAT WAS HOPED FOR IN AN ACHIEVE-MENT-RELATED ENTERPRISE (frustration). *Example*: failure to pass an examination

16 = OBJECT LOSS (selling, theft, loss). *Examples*: loss of a piece of jewelry; selling one's car

18 = SADNESS ABOUT RITUALS. *Example*: the anniversary of one's mother's death

19 = SICKNESS OF CLOSE ORGNANISMS IMPORTANT TO SUBJECT AND OF SELF. *Examples*: sickness of one's dog; friend has heart attack

23 = GENERAL DEPRESSION, ALIENATION (for no specific reason)

FEAR = 3

00 = uncodable

01 = BAD NEWS (immediate social context). *Example*: anticipation of losing one's job

02 = BAD NEWS (mass media). *Example*: anticipation of bad news in newspapers or on TV

03 = FEAR OF PROBLEMS IN RELATIONSHIPS WITH FRIENDS AND PERMANENT PARTNERS, ANIMALS, AND PLANTS. *Example*: fear of quarrels, estrangement, etc.

04 = FEAR OF PROBLEMS IN RELATIONSHIPS WITH BLOOD RELATIVES AND IN-LAWS. (see 03)

05 = FEAR OF PROBLEMS WITH GROUPS (actual and reference). *Example*: anticipation of problems with the members of one's football team

06 = FEAR OF TEMPORARY SEPARATION FROM FRIENDS AND PERMANENT PARTNERS, ANIMALS, AND PLANTS (indication that the person will come back)

07 = FEAR OF TEMPORARY SEPARATION FROM BLOOD RELATIVES AND IN-LAWS (indication that the person will come back)

08 = FEAR OF PERMANENT SEPARATION FROM FRIENDS, ANIMALS, AND PLANTS

09 = FEAR OF PERMANENT SEPARATION FROM BLOOD RELATIVES AND IN-LAWS

10 = FEAR OF DEATH OF FRIENDS AND PERMANENT PARTNERS, ANIMALS, AND PLANTS

11 = FEAR OF DEATH OF BLOOD RELATIVES AND IN-LAWS

12 = FEAR OF PHYSICAL AGGRESSION BY OTHERS. *Examples*: sexual assault, robbery, attack by hooligans

13 = FEAR OF SOLITUDE.

14 = FEAR OF THE UNKNOWN (something unspecified).

15 = FEAR OF FAILURE IN ACHIEVEMENT-RELATED SITUATIONS.

16 = FEAR OF LOSS OR DAMAGE OF OBJECT OR MONEY. *Example*: burglary

17 = FEAR OF TRAFFIC (accidents). *Examples*: driving too fast; being endangered by others

18 = FEAR OF RITUALS AND ANNIVERSARIES. *Example*: fear of the anniversary of a loved one's death

19 = FEAR OF OWN SICKNESS (illness, tests, or treatments). *Example*: believing one is seriously ill or in danger of death
20 = FEAR OF PAIN
23 = FREE-FLOATING ANXIETY
24 = FEAR OF SUPERNATURAL EVENTS, AND THE "UNHEIMLICHE." *Examples:* horror films, seances, witchcraft, weird situations
25 = CONSCIOUS RISK TAKING. *Example*: rock climbing
26 = PHOBIA (situations such as fear of closed spaces, animals, high altitudes, going out)
27 = FEAR OF ADVERSE EFFECTS FROM EXTERNAL FORCES. *Examples*: thunderstorms, bad weather at sea, dangerous machine not functioning

ANGER = 4
00 = uncodable
01 = BAD NEWS (immediate social context). *Example*: your sister having been humiliated by her boss
02 = BAD NEWS (mass media)
03 = ANGER AT FAILURE OF FRIENDS, ANIMALS, PLANTS TO CONFORM TO SOCIAL NORMS, TO BE CONSIDERATE ABOUT PERSONS AND PROPERTY
04 = ANGER AT FAILURE OF BLOOD RELATIVES AND IN-LAWS TO CONFORM TO SOCIAL NORMS, TO BE CONSIDERATE ABOUT PERSONS AND PROPERTY
05 = ANGER AT GROUPS (actual or reference). *Example*: one's club behaves badly during an outing
06 = ANGER ABOUT TEMPORARY SEPARATION FROM FRIENDS, ANIMALS, PLANTS (indication that person will come back)
07 = ANGER ABOUT TEMPORARY SEPARATION FROM BLOOD RELATIVES AND IN-LAWS (indication that person will come back)
08 = ANGER ABOUT PERMANENT SEPARATION FROM FRIENDS, ANIMALS, PLANTS
09 = ANGER ABOUT PERMANENT SEPARATION FROM BLOOD RELATIVES AND IN-LAWS
10 = ANGER ABOUT DEATH OF FRIENDS, ANIMALS, AND PLANTS
11 = ANGER ABOUT DEATH OF BLOOD RELATIVES AND IN-LAWS
12 = ANGER AT FAILURE OF OTHERS TO CONFORM TO SOCIAL NORMS AND TO BE CONSIDERATE ABOUT PERSONS AND PROPERTY
15 = FAILURE TO REACH GOALS OR TO ACHIEVE AN OBJECTIVE. *Examples*: anger about failing an examination
16 = DAMAGE TO PERSONAL PROPERTY BY OTHERS AND ONESELF. *Example*: anger about losing money
17 = ANGER IN TRAFFIC (about inconsiderate, norm-violating behavior by others)
18 = ANGER ABOUT RITUALS AND ANNIVERSARIES. *Example*: anger about having to attend an aunt's birthday party
20 = ANGER ABOUT A PHYSICAL HURT. *Example*: an assault

23 = FREE-FLOATING ANGER (bad mood for no specific reason)

28 = ANGER ABOUT INAPPROPRIATE REWARDS FOR SELF (feeling unjustly treated). *Examples*: Failure to get a deserved reward; being the object of unfair accusation

29 = ANGER AT DAMAGE TO COMMON PROPERTY. *Examples*: damage to public buildings; vandalism

30 = UNEXPECTED, UNNECESSARY INCONVENIENCE, TIME LOSS. *Example*: time loss caused by failure of machines to work properly

3. Codes for nonverbal and physiological concomitants of emotions

Experienced subjective quality (ESQ)

XX1 Normal	Code ESQ only if mentioned explicitly
XX2 Aroused positive	by subject! Check other more specific
XX3 Aroused negative ("tight, nervous, tense")	codes first!
XX4 Increase (Fast/Much/Strong)	In case of uncertainty: Aroused
XX5 Decrease (Slow/Little/Weak)	positive/negative dominates increase!
XX6 Controlled	
XX7 Changed (unspecified)	

Associated emotions

XX1 Happiness	
XX2 Sadness	Code Assodiated emotions only if
XX3 Fear	mentioned explicitly by subject!
XX4 Anger	
XX5 Surprise	
XX6 Disgust	
XX7 Contempt	

3.1 Speech

101	Silence, Say nothing		
11X	Experienced subjective quality (ESQ, see above)	12X	Associated emotions (see above)
181	Hesitant	100	Not specified
182	Change in articulation	109	Other
183	Change in rhythm		

3.2 Voice

21X	ESQ (see above)	If possible code ESQ for:	
		23X	Loudness
22X	Associated emotions (see above)	.	
		.	(1 to 7)
		24X	Pitch

			(1 to 7)
281	Tense, choked	285	Warm
282	Harsh		
283	Trembling	200	Not specified
284	Whistling	209	Other

3.3   Facial expression

331	Laugh	334	No smile
332	Smile	335	Cry
333	Painful smile	32X	Associated emotions (see above)
31X	ESQ (see above)		
381	Pressing, biting lips	385	Other action in lower face
382	Clenched teeth	386	Action around nose (wrinkle, etc.)
383	Pulling lip corners down	387	Action around forehead
384	Mouth open	388	Other muscular action
300	Not specified	309	Other

3.4   Gaze

431	Stared	434	Closed one's eyes
432	Sought eye contact	435	Looked at objects
433	Avoided eye contact		
41X	ESQ (see above)	42X	Associated emotions (see above)
400	Not specified		
409	Other		

3.5   Movements and posture of bodily parts

Behaviors of head, arms, feet, trunk; person staying in one place (for movement of whole body see 3.6):

531   Turning toward other (head or trunk)
532   Turning away from other (head or trunk)
533   Touching positive (to hug, caress, also to kiss)
534   Touching negative (to hit, beat)
535   Instrumental action positive (putting away something carefully, etc.)
536   Instrumental action negative (throwing, also kicking objects, slamming door, etc.)
537   Rest, relaxing, lean back
538   Unrest, not to be able to sit quietly, move back and forth
539   Tense, attending movements (lean forward, etc.)
51X   ESQ (see above)

52X   Associated emotions (see above)

551   Eating, drinking
522   Sleeping

500   Not specified
509   Other

If necessary, specify further:

Head

561   Head down
562   Head up
569   Head other

Feet, legs

581   Legs pulled up
582   Stamp one's foot
589   Feet, legs, other

Arms, hands, gestures

571   Adaptors (manipulation of
      body or objects)
572   Illustrators (speech-related
      gestures of head, hands, arms)
573   Emblems (head shaking, clen-
      ched fist, gesture of kicking, etc.)
574   Hands in pockets, arms crossed
575   Arms, hands, other
591   Trunk movements, other

3.6   Body movement, displacement, and posture

(When walking, taking a chair, posture related to *whole* body; for bodily parts, see 3.5):

631   Approaching, turning
      toward somebody to contact
      (walking, not only 531!)
632   Distancing, turning away
      from somebody (walking, not
      only 532!)
633   Leaving the situation, slow
      to normal
634   Running away
61X   ESQ (see above)

641   Collapsed posture
642   Freezing
643   Sitting down
644   Erect posture, attending, tense
645   Walking up and down
646   Jumping, Dancing around

600   Not specified
609   Other
62X   Associated emotions (see
      above)

3.7   Behavioral tendencies

(not actually done but rather "feel like . . ." or "need for . . ." or "have a desire to . . ."):

Bodily parts (see 3.5)

731   Turning toward other (head or trunk)
732   Turning away from other (head or trunk)
733   Touching positive (to hug, caress, also to kiss)
734   Touching negative (to hit, beat)
735   Instrumental action positive (putting away something carefully, etc.)
736   Instrumental action negative (throwing, also kicking objects, slamming
      door, etc.)
737   Rest, relaxing, leaning back
738   Unrest, not to be able to sit quietly, move back and forth
739   Tense, attending movements (lean forward, etc.)
751   Eating, drinking   700   Not specified
752   Sleeping   709   Other

Whole body (see 3.6)

781 Approaching, turning toward somebody to contact (walking, not only 731!)
782 Distancing, turning away from somebody (walking, not only 732!)
783 Leaving the situation, slow to normal
784 Running away

791 Collapsed posture
792 Freezing
793 Sitting down
794 Erect posture, attending, tense
795 Walking up and down
796 Jumping, dancing around

3.8 General sensations

831 Pleasant — Rest
Harmony, ease, complete absorption, feeling delight, relaxed, rest, satisfaction, to feel well
841 Pleasant — Arousal
Refreshed, lighthearted, "winged," watchfulness, full of energy, animated, boiling over with happiness, pleasant arousal of the whole body
851 Unpleasant — Rest
Feeling tired, drowsiness, feeling heavy, weakness, laxity, slackness, decreasing readiness to react, dejected, disappointed
861 Unpleasant — Arousal
Tense, restless, not concentrated, being nervous, to feel like exploding, impatience
800 Not specified   809 Other

3.9 Vegetative sensations and symptoms

General

931 Pleasant
932 Unpleasant (slight pain, etc.)
933 Severe pain   900 Not specified
934 Headaches   909 Other

Body temperature and skin sensations

941 Pleasant
942 Unpleasant
943 Cold (coldness, to feel cold, to be pale
944 Warm (heat, raising of body temperature, rush of blood to the brain, head feels hot)
945 Blushing

Chest and Heart

961 Pleasant
962 Unpleasant
963 Rising blood pressure, heart beats faster
964 Heart beats slower
965 Chest (chest pain, sense of weight, anguish, feeling squeezed)

946 Perspiration, sweaty palms
949 Other (goose pimples, pins and needles in the arm)

966 Difficulty in breathing, breath stops
967 Deep breathing
969 Other

Mouth

951 Pleasant
952 Unpleasant (dry mouth, etc.)
959 Other

Muscles

981 Pleasant
982 Unpleasant
983 Trembling, weak knees
984 Tension of the muscles, muscle cramps
985 Other

Stomach

971 Pleasant
972 Unpleasant or other odd feelings
973 "Butterflies in the stomach"
974 Pressure on the stomach
975 Churning stomach, feeling sick in the stomach
976 Hunger, thirst
979 Other

4. Combined nonverbal and physiological symptoms/reactions

As the symptom/reaction codes consists of a multitude of categories, it may be necessary to combine categories into larger symptom/reaction groups. The symptom/reaction groups that were used in the previously mentioned studies are specified in the following table and the relevant categories are indicated by their respective code numbers (see Section 3).

Variable Code	Name of variable	Codes combined
Speech		
SPEEQN	Speech subjective quality normal	111, 116
SPEEQC	Speech subjective quality changed	112–115, 117
SPEESY	Speech reactions mentioned	181–183, 100, 109
Voice		
VOIQN	Voice subjective quality normal	211, 216, 231, 236
VOIQC	Voice subjective quality changed	212–215, 217, 232–235, 237
VOISY	Voice reactions mentioned	281–285, 200, 209
Facial expression		
FACQN	Face subjective quality normal	311, 316
FACQC	Face subjective quality changed	312–315, 317
LAFSMI	Laughing/smiling	331, 332
CRY	Crying	335
FACSY	Face reactions mentioned	381–388, 300, 309
Gaze		
GAZESY	Gaze reactions mentioned	431–435

Variable Code	Name of variable	Codes combined
Body part movements		
MOVQN	Normal movements of body parts	511, 516
MOVQC	Changed movements of body parts	512–515, 517
PERSMOV	Interpersonal movement	531–534
INSTACT	Instrumental action	535–536
UNREST	General unrest	538–539
HANDSY	Hand movements mentioned	571–575
Whole body movements and postures		
BODYQN	Normal body movements	611, 616
BODYQC	Changed body movements	612–615, 617
AVOID	Avoidance/distancing	632–634
FREEZ	Freezing	642, 644
EXPAN	Expansive movements	645, 646
Sensations		
PLEARES	Pleasant rest sensations	831
PLEAROU	Pleasant arousal sensations	841
UNPLRES	Unpleasant rest sensations	851
UNPLROU	Unpleasant arousal sensations	861
Vegetative symptoms		
COLDTEM	Symptoms of coldness	943, 949
WARMTEM	Symptoms of warmth	944, 945
PERSPIR	Perspiration	946
BLOPRES	Blood pressure rise	963
CHESBRE	Chest/breathing problems	965, 966
STOTROU	Stomach symptoms	972–975
MUSCLSY	Muscle symptoms	983, 984

5. Combined antecedent codes—antecedent groups

As for the symptom/reaction codes, for statistical purposes some of the antecedent codes can be combined into larger groups. These combinations are based on frequencies of occurrence and on content of categories and are presented in the following table together with the categories included in each group. Most of the groups can be used for all four emotions, but some are emotion-specific.

Variable Code	Antecedent group	Categories included
NEWS	News	01, 02
RELA	Relationships	03, 04
INST	Social institutions	05, 18
TEMP	Temporary meeting/separation	06, 07
PERM	Permanent separation	08, 09
ALPH	Birth/death	10, 11

Variable Code	Antecedent group	Categories included
BODY	Pleasure/pain	19, 20, 21
STRANG	Interactions with	
	strangers	12
ACHI	Achievement	15

only for fear:

SUPER	Supernatural	24
RISKI	Risk-taking/External forces	25, 26, 27
TRAF	Traffic	17
NOVEL	Novelty	14

only for anger:

JUST	Injustice	28
INCON	Inconvenience	30

APPENDIX C: QUESTIONNAIRE USED IN THE "INTERNATIONAL SURVEY ON EMOTION ANTECEDENTS AND REACTIONS" (ISEAR)

Instructions to Subjects

In this study we are concerned with the different types of emotional experiences that people have in everyday life. We would like you to recall occasions on which you have experienced one of the following emotions: JOY, FEAR, ANGER, SADNESS, DISGUST, SHAME, GUILT. For each of these emotions, please think of a situation which aroused this feeling in you and for which you vividly remember both the circumstances and your reaction. Your responses will of course remain completely anonymous.

In this questionnaire there are *two pages* of questions for each of these emotions. Please answer *all* the questions for each of the emotions specified on the top of the page. For those questions where there are *several answer alternatives*, please *circle* the appropriate alternative as follows:

1. not at all   2. a little   3. very much   0. not applicable

If none of the alternatives applies to the respective situation, or if the question is not appropriate, please circle the answer category "not applicable."

The Questionnaire

Emotion: _____

1. Please *describe a situation or event* — in as much detail as possible — in which you felt the emotion given above.

_____

_____

2. *When* did this happen?
    1. days ago   2. weeks ago   3. months ago   4. years ago
3. *How long* did you feel the emotion?
    1. a few minutes   2. an hour   3. several hours   4. a day or more
4. *How intense* was this feeling?
    1. not very   2. moderately intense   3. intense   4. very intense
5. Below you find a list of *bodily symptoms and reactions* which often occur in such situations. Please make a check next to *each one* you experienced in the situation.

Bodily symptoms

0. _____ Do not remember
1. _____ Lump in throat
2. _____ Change in breathing
3. _____ Stomach troubles
4. _____ Feeling cold, shivering
5. _____ Feeling warm pleasant

6. _____ Feeling hot, cheeks burning
7. _____ Heart beating faster
8. _____ Muscles tensing, trembling
9. _____ Muscles relaxing, restful
10. _____ Perspiring, moist hands
11. _____ Other symptoms

Expressive reactions

0. _____ Do not remember
1. _____ Laughing, smiling
2. _____ Crying, sobbing
3. _____ Other changes in facial expression
4. _____ Screaming, yelling
5. _____ Other changes in voice
6. _____ Change in gesturing

7. _____ Abrupt bodily movements
8. _____ Moving towards people or things
9. _____ Withdrawing from people or things
10. _____ Moving against people or things, aggression
11. _____ Other expressive reactions

Verbal reactions

1. _____ Silence
2. _____ Short utterance
3. _____ One or two sentences
4. _____ Lengthy utterance

5. _____ Speech melody change
6. _____ Speech disturbances
7. _____ Speech tempo changes
8. _____ Other verbal reactions

6. Did you try to *hide* or to *control* your feelings so that nobody would know how you really felt?
    1. not at all   2. a little   3. very much   0. not applicable
7. Now please think back to the situation or event that caused your emotion. Did you *expect* this situation to occur?)
    1. not at all   2. a little   3. very much   0. not applicable
8. Did you find the event itself *pleasant or unpleasant*?
    1. pleasant   2. neutral   3. unpleasant   0. not applicable
9. *How important* was the event for your *goals, needs, or desires at the time it happened*? Did it *help* or *hinder* you to follow your plans or to achieve your aims?
    1. it helped   2. it didn't matter   3. it hindered   0. not applicable

10. Would you say that the situation or event that caused your emotion was *unjust* or *unfair*?

    1. not at all   2. a little   3. very much   0. not applicable

11. Who do you think was *responsible* for the event in the first place? Check one, the most important, of the following:

    0. _____ Not applicable   6. _____ Authority figures
    1. _____ Yourself   7. _____ Natural forces
    2. _____ Close relatives   8. _____ Supernatural forces
    3. _____ Close friends   9. _____ Fate
    4. _____ Colleagues/acquaintances   10. _____ Chance
    5. _____ Strangers

12. How did you evaluate your *ability to act on or to cope with the event and its consequences* when you were first confronted with this situation? Check one, the most appropriate, of the following:

    1. _____ I did not think that any action was necessary.
    2. _____ I believed that I could positively influence the event and change the consequences.
    3. _____ I believed that I could escape from the situation or avoid negative consequences.
    4. _____ I pretended that nothing important had happened and tried to think of something else.
    5. _____ I saw myself as powerless and dominated by the event and its consequences.

13. If the event was caused by your own or someone else's behavior, would this behavior itself be judged as *improper or immoral* by your acquaintances?

    1. not at all   2. a little   3. very much   0. not applicable

14. How did this event affect your *feelings about yourself*, such as your *self-esteem* or your *self-confidence*?

    1. negatively   2. not at all   3. positively   0. not applicable

15. How did this event change your *relationships* with the people involved?

    1. negatively   2. not at all   3. positively   0. not applicable

APPENDIX D: SPANISH VERSIONS OF THE "EMOTIONAL EXPERIENCE" QUESTIONNAIRES

ESTUDIO DE LAS REACCIONES EMOCIONALES

El presente estudio es parte de una investigación sobre los hechos y situaciones que provocan reacciones emocionales. Le pediremos que describa situaciones y acontecimientos que le hayan provocado determinadas reacciones emocionales. En las páginas siguientes encontrará cuatro emociones. Cada una de las emociones está definida por dos palabras diferentes. Por favor describa para cada emoción un acontecimiento o situación que, en las últimas semanas hayan provocado la emoción con más o menos intensidad.

Le pediremos nos dé la siguiente información para cada hecho:

Cuándo pasó?	Cuánto hace que ocurrió?
Dónde pasó?	Por favor, describa el lugar donde ocurrió el hecho. Fue en su salón, en un restaurante, en público, etc?.
Quién estuvo implicado?	Por favor, indique quién estaba implicado en la situación y sus relaciones con esa persona.
Qué pasó?	Por favor, describa la naturaleza, causa y desarrollo del acontecimiento.
Cuanto tiempo le duró?	La sensación continuó durante algunos minutos o dias?

También le preguntaremos algunas cuestiones sobre qué dijo y, por otra parte, cómo reaccionó. Además le preguntaremos una serie de cuestiones sobre sus sensaciones y su conducta durante el hecho.

No es necesario que intente unicamente describir las situaciones extremas, en las que sus reacciones emocionales hayan sido muy fuertes y evidentes. Es igualmente importante recordar aquellos hechos en los que reaccionó emocionalmente sin que nadie se diera cuenta.

Tal vez tenga dificultades en recordar enseguida un acontecimiento para cada emoción. Inténtelo nuevamente buscando en su memoria los hechos que pasaron durante la últimas semanas e intente pensar una situación concreta.

Piense en una situación en la que haya experimentado

_____

_____

Descripción de la situación

Dónde ocurrió la situación?

_____

Quién estuvo implicado?

_____

_____

Que pasó exactamente?

_____

_____

_____

_____

_____

_____

Cuantó tiempo duró la sensación?

_____

De qué modo terminó la situación?

_____

_____

_____

Descripción de su reacción emocional

En su opinión qué palabras describen mejor su emoción?

_____

Con qué intensidad sintió la emoción? (Por favor, ponga un círculo en el número apropiado)

Nada en absoluto   0   1   2   3   4   5   6   7   8   9   Muchisimo

Qué dijó?

___

Cuáles fueron sus reacciones corporales (por ejemplo, temblores, se le revolvió el estomago) y sus reacciones no verbales (por ejemplo expresiones faciales, calidades de la voz o gestos)?

___

Control de la emoción

Cuantó intento controlar lo dijó

Nada en absoluto   0   1   2   3   4   5   6   7   8   9   Muchisismo

Qué hizo?

___

Cuánto intentó controlar sus reacciones no verbales?

Nada en absoluto   0   1   2   3   4   5   6   7   8   9   Muchisimo

Qué hizo para esto?

___

Qué haría de manera diferente si se encontrara otra vez en una situación como esa?

___

EMOTIONS: JOY = ALEGRIA   HAPPINESS = FELICIDAD
           ANGER = COLERA   RAGE = RABIA
           FEAR = MIEDO   FRIGHT = SUSTO
           SADNESS = TRISTEZA   GRIEF = PESAR

CUESTIONARIO DE EXPERIENCIA EMOCIONAL

Este trabajo pretende estudiar los diferentes tipos de experiencias emocionales que las personas tienen en su vida cotidiana. Tendrá que recordar momentos en los que hay experimentado una de las siguientes emociones: ALEGRIA, MIEDO, COLERA, TRISTEZA, DISGUSTO, VERGUENZA, CULPA. Para cada una de estas emociones pensará en una situación que despertó en Vd. esta sensación y en la que recuerde perfectamente tanto las circustancias como su reacción. Sus respuestas serán anónimas.

Este cuestionario consta de *dos páginas* de preguntas para cada una de las emociones. Por favor, responda a *todas* las preguntas para cada una de las emociones especificadas en la parte superiod de la página. Para aquellas preguntas que tienen *varias alternativas de respuesta*, por favor, senale con un *círculo* la alternativa apropiada como en el siguiente ejemplo:

1. de ninguna manera   2. un poco   3. mucho   0. no apropiada

Si ninguna de las alternativas se aplica a la situación correspondiente o si la pregunta no es apropiada, marque con un círculo la categoria de respuesta "ni apropiada".

_____

_____

Antes de comenzar a describir las situaciones, por favor responda a las siguientes preguntas:

SEXO: 1. Hombre   2. Mujer   (senalelo con un circulo)

EDAD: _____ anos

RELIGION: _____ Es practicante?   1. si   2. no

NACIONALIDAD: _____

PAIS DONDE CRECIO: _____

LENGUA NATIVA: _____

OCUPACION DE SU PADRE: _____

OCUPACION DE SU MADRE: _____

ESTUDIOS (Facultad): _____

Emoción

1. Por favor, describa una situación o acontecimiento —*con el mayor detalle posible*— *en el que* sintió la emoción senalada arriba.

_____

_____

_____

_____

2. Cuándo ocurrió?
   1. hace dias   2. hace semanas   3. hace meses   4. hace anos

3. Cuánto duró la emoción?
   1. minutos   2. una hora   3. varias horas   4. un día o más

4. Qué *intensidad* tuvo la sensación?
   1. no mucha   2. moderadamente intensa   3. intensa   4. muy intensa

5. A continuación encontrará una lista de *sintomas corporales y reacciones* que ocurren a menudo en estas situaciones. Por favor, elija entre todas aquellas que experimentó en la situación.

Sintomas corporales
0. _____ No recuerdo
1. _____ Nudo en la garganta
2. _____ Alteración del ritmo respiratorio
3. _____ Molestias de estómago
4. _____ Sensación de frio, tiritar
5. _____ Sensación cálida, agradable
6. _____ Sensación de calor, mejillas sonrojadas
7. _____ Aceleración del ritmo cardíaco
8. _____ Tensión muscular, temblor
9. _____ Relajación muscular, sosiego
10. _____ Sudar, manos sudorosas
11. _____ Otros sintomas

Reacciones expresivas:
0. _____ No recuerdo
1. _____ Reir, sonreir
2. _____ Llorar sollozar
3. _____ Otros cambios de expresión facial
4. _____ Chillar gritar
5. _____ Otros cambios en la voz
6. _____ Cambios gestuales
7. _____ Cambios corporales bruscos
8. _____ Avanzar hacia personas o cosas
9. _____ Alejarse de personas o cosas
10. _____ Agredir a personas o cosas
11. _____ Otras reacciones expresivas

Reacciones verbales:
1. _____ Silencio
2. _____ Expresión corta
3. _____ Una o dos frases
4. _____ Expresión larga
5. _____ Cambios en la melodia del habla
6. _____ Perturbaciones en el habla
7. _____ Cambios en el ritmo del habla
8. _____ Otras reacciones verbales

6. Trató de *ocultar o controlar* su emoción para que nadie ra cómo se sentía?
1. de ninguna manera   2. un poco   3. mucho   0. no apropiada.

7. Ahora intente recordar la situación o acontecimiento que causó su emoción. *Esperaba que dicha situación* ocurriera?
1. de ninguna manera   2. un poco   3. mucho   0. no apropiada.

8. Cómo encontró el acontecimiento en si mismo, *agradable o desagradable*?
1. agradable   2. neutro   3. desagradable   0. no apropiada

9. De qué manera *influyó el acontecimiento en sus* objetivos, necesidades o deseos en el momento en que ocurrió? Ayudó o entorpeció *la continuación* de sus planes o el logro de sus objetivos?
   1. ayudó   2. no influyó   3. entorpeció   0. no apropiada

10. Diría que la situación o acontecimiento que provocó su emoción fue *injusta*
    1. de ninguna manera   2. un poco   3. mucho   0. no apropiada

11. Quién considera que fue el *responsable* en primer término del acontecimiento? Elija uno, el más importante:
    0. _____ No apropiada
    1. _____ Usted
    2. _____ Parientes cercanos
    3. _____ Amigos cercanos
    4. _____ Companeros/conocidos
    5. _____ Extranos
    6. _____ La autoridad
    7. _____ Fuerzas naturales
    8. _____ Fuerzas sobrenaturales
    9. _____ El destino
    10. _____ La suerte

12. Cuando se enfrentó a esta situación Cómo valoró su *capacidad para actuar o afrontar el hecho y sus consecuensias*? Elija la respuesta más apropiada.
    1. _____ No creí necesaria ninguna actuación (acción)
    2. _____ Creí poder dominar la situación o cambiar las consecuencias.
    3. _____ Creí poder huir de la situación o evitar sus consecuencias negativas.
    4. _____ Consideré que no había ocurrido nada importante e intenté pensar en otra cosa.
    5. _____ Me ví impotente y dominado por el acontecimiento y sus consecuencias

13. Si el acontecimiento fue provocado por su conducta o por la de otra persona. Juzgaían sus amistades esa conducta como *impropia* o inmoral?
    1. de ninguna manera   2. un poco   3. mucho   0. no apropiada

14. Cómo afectó el acontecimiento a su autoestima o a la confianza en si mismo?
    1. negativamente   2. de ninguna manera   3. positivamente
    0. no apropiado

15. De qué manera modificó este acontecimiento sus *relaciones* con las personas implicadas?
    1. negativamente   2. de ninguna manera   3. positivamente
    0. no apropiado

EMOTIONS: JOY = ALEGRIA   GUILT = CULPA
          ANGER = COLERA   DISGUST = ASCO
          FEAR = MIEDO   SADNESS = TRISTEZA
          SHAME = VERGUENZA

APPENDIX E: SELECTED REPORTS ON EMOTIONAL EXPERIENCES FROM THE "EMOTION IN SOCIAL INTERACTION" PROJECT (REPORTS FROM WEST GERMAN SAMPLE)

In this appendix a small "library of situation descriptions" typical of the descriptions collected in the European study reported in Scherer, Wallbott, and Summerfield (1986) is presented. These descriptions were reported by subjects of the West German sample and have been translated from German into English. Only situations typically eliciting the respective emotion were selected (for detailed results see Scherer, Summerfield, & Wallbott, 1986):

- for JOY: situations centered around relationships with other persons; temporary meetings with other persons; success experiences in achievement-related situations; and body/mind–centered pleasures.

- for SADNESS: situations involving relationships with other persons, especially the breaking up of relationships; death and severe illness of close beings; body-mind–centered situations, for instance own illness; and bad private or public news.

- for FEAR: situations in traffic; encounters with strangers; novel, unknown situations; and situations in which risks are consciously taken.

- for ANGER: situations involving friends and relatives violating norms or agreements; situations in which the person feels unjustly treated; encounters with strangers not obeying norms and conventions; and situations involving inconvenience for the person.

The reports are presented in the following format:
- Subject-number   Target emotion

- A: _____   Answers to the questions:
    - Where did the situation occur?
    - How long ago was it?
    - Who was involved?
    - What exactly happened?
    - How long did the feeling last?
    - In what way did the situation end?
- B: _____   · What did you say?
- C: _____   · What did you do (to control what you said)?
- D: _____   · What were your bodily reactions and your nonver-
      bal reactions?
- E: _____   · How strongly did you try to control your nonver-
      bal reactions?
- F: _____   · What would you do differently, if you found
      yourself again in such a situation?

(No information = subject did not answer the respective question)

(Names of persons, cities, etc., are replaced by "XXX" in order to guarantee anonymity of subjects)

(for a complete version of the questionnaire see Appendix A)

026   JOY
A   4 months ago, in summer. I spent my holidays in the States. I got on
A   really well with one boy and two girls there, so that I felt really
A   good the whole time of my stay, which was 4 weeks. Every time I was
A   excited to see them again. I was well because I had a lot in common
A   with them and similar ideas. The emotion lasted for 4 weeks and
A   ended when I had to go back to Germany.
B   Talked a lot, laughed.
C   I didn't want to show my happiness too much, and sometimes tried to
C   stay earnest.
D   Great feeling in my body, nonverbal: talked very much, laughed,
D   expressed.
E   See above.
F   Nothing.

029   JOY
A   The situation happened a few weeks ago, about 3 weeks. By accident
A   I met an ex-boyfriend in town. We immediately decided to spend the
A   day together. We realized, that we had developed in the same
A   direction, though we had split up long ago. We still were on the
A   same "level." The exchanging of our experiences was an enrichment
A   to me and also strengthened my self-confidence. After a long walk
A   and an evening meal, we parted. He continues his life, I continue
A   my life. The emotion lasted some days.

B   I said quite a lot of things that seemed important to me, which I
B   can't summarize here.
C   I let it all happen.
D   Bodily reactions like trembling or pressure on my stomach only
D   occurred in the beginning, when we met. Later nonverbal reactions
D   occurred (intense eye contact). My voice especially changed, when I
D   realized that I hadn't completely coped with some of the things I
D   was talking about.
E   I didn't play any "role."
F   Nothing.

031   JOY
A   In the evening, about a week ago. On the way to sports by bike I
A   found the weather and the air so wonderful. It was very mild after
A   having been freezing the days before, so that I would have loved to
A   scream. The emotion lasted all the way to the gymnastics-hall and
A   back, about 20 minutes. Then I went home feeling well.
B   I sang.
C   No information.
D   Good feeling all over my body, feeling very light, as if I was
D   gliding.
E   I didn't really pay attention to that.
F   Cycle longer.

033   JOY
A   On a Saturday, about 6 weeks ago. My husband and I had been looking
A   for a flat in XXX for 5 weeks without any success. On that
A   Saturday we got the message that we were allowed to move into a
A   very nice flat. The joy was lessened when I realized the price of the
A   flat, which was quite high. The emotion lasted for hours.
B   I was so glad, because we had so much bad luck up to then. My
B   husband is a foreigner, and that is why we had been rejected so many
B   times. But I had the impression that he (the landlord) didn't seem
B   to mind what nationality one is.
C   Tried not to become too excited, talk on a formal level (when to
C   move in, what furniture was there, etc.).
D   Being silly, pinched my husband in his arm, face like a sheep.
E   Put my hands in my pockets.
F   Behave a bit more calm.

036   JOY
A   This week, 4 days ago. I had been ill for a week and was in my home
A   town, not where I study. At the beginning of the week a fellow
A   student, whom I liked to get in contact with, but who had appeared
A   quite cool up to then, phoned me at my home. She asked where I was
A   and offered to get papers for me and lend me her notes later.
A   First I was very surprised, then I was really happy about her inter-
A   est and her offer. I will get in closer contact to her. The emotion

A   lasted some hours.
B   I told her about my joy and thanked her.
C   No information.
D   Excited in a positive sense, laughing, more desire to move.
E   No information.
F   I would react the same.

039   JOY
A   At about midnight, 6 months ago. My girlfiend and I began to talk.
A   We went on for hours. Very often we found ourselves to have similar
A   opinions. A wonderful feeling of harmony and understanding arose,
A   because we were talking about very personal affairs. As I mentioned
A   above, the next morning the feeling went away pretty soon, because
A   of our daily duties and worries. The emotion lasted one or two
A   hours, then I fell asleep.
B   I didn't especially say anything, but our feelings were recognizably
B   the same.
C   I occasionally tried to let my girlfriend speak first. Sometimes,
C   when this lasted too long, I just dropped what I was going to say.
C   Also I tried not to become too personal.
D   Maybe I felt some calmness in my body.
E   No special effort.
F   Nothing.

040   JOY
A   In the late afternoon, about 3 years ago. I assumed I was pregnant.
A   After great difficulties I told my boyfriend about it. I had no idea
A   how he would react. I was totally surprised when he said: "That
A   would be great, I would be very happy." I was not pregnant, though.
A   The emotion lasted a few hours.
B   "Really? This makes me feel a lot better, I'm so glad."
C   I didn't express my joy in words as much as I could have done.
D   Feeling of relaxation, the tension went, laughing, hugging,
D   squeezing him tightly, being affectionate.
E   No information.
F   I would verbalize my joy. In other words really speak out what I
F   feel and keep nothing back.

042   JOY
A   Yesterday morning. One of my best friends was very depressed. We
A   spoke about it. During the conversation I realized more and more
A   that her problems were very similar to my hidden problems and I felt
A   I understood very well. This made me feel happy,
A   because actually this "being understood" is both our main problem. I
A   went home to make biscuits and to write little letters to give to my
A   friend, as she was going to leave for two weeks. When I gave the
A   things to her in the evening we were both very happy, to have built
A   up even more understanding on both sides. The emotion lasted all day

A   and was interrupted today by a very difficult relation to someone
A   else.
B   "I often feel similar to you," and I remembered occasions when
B   I had told her so before.
C   By thinking hard.
D   Reflecting, I looked her in the eyes and the face very intensely, I
D   embraced her.
E   I didn't do anything to it, it just came the way it did.
F   Nothing really.

043   JOY
A   6 days ago in a friend's flat. From where I study I drove quite a
A   long distance (600 km) to go to my friend's house-warming party. I was
A   very happy, because I hadn't seen her for a long time (because of
A   the distance). She hadn't expected me to really come. We put our
A   arms around each other and hugged each other. Then I had to go
A   back. I will see her again at Christmas, because we come from the
A   same town. I'm already looking forward to that. The emotion is still
A   lasting.
B   That it is great to see her again, that I'm happy.
C   No information.
D   Joy flooded through all my body. Tingling in my arms, laughing.
E   No information.
F   Nothing.

046   JOY
A   In the afternoon, a week ago. I had got stuck in my work for my
A   masters degree (teacher) as I drove to the university library and
A   looked up a thesis about a similar subject. When I saw the structure
A   of this thesis I was more back to reality and realized that my
A   expectations had been too high. This was a great relief to me. Then
A   I drove to the psychological department and learned that I had
A   passed the test-theory exam, for which I had learnt only short but
A   very intense. This gave me a good feeling.
B   Thank God, great.
C   I didn't say that I was surprised.
D   First pressure in my stomach, when I was on my way to the notice-
D   board and hadn't got the results yet. Then the pressure in my
D   stomach stopped and there was an easy feeling.
E   Wasn't necessary, because they weren't so noticeable.
F   The same.

047   JOY
A   In the evening about a month ago. We (I) had had our first perfor-
A   mance with our theater-group in a pub. Of course we were all very ex-
A   cited, especially because the dress rehearsal had not been very suc-
A   cessful. But we weren't too bad during the performance itself and

A   were given many compliments, especially I was complimented, which
A   was very important and motivating for me. We had a little cele-
A   bration together, during which I noticed, that I was rather quiet
A   (maybe because of my joy?). The emotion lasted some days, maybe 3–4.
B   Not very much, rather few words, I don't know exactly.
C   I guess I wasn't very much controlled and therefore I can't
C   remember.
D   I was relieved and tired, but quite exhausted.
E   As mentioned above.
F   Not very much, it wasn't very much a mental affair.

048   JOY
A   In the evening, two weeks ago. By accident we met a friend from our
A   home town (old schoolmates and friends that I had gone to school
A   with). I was very happy to see him, because I hadn't seen him for a
A   long time. We began to talk, only short, but this was important,
A   because there were some conflicts in the past that had to be spoken
A   out and cleared. But even this short talk was enough to evoke a
A   feeling of joy or happiness in me. It ended when the friend went
A   home. The emotion lasted for some days.
B   That I was very happy to meet him.
C   I thought about how to start talking about our old problems, so that
C   we would come to an agreement.
D   Quicker heartbeat, happy smile.
E   In suppressing spontaneously hugging him, when we said hello.
F   I would not suppress the impulse mentioned above and try to speak
F   about our problems in an uncontrolled way.

051   JOY
A   In September, 2½ months ago. A very good friend from the USA came
A   to see me and my fiancee unexpectedly. We talked a lot and felt very
A   close together. Then my friend continued his journey the next
A   morning. The emotion lasted some days.
B   I can't remember my words too well, I didn't regard this as so
B   important.
C   I adjusted to my friend as far as possible.
D   I found my language very colorful, felt sort of "burning" in my
D   chest, felt wide awake, attentive.
E   No information.
F   Nothing.

052   JOY
A   Yesterday at a wine-bar, after an unsatisfying conference. My
A   friend and I just went into the bar before a lecture. There I
A   met an old man, who was talking about his dog. We were then
A   talking about all sorts of things. He invited us to a glass of
A   wine and so we stayed longer than planned. The situation ended

A   when we left the place and I tried to write a report at home. I
A   also had to make a drawing from very poor data.
A   The emotion lasted for 4 hours.
B   A lot.
C   Said my opinion.
D   Gestures with my hands during the conversation.
E   Didn't pay attention to it.
F   Nothing.

053   JOY
A   2 years ago, when I had heard the results of my written examina-
A   tions. The principal (my maths-teacher) told me my results. The
A   emotion lasted for some days.
B   I said I hadn't expected the results to be so good.
C   I only said what I mentioned above. I wouldn't have liked to
C   go out and scream.
D   Relief, relaxation, laughing, rather a high pitched voice.
E   I didn't embrace the principal, which I would have loved to
E   do. Instead I stood still.
F   I would show my joy more.

059   JOY
A   Discharge from the hospital, 3 weeks ago. I was happy to
A   leave all my fears and all the inconveniences of the
A   hospital behind me and to be in my girlfriend's arms.
A   Then everyday life began again.
A   The emotion lasted for about 2 days.
B   Glad to be out of hospital, to be together with "her,"
B   alone. Actually no words were necessary.
C   Sobbed.
D   Need to lean on her.
E   Celebrated.
F   Nothing.

064   JOY
A   Three months ago, at the beginning of this year. I was alone
A   on the beach (in Italy) after some rain. I wandered along the
A   storming sea with the wind blowing.
A   The emotion lasted for one hour, till the end of my walk.
B   Nothing.
C   No information.
D   Nothing.
E   No information.
F   Nothing.

079   JOY
A   On Christmas-eve, a week ago. My mother and I were sitting in front
A   of the burning Christmas-tree (Only the candles were burning, good

A   look). I wanted to play a record with Christmas-carols, but the
A   record-player wouldn't work. So we decided to sing ourselves (which
A   we never do, otherwise). This singing was wonderful. When we
A   couldn't think of any more carols, we stopped singing and unwrapped
A   our presents. The emotion lasted for some minutes (while singing).
A   But it stayed for a few more days, less intense.
B   "This was lovely."
C   I didn't say all I thought and felt.
D   Warmth in my stomach, relaxation of my cramped muscles (especially
D   in my stomach), trembling voice, my eyes went wet, and I swallowed,
D   so that I wouldn't cry.
E   I tried to suppress my tears (because I felt a little shy).
F   Probably nothing. Maybe I would show my mother more how touched I
F   was.

083   JOY
A   During a journey through France, about 14 weeks ago. First my
A   girlfriend and I toured through France, then we went on to the
A   mountains to see the Mont-Blanc for a few days. I am a passionate
A   skier and I love the Alps, so that the view of the sun-flooded
A   glacier made me happy. It ended when we drove off in rain. The
A   emotion lasted for 3 days.
B   This is one of the most beautiful views that nature can give me.
C   No information.
D   A deep inner feeling of well-being together with a strong force
D   to tell others about it. Deep breathing.
E   No information.
F   No information.

027   SADNESS
A   Two days ago, in the house in the afternoon. My girlfriend complained
A   that I would read so much, and that she herself would rather go out
A   and do something, but she was afraid to force me. I said that I
A   approved of this, she should do so, but I would only occasionally
A   join her. She found this abnormal and said, "How is this going to
A   work out?" I turned around and started doing the dishes. I had the
A   impression that she had only said this for tactic reasons. Then we
A   arranged matters soon.
B   When we had settled the quarrel, I asked whether she had really
B   meant what she had said.
C   I didn't say anymore.
D   I wouldn't let her see my face. My hands doing things.
E   I wouldn't let her see my face.
F   I would talk to her directly and take it all less seriously, less
F   personally, just as a thought.

029   SADNESS
A   This year, 6 months ago. I had bought 2 little turtles. Later a

A   conversation with my boyfriend followed. After having bought these
A   animals, I informed myself about how to keep and feed them, etc.
A   A few days later I realized that one of the animals seemed to be
A   ill. I tried to keep it alive as best as possible, but it still
A   died. The event made me reflect about death. This was very helpful
A   to me, also in other aspects. The emotion lasted for some days.
B   The situation was mainly nonverbal. Later I told my boyfriend
B   about it.
C   I tried to face the fact of death, especially in
C   talking to my boyfriend about it.
D   Pressure on my stomach. When I talked to my boyfriend about it,
D   he noticed a change of my facial expression.
E   I tried to take the time to be able to watch my nonverbal reactions
E   during the conversation.
F   I doubt that I will ever be in a similar situation again.

030   SADNESS
A   In the morning, three weeks ago. After a long period of treatment
A   I was forced to have my ill cat treated again, to give her another
A   chance. When I gave the cat into the nurse's hands, there was a 50%
A   chance for her to stay alive If she was treated at the veterinar-
A   ian hospital. The cat died after six days in hospital. I calmed
A   myself down with the argument that this was surely best for her.
A   The acute emotion lasted for 15 minutes. I'm still sad now.
B   Oh my dear little tiger, it has to be done. When can I ask how she
B   is?
C   I thought it is the best I could do, and talked to a friend about
C   it.
D   I spoke slowly and in a dark voice. My reactions were a little
D   delayed. I looked earnest, my jaws close together.
E   Frequent swallowing, to prevent crying.
F   Not to go into this situation alone.

034   SADNESS
A   In the evening three weeks ago. My, as I had thought, girlfriend
A   told me that she had got a boyfriend, with whom she had been to-
A   gether for longer than with me. I was only boyfriend number two.
A   The situation is not over yet. The emotion lasted for weeks.
B   I said, it is up to you, whom you want to decide to go out with, I
B   will behave more passively from now on.
C   I said hardly anything at all, and I thought about what I was
C   going to say.
D   An awful calmness, which had the effect that I reacted more
D   passively from then on and hardly spoke anything.
E   I didn't try to control my nonverbal behavior.
F   I still don't know how to react in my present situation.

036   SADNESS
A   In the last week of October, about 4 weeks ago. I had developed
A   an intense and intimate relation to a boy that I had known for
A   about 3 months. At first this relation had been wanted from both
A   sides, then he drew back from me. One evening he told me that he
A   wanted to end this relationship or change it to a less binding
A   level. First I felt very disappointed, which then turned into sad-
A   ness, because I had wanted to continue this relationship and ex-
A   tend it. After about a week I tried to talk to him and change his
A   mind. There was no result, because he blocked himself up. I will
A   accept his suggestion and keep up friendly contact to him. The
A   emotion lasted some days, then became weaker.
B   I told him that I would like to continue our relation and that I was
B   very sad about his decision.
C   I tried to stay calm and not to look at him.
D   Strong inner trembling, outside concentration and controlled
D   behavior at first, later increasingly visible excitement, which I
D   couldn't control any more. Crying.
E   I tried to build up distance.
F   I would accept my feelings and show them.

037   SADNESS
A   In spring, before a lecture, 2½ years ago. My mother, my fiancee
A   and I were involved. 5 minutes before the beginning of a lecture I
A   was informed that my father had died after a heart attack, while
A   going for a walk in the woods that morning. I could only just pack
A   my most important things and get on my way to the place, which was
A   200 km away. My father was buried 4 days later (= official end of
A   the situation). The emotion was very intense for the first days, it
A   is still there, but not as intense.
B   No information.
C   No information.
D   Sweating, severe trembling, freezing, crying (badly).
E   No information.
F   I guess I would react the same in this situation and not try to do
F   anything different.

038   SADNESS
A   In the evening, 7 weeks ago. The mother of a boy who was going out
A   with my friend phoned me (I was alone in the house). She told me
A   that my friend had died in an accident. I couldn't believe this at
A   the time and went to bed with the feeling that it would all prove to
A   be a mistake. The emotion lasted some days (partially up to now).
B   This can't be true, it must be a mistake, are you sure you heard it
B   clearly.
C   No information.
D   My whole body was shaking, fast heartbeat, difficulty in breathing,

D   not being able to say anything for a moment.
E   No information.
F   Can't be answered here.

039   SADNESS
A   In the evening, a few weeks ago. My mother and I had a conversation
A   on the phone. She mentioned an opinion that I didn't agree with.
A   This was about something very important to me. I live quite far away
A   from home and can't speak to her very often. On the phone it is
A   always difficult to speak properly. A strong feeling of helpless-
A   ness, sadness, and not being able to do anything came over me. I
A   wrote a long letter to my mother to explain my point of view. She
A   answered. This gave me satisfaction to some extent. The emotion
A   lasted for some hours. But it was even there after some days.
B   See above.
C   I tried to mention my central points of view on the phone, staying
C   quite rational.
D   Absence, reflecting.
E   No information
F   I would do the same.

047   SADNESS
A   In the afternoon, a few days ago. I went for a walk alone, to come
A   to myself and to concentrate on some questions about my person. Many
A   things went through my head: my relationships, sexuality, problems
A   at work, psychosomatic diseases (asthma . . .). I came home finding the
A   mood of my flat mates quite miserable but didn't tell them so. I
A   had got to do preparations for my group of children and was tired.
A   The emotion is still lasting but isn't present all the time.
B   Nothing, I was alone during my sadness. Later I was unable to speak
B   about it.
C   I didn't say anything, as I mentioned before, but my silence was
C   controlled.
D   I probably had a very sad facial expression.
E   I can't say.
F   I don't know exactly. I still can't deal with my sadness. I fall
F   and sink

051   SADNESS
A   Ten years ago. My grandma had died in our house the day before. The
A   situation of the undertaker's people coming to fetch my grandma's
A   body is still very clear in my memory. I kept thinking about it
A   for a long time. Especially this picture of my grandma's death is
A   still very vivid, even today. The emotion lasted for some days and
A   went only very slowly.
B   Nothing.
C   No information.

D   Shaking, lump in my throat, wanting to cry, paleness, pressure on
D   my chest and stomach.
E   I swallowed, because of the feeling in my throat.
F   I guess nothing.

052   SADNESS
A   Yesterday evening, at a fellow student's flat. She told me
A   about her practical work in organics. She told me about the
A   substances they were dealing with, and what kinds of damage
A   they caused. She told me how she had burnt her hand, the fluid
A   had been cauterizing and what had happened to the others. Their
A   hands had been cauterized and they had inhaled cauterizing fumes.
A   It ended with me thinking about my own practical work the
A   following semester.
A   The emotion lasted about an hour.
B   I asked about protective precautions, which usually don't help
B   much, though.
C   I expressed my horror.
D   Unpleasant feeling.
E   Pressed my hands together tightly, to have another feeling.
F   Nothing.

053   SADNESS
A   About 8 weeks ago. My cousin phoned me to tell me that I had not
A   been chosen for studying medicine. I heard my mother in the back-
A   ground. One semester later I applied for psychology.
A   The emotion lasted for several days to weeks.
B   I said that it wasn't so bad and that I would manage to study
B   medicine one day, and that I would now apply for psychology.
C   I immediately forced myself to believe that it doesn't matter.
D   Cramped, resignation in my face.
E   I suppressed my reactions, which would have been motor reactions
E   (Stamp on the floor).
F   Nothing, rather show my anger more open.

064   SADNESS
A   This year in September, two months ago. A good friend of mine,
A   who was suffering from cancer, died with full consciousness. She
A   was mentally present nearly up to the end, and was suffering
A   severe pain all the time and was hardly able to breathe.
A   The emotion is still there. The situation has not come to
A   an end (strictly speaking).
B   Nothing.
C   No information.
D   Sweat on my forehead. Blocking.
E   Tried to hold back my tears.
F   Nothing, I can't say, anyway.

068	SADNESS
A	Middle of November, 4 weeks ago. I had applied for an
A	apprenticeship. I knew one of the teachers quite well, liked him
A	very much. I had taken great care in writing an application and
A	was very motivated to take part. Then I received a letter from my
A	acquaintance saying that I shouldn't feel rejected. Twice as many
A	people had applied than places were available. They had to select.
A	I was the first one to be rejected. (First one on the waiting list.)
A	I was disappointed and sad. I told it to some friends. After some
A	days I wrote to my friend that it was very disappointing for me, but
A	that I would like to participate if anyone had lost interest.
A	The emotion lasted some days.
B	No information.
C	I stayed seated. Later I found some relief in telling others about
C	it (with a little distance).
D	I was slightly depressed, I drew my head back, lay on my bed for
D	a short while, until some anger and disappointment arose in
D	addition. For a short time unsure what to do, no energy, tension
D	inside me (ambivalent!).
E	No information.
F	Tell a close friend about the matter earlier.

069	SADNESS
A	6 days ago, in December. My girlfriend and I hadn't seen each
A	other for two weeks. When we met again, she told me that she
A	had fallen in love with another man. She split up with me.
A	The situation is not over yet.
A	The emotion lasted for days.
B	I showed my helplessness and that I couldn't understand.
C	It was difficult for me.
D	I couldn't sleep, pressure in my stomach, no appetite,
D	couldn't concentrate very well, I can hardly laugh.
E	It was impossible to control my thoughts.
F	Nothing, I hope that I will never be in such a situation
F	again.

071	SADNESS
A	On a working day, one week ago. My brother (11 years old, 5th grade)
A	told me on the phone about failing an exam. The week before I
A	had helped my brother quite a lot to increase his school knowledge.
A	I came home to my mother quite often, to be able to study with my
A	brother. The emotion lasted for one day. Then I forgot about it.
B	I told my brother not to worry unnecessarily, it would work out
B	better next time.
C	Rationally telling myself that I mustn't also tell him that I am
C	not satisfied with him.
D	I smoked more, I guess I was less relaxed, stiffer.

E   I didn't control them much more (on the phone) than usual.
F   No information.

075   SADNESS
A   A week ago. I received a letter from my sister, telling me that the
A   parcel I had sent to her had arrived very late and that the contents
A   were broken. The emotion lasted for some hours. I made up my mind to
A   send a similar parcel soon, which was packed with more care.
B   That it was a shame that the nice present had broken, that I was
B   sad about this bad luck.
C   No information.
D   Depressed voice with a sad sound.
E   No information.
F   Nothing.

085   SADNESS
A   In the morning. Mid-November, about 6 weeks ago. I and my girlfriend
A   stopped our intense relationship. The emotion lasted several weeks.
A   We have now more or less accepted that our expectations of a
A   partnership differ too much.
B   Tried to explain why I don't want the relationship.
C   I thought about what I would say in advance, to avoid permanent
C   misunderstandings.
D   (a) general exhaustion, no fun in any occupation, pressure on my stomach;
D   (b) bad-tempered, cramped face, folds on my forehead.
E   Tried to get out of my exhaustion, by going on walks a lot, talking
E   to people.
F   Control less of what I said and did. If possible not to elicit
F   such a state anymore.

027   FEAR
A   Late at night, light rain, yesterday. I was driving downhill on my
A   bike. I gained speed. Suddenly I realized that I was losing
A   control and started sliding. I fell but didn't get hurt. The
A   emotion lasted for some seconds.
B   I breathed noticeably.
C   No information.
D   I stood up again and got ready, concentrated.
E   Concentration.
F   Nothing.

029   FEAR
A   One year ago, in winter. My boyfriend and I were on our way in the
A   car. He was driving. It was a broad road, with traffic coming on both
A   sides. The road was probably covered with ice, the car started to
A   slide, and turned around three times. This surely only lasted a
A   few seconds, but to me it seemed endless. In the end, nothing

A   happened. We told each other what we had felt at the time, after
A   having left the car, in which we had sat without saying a word. The
A   emotion lasted until a few minutes after I had left the car.
B   Nothing.
C   I simply started talking.
D   Trembling, after getting out of the car. Trembling of my legs. No
D   fluent talking.
E   I was glad that nothing had happened to me, I concentrated on this
E   feeling.
F   I can't say.

030   FEAR
A   In the morning, two weeks ago, on my way to university. There was
A   ice on the roads that morning. When I slowed down before a slight
A   bend, my car began to slide. I bumped straight into the bordering
A   of the road and came to a standstill right at the edge of the
A   slope. A man helped me and pushed me away, so that I wouldn't
A   slide down the slope after all. Very slowly I drove the 20 km which
A   were left, till I reached the university. The acute emotion lasted
A   4–10 seconds after that one hour.
B   Oh!
C   I told myself to keep calm, to think how to react best.
D   Opened my eyes wide, stiff body, holding tight to the steering
D   wheel. I went pale.
E   See above.
F   I would press the clutch pedal, not brake again, "prevention."

033   FEAR
A   In the evening, about a week ago. I was hitchhiking home from the
A   university. The driver gave me a lift and drove at a speed of
A   150 km/h on the wet road. As I had already been in three severe
A   accidents I was terribly frightened that we would slide and some-
A   thing would happen. The situation ended when I got out of the car.
A   The emotion lasted some minutes.
B   Whether he could drive more slowly.
C   I tried to say in a calm voice that it is very dangerous in
C   general to drive so fast, and explained what could happen, etc.
D   Stomachache, I sat back in my seat and held on tight. I was
D   only able to look at his dashboard.
E   No information.
F   Nothing.

034   FEAR
A   6 months ago, during the day. Two friends of mine and I were at a
A   holiday-park with a huge roller coaster. My friends wanted to take a
A   ride on this roller coaster. I wanted to go too, because it was new
A   to me, but I was scared to death, especially at the sight of one big

A	loop. I still got on it, despite all my fears, because I didn't want
A	to say no. The emotion lasted some minutes.
B	Verbally I pretended not to be affected at all.
C	I tried to react as normally as possible.
D	Trembling, pressure on my stomach, sickness, nearly fainting.
E	I didn't speak much and tried to keep control over myself.
F	Now I know that I needn't be scared of such a situation.

036   FEAR

A	At the beginning of November, about 3 weeks ago. I was driving on
A	the motorway in my car. It was dark and raining heavily. When other
A	cars, especially lorries, overtook me my windscreen was covered with
A	water by the overtaking vehicle, so that for a moment I couldn't see
A	anything. I was scared to have an accident and to be killed or badly
A	injured. It ended after arriving at my flat. The emotion lasted for
A	20 minutes.
B	No information.
C	No information.
D	Trembling, excitement, sweating, tension, cramping of muscles, tried
D	to see more by partially closing my eyes.
E	I tried to concentrate on the road and to listen to the music in the
E	radio, to relax.
F	Not let myself be forced to speed up to a certain speed because of
F	others. Drive very slowly, maybe stop and wait till the rain gets
F	less.

037   FEAR

A	6 months ago, on a summer morning. My wife and I were being inspect-
A	ed very thoroughly before a flight to some Eastern country. The
A	actual feeling of fear came up when the plane took off and gained
A	more and more height. Then the bodily reactions due to this feeling
A	went away and I could feel relaxation coming. The feeling of fear
A	lasted several minutes and than vanished completely.
B	Nothing, I only concentrated on my present state.
C	No information.
D	Cold sweat on my forehead, pressure on my stomach, slight dizzi-
D	ness.
E	lasted several minutes and then vanished completely.
E	myself that I couldn't do anything if the plane was going to come
E	down; (b) diminishing my fear-causing thoughts.
F	I would start a conversation with my neighbor.

042   FEAR

A	About 2 weeks ago, late at night. I was alone in the flat. Suddenly
A	fear came over me that I was to spend the night alone in the house.
A	(This doesn't usually worry me at all.) It was an unknown feeling to
A	me. I put the chain in front of our door-lock, which I never do

A normally, and I don't think it's a very good idea. The emotion
A lasted till I fell asleep (about 3 hours).
B Nothing.
C I didn't say anything.
D I felt quite cold and was restless, didn't really know what to do
D with myself.
E I tried to tell myself that all my fears were totally unnecessary
E and that there was no reason for it.
F I don't know exactly. Maybe phone someone up, to be able to speak to
F someone.

045 FEAR
A In the evening, about 16 hours ago. Before our evening meal we
A played around with each other, tickling . . . He pulled me up by my
A feet as he often does. When he let me down again, I could have
A rolled backwards. But I'm always terribly scared to break my neck in
A doing so, at the same time I was frightened that he might not
A realize the danger of this exercise. I shouted: be careful, it
A hurts. He let me go. I was able to get back on my feet safely. The
A emotion lasted some minutes.
B "Careful, it's hurting."
C I didn't want to scare him. I know my fears so I usually react be-
C fore it starts to hurt.
D Heat, fright, heartbeat.
E Not possible, there was no time.
F I would explain that I tend to be scared to fall in a bad way when
F we do such games.

051 FEAR
A 2 weeks ago. I was waiting for the hearing at court where they were
A going to decide whether I would have to join the German army. My
A brother and I had to wait for more than an hour before the hearing
A began. We were alone in a large waiting room. Then we were called to
A come in. The emotion lasted for some minutes.
B I talked about all sorts of things (without any order).
C I sat down, tried to read, encouraged myself.
D Wet and cold hands, heart beating, wanting to go to the toilet,
D trembling of hands, wanting to walk around, restlessness.
E Warmed my hands at the heat, encouraged myself to keep calm,
E breathed deeply.
F Nothing.

052 FEAR
A Yesterday during a report in a seminar. My friend and I were
A going to give a report in a seminar. We were the first ones. I
A was scared anyway, because I had never done this before. My
A friend was asked questions by the professor, to which she

A   couldn't know the answer. It confused her even more. I was
A   afraid that the same would happen to me. I was right. After
A   I had finished the report the professor explained that our
A   difficulties were those of all beginners and he was content,
A   surprisingly.
B   I tried to talk about other things.
C   By reading in my papers again.
D   Pressure in my stomach, moving about with my hands, and holding
D   on to a pencil nervously.
E   I desperately tried to put down my pencil.
F   Better preparation.

058   **FEAR**
A   Last night, about 9:30 P.M., 25 hours ago. The secretary
A   of my husband's colleague phoned us and reported an
A   anonymous phone call from a man who wanted to know her
A   manager's name and address. He said he needed money.
A   He knew that she was employed at that bank but had
A   confused the different departments. The secretary reacted
A   sensibly and told him to come to the bank during the
A   usual opening hours. She didn't tell him the name of
A   the department where she was really employed. After
A   some hesitation she decided to inform at least one of
A   the three directors and to ask what to do. Whether to
A   inform the police or the director of the bank he had
A   mentioned. The anonymous man had called 5 more times
A   but without speaking. On the phone only his breathing
A   was to be heard. Bank robberies or attacks on bank
A   managers are no more seldom nowadays. We live outside
A   the town in an area with many large grounds and
A   partially large old trees. I switched on all the
A   lights outside and looked for footprints on the white
A   snow. I wouldn't go out of the house. I was afraid
A   that there might be an attack. My husband had a long
A   phone call with the secretary, told her what to do, and
A   calmed her down. I heard that he himself didn't think
A   it impossible that we might be attacked. He said that
A   his behavior was accordingly, which I hadn't known up
A   to then. I calmed down again, because I was able to
A   overlook our whole property as a result of all the
A   lights. There were no footprints. Before going to sleep
A   all kinds of safety precautions came to my mind.
B   Inform the police by any means.
C   Nothing.
D   A little fast heartbeating, no other reactions.
E   Nothing.
F   Nothing, but I would have asked the director of the

F   police, whom we knew, for advice if I had been alone.

059   FEAR
A   End of October, 6 weeks ago. I had to go to hospital because
A   I was suffering from angina tonsiliaris. After a week it
A   became clear that my life was in danger, because some
A   bacteria had infected my blood. These bacteria mainly
A   attacked my heart. By means of strong pills and other medical
A   methods my blood was cleaned. My fear decreased a lot but
A   hasn't gone completely. I'm afraid of it happening again,
A   which is possible, according to what the doctors say.
A   The emotion lasted for several days (one week).
B   As I didn't tell my parents and my girlfriend all of it, I
B   didn't want to say much.
C   I turned to other subjects, talked about everyday things,
C   read novels.
D   Stomachache, nervousness, uncertainty, shaky voice.
E   Mostly let the others talk.
F   I have no idea. If I want to continue living, it mustn't
F   come again.

060   FEAR
A   In the evening, at about 5:00 P.M., about 2 years ago. On the
A   day before memorial Sunday for the dead, my father and I
A   went to the cemetery to take care of my grandfather's grave.
A   We were very busy working, when suddenly the church
A   bells began to ring. I was scared to death, because it was
A   quite dark already. The same happened to my father. The
A   emotion lasted only a few seconds. We were very much relieved,
A   when we realized that it was only the church bells ringing
A   at 5:00 P.M.
B   We didn't say anything at that moment, we couldn't say anything.
C   I tried to find an explanation, but somehow I was unable to
C   speak, although I tried.
D   A scary tingling feeling went through my body. I was shaking.
D   My mouth was nearly paralysed. I couldn't say a word.
E   I tried to understand what was going on, but it took a while.
E   I tried to overcome my stiffness.
F   I would hardly be able to do anything different, because such
F   situations come so suddenly, that one can't adjust to it.

062   FEAR
A   Going home at 12:30 at night, a week ago. I was on my
A   way home and thought about a man of my age, who had been
A   robbed by 4 young people and beaten up. So I turned
A   around from time to time to make sure that I was alone.
A   The situation ended when I arrived at home.

A   The emotion lasted for about half an hour, all the way
A   home.
B   Nothing.
C   Nothing.
D   Goose pimples, sensations in my stomach region. Speeding
D   up, clenched my fists, tension of my muscles.
E   I tried to tell myself that it is childish to be afraid,
E   because it depends on the situation.
F   Control myself more. Think more about other things.

063   FEAR
A   2 months ago in the forest. I had been walking for a long
A   time and was on my way home in the dark. Some lightning
A   came up and soon turned into a heavy thunderstorm.
A   The emotion lasted for 15–30 minutes, until I came home
A   and was safe from the lightning.
B   When I reached home I kept saying silly things to myself in
B   relief.
C   No information.
D   I felt my fear in the solar plexus region. And at home I was
D   shaking, but this was probably the result of running too fast.
E   No information.
F   Nothing.

070   FEAR
A   2 days ago. Two jet planes were flying right above my head making
A   a terrible noise. I thought this was war and was paralyzed for
A   some seconds and trembling. After some minutes the trembling
A   stopped. The emotion lasted for some seconds.
B   "Shit, help."
C   Did nothing.
D   Shaking all over my body.
E   I was sweating.
F   The same.

075   FEAR
A   5 hours ago, today. For the first time after a long period I was
A   skiing down a sloppy way. I was scared to gain too much speed or
A   maybe that a car or a pedestrian would come near me and that I
A   wouldn't be able to stop in time. The emotion lasted for some
A   minutes (about 30 minutes). I managed to ski down the hill without
A   any trouble. I didn't reach too much velocity; I was able to stop
A   and slow down, no one came near me.
B   Nothing.
C   No information.
D   Tense leg and foot muscles.
E   Tried to relax my legs, and to trust my abilities.
F   Worry less, try to relax more, trust myself more.

077	FEAR
A	Summer, 1979, 2½ years ago. My parents and I were using a
A	ski lift to Molten in Austria. Suddenly there was a power-cut and
A	we fell back a few centimeters. There I was honestly scared to lose
A	my life. I think for the first time. The emotion lasted for some
A	minutes. The generator was switched on and our ride continued
A	immediately.
B	"No," a scream of resentment.
C	No information.
D	Holding on to the interior of the cabin (pole) and to my mother's
D	arm.
E	No information.
F	I would not do anything different.

079	FEAR
A	12:30 a.m. shortly after leaving a student's dancing party. A
A	little more than three years ago (in autumn). After the party I
A	walked to my car, which I had parked a little further toward the
A	center of the town. I was alone. I was already half in my car
A	when a shadow appeared behind me.
A	A (white) American soldier stood very close to me, and said
A	(in English): "Be quiet, otherwise I have to hurt you." He
A	wanted to be brought to a town 40 km away from here. He wouldn't
A	do me any harm if I did this. I started a short conversation with
A	him, he obviously gained faith in me. Then I said: "Okay, get in
A	at the other side." He walked around the car (the other door was
A	locked), I slammed my door shut, turned my car, and drove away in
A	a hurry. The emotion lasted for a few minutes.
B	A short, low sigh. Then totally calm reaction.
C	Thought, not to let him become suspicious.
D	Later: trembling, especially in my knees, cold hands.
D	During the situation itself—except for the first second—I
D	felt no fear.
E	During the situation I was very cool and rational, felt no fear,
E	except for the first moment, I didn't have to change myself very
E	much. It was only later that I didn't try to suppress the
E	shaking.
F	Nothing. I was glad to have been so "cool."

085	FEAR
A	24 hours ago, yesterday afternoon. A friend and I were going for a
A	walk, when suddenly a German shepherd dog approached us and
A	started barking dangerously. He seemed to want to jump up on us,
A	he followed us for about 50 meters. Then he let us go. The emotion
A	lasted for 5–10 minutes.
B	Nothing.
C	No information.

D   Tension in leg and arm muscles. Walking on with tension. Earnest
D   facial expression.
E   I tried to slowly move on and to show no fear. I looked into the
E   dog's eyes when possible.
F   Stop and maybe shout at the dog.

026   ANGER
A   Two days ago. I and another boy had made an appointment to meet for some
A   report we were going to give on that same day. I waited all morning,
A   but he didn't turn up. (It was the second time that he had acted
A   this way.) In the afternoon he didn't come to the seminar and I had to
A   present my part alone. I haven't met him since. The emotion lasted for
A   one day.
B   If I saw him now, I guess I wouldn't be able to keep control over
B   myself.
C   I told others about my anger, and so I feel better now.
D   No bodily reactions, nonverbal: dark voice, earnest face, furious
D   altogether.
E   Tried to relax and consider it all as "fate."
F   Make him stick to his word.

028   ANGER
A   4 years ago, during the day of the 31st of December. I asked my father
A   whether I was allowed to go to a certain party. He only unwillingly
A   looked up from his newspaper and looked at me with the utmost
A   astonishment. Looking down on me he asked me what kind of people I
A   was going to celebrate with and then went on about the reasons why
A   he wouldn't let me go, clearly showing me his dominant position. I
A   left the room while he was still talking, because I could see that
A   it would be useless to try to persuade him. Also, I didn't want him
A   to see my tears that came up as a result of my aggression and the
A   feeling of helplessness. The emotion lasted for a few hours in its
A   full intensity. But there is still a latent anger or aggression
A   toward my father, up to this day.
B   I tried not to be personal in my arguments, tried to make him
B   compare me with others of my age, my brother, when he was my age,
B   kept asking why, not receiving a distinct answer.
C   I tried to suppress all my feelings toward—better against—my
C   father, telling myself that otherwise I wouldn't get anywhere at
C   all. I intentionally responded to all his arguments.
D   Crying, sobbing (like often in similar situations),
D   difficulties in breathing, desire to break something (—which I
D   never did).
E   I remember having tried, but I don't think I managed very well.
E   Anyway, my father never made any remarks.
F   Today I would leave the room, if I find no sense in further
F   discussions. But I would carry out my will. I wouldn't feel so much

F   dependence and rage at all. I still wouldn't be able to talk about
F   my true hate.

029   ANGER
A   Some months ago, in summer. Some people that I had been friends with
A   for a long time and I had decided to go swimming. The weather was
A   fine. But they didn't turn up, at least not at the appointed time.
A   I waited 2 hours. I was very angry when they eventually stood in
A   front of my door. We discussed the matter. During the conversation
A   I realized that my reactions were quite strong. This might be due to
A   former experiences. The emotion lasted for some hours.
B   "There you are at last. I'm not in the mood for going out any more. I
B   will stay here."
C   I sat down at my desk and started turning pages in the book that I
C   had just begun to read.
D   My voice was a little louder than usual. My gestures weren't as well
D   controlled as usual. I can't tell very well in general, how my
D   facial expression is.
E   I tried to concentrate on certain objects,
F   Maybe I should not have played the role of an offended person?

030   ANGER
A   In the evening, 10 days ago. After our evening meal our being-to-
A   gether turned into a drinking bout. I don't like such excessive
A   drinking and was very cross and angry that my boyfriend does it
A   over and over again, although he knows how much it annoys me.
A   I insisted on having a quiet night, tried to become tired and
A   went to bed alone. The others continued drinking. The emotion
A   lasted for 5 days.
B   You know what it's about. I don't want to get any angrier—I will
B   go to bed.
C   I thought, it wouldn't help to cry or shout.
D   I didn't express anything further. But I was very upset, and talked
D   rather slowly and earnestly.
E   I did exactly the opposite of what I actually felt. Instead of
E   pushing my boyfriend away I leaned on him.
F   Nothing.

031   ANGER
A   About three weeks ago in the evening, during and after supper.
A   My grandfather, my father, and I were discussing problems of
A   preventing war, and peace, e.g., how far is it
A   possible to make peace come true. During the conversation the
A   discussion grew more and more aggressive between my grandfather and
A   me. I was always pushed into a position of defending myself.
A   Eventually my grandfather shouted at me and left the room. I was so
A   angry, about my grandfather's behavior that I started crying. My

A   father and I continued the conversation and he (my father) calmed
A   me down. The emotion lasted 2–3 hours.
B   I protested and told him my opinion and let him know how excited I
B   was.
C   Forced myself to be calm, tried to relax.
D   Sickness, lump in my throat, pressure on my stomach, trembling.
E   I'm sorry, I don't really know anymore. Probably by trying to
E   convey a certain impression that I wanted to show.
F   React more calmly. Show less involvement, accept others' opinions
F   more.

033   ANGER
A   A few days ago, after supper. Our flat-mates, my husband and I were
A   involved. We had to clean the flat. The "nicer" work had already
A   been given away to others, so that it was left to me to clean the
A   loo. My husband was going to do our room. When I had finished
A   cleaning the loo, he was still sitting at the table, making jokes
A   about those who were cleaning. I was very angry, but then I still
A   started tidying up our room. I shouted at my husband that he was
A   always making the whole mess and then not cleaning it up. A very
A   important letter that I couldn't find anymore gave rise to all
A   this. My husband found my shouting unbearable, but then he admitted,
A   that his behavior hadn't been so good. The emotion lasted about 2
A   hours.
B   That I can't bear this mess.
C   I tried to keep my voice down, not to shout.
D   Trembling, very red face, feeling hot.
E   I held on to the cupboard.
F   I wouldn't clean up anymore. I would tell him immediately that it
F   was now his turn to do his job.

034   ANGER
A   Since 10 weeks ago, still lasting. One of my flat-mates is French and
A   listens to shortwave or mediumwave radio all the time, which has
A   a terrible high-frequency whistling tone all the time. He seems to
A   be immune to it, but to me it is a pain, which is annoying me more
A   and more. My flat-mate is careful now to listen to the radio
A   with his door closed and not so loudly anymore. The emotion lasted for
A   some hours.
B   "If you don't turn your radio down immediately I will throw it out
B   of the window whenever I get hold of it next."
C   I didn't try to control what I said.
D   Cramped position, aggressive mood, furious look.
E   I just let my feelings come.
F   I am still in the same situation, only my flat-mate has understood
F   that it is not bearable for us (also for the other flat-mates) to
F   have such a whistling tone coming out of the radio.

037   ANGER

A   In Autumn, two days ago, in the evening. We received a bill for a

A   newspaper subscription, although it had already been paid. On the

A   letter requesting payment it said that this letter was of no

A   meaning if the bill had already been paid, but still I was

A   very angry about it, especially that such companies are not able to

A   organize such things properly. After talking to my wife I eventually

A   calmed down. The emotion lasted about half an hour.

B   I told myself that such letters were absolutely stupid. Also I

B   talked to my wife about it in a less angry tone.

C   No information.

D   Increase of breathing frequency, quicker heartbeat, more blood came

D   into my head.

E   No information.

F   Maybe write a letter to the editor. Think more rationally, e.g., I

F   would tell myself that it is useless to get angry about such comput-

F   erized letters.

038   ANGER

A   In the evening, about a year ago. I had found out that my boyfriend

A   had started a relationship with another girl about 2 weeks previously and

A   hadn't told me the truth because of that. I spoke to him about it.

A   He gave up the other relationship, and we got on with each other again.

A   The emotion lasted for 2–3 days.

B   I guess I didn't say anything at first.

C   Before I talked to him, I thought about the situation.

D   First trembling all over my body, after a while of reflecting I be-

D   came relatively calm.

E   No information.

F   I don't know.

042   ANGER

A   In the evening, two days ago. I was at a discussion where the audience

A   was allowed to ask questions to the participants of the dis-

A   cussion. The questions which were asked were ignored by the partici-

A   pants, who answered completely different matters. Later the actual

A   questions couldn't be answered, because the time was over. I talked

A   to some friends about it, who thought similarly to me. We told our

A   opinion to the initiators of the discussion. The emotion lasted all

A   day, till night (about 3 hours). The next morning the emotion was

A   still there but much weaker.

B   These people just wouldn't listen to our questions and didn't

B   answer accordingly.

C   I just talked without thinking, only occasionally wondering

C   whether I didn't do those people wrong.

D   I had the feeling I would burst, my gestures were a lot more

D   frequent than usual. I also felt a bit of trembling.

E   I didn't make any effort to concentrate on that.
F   I would try to talk to these people immediately and try to under-
F   stand their situation.

043   ANGER
A   At the parking lot of the campus, about 3 weeks ago (maybe longer).
A   I came back to my car, drove off, and wondered why there was so
A   little fuel in my tank. (I had just filled it up before.) There
A   was a smell of fuel. I stopped to check and saw that my tank-lid
A   was broken open and the fuel had been stolen. I had to go and
A   have it repaired the next day and pay for it. It cost me a
A   lot of time. I'm still waiting for the money from the insurance company.
A   I informed the police, although I know it is of no use except that
A   the insurance company will be more likely to believe me. I hope it doesn't
A   happen again. The emotion lasted for 2 days, partially it is still
A   lasting.
B   I was uttering "damn" or something like that.
C   No information.
D   Increase of adrenaline in my blood, blood came into my head, I hit
D   the roof of my car with my hand.
E   I didn't hit the wing of the car. (After all, it isn't the car's
E   fault.)
F   Nothing.

044   ANGER
A   4 years ago. I was going to improve my chemistry mark at school that
A   spring. I worked like mad to reach my goal. At the end of the term I
A   only got a "4," because the teacher couldn't stand me. This made me
A   grow angrier than I ever had been before in my life, because I had
A   the impression that my work was simply being ignored. I tried all
A   possibilities which were open to me as a pupil. (Tutoring teacher,
A   principal, president of the country government.) Nevertheless, I had
A   to realize that the rights of a pupil exist only in the books but not
A   in reality. The emotion lasted for about 3 weeks, but I'm still
A   angry.
B   I wished lots of terrible things would happen to my teacher.
C   I tried to see the case from his point of view.
D   Trembling, voice louder.
E   I thought, this excitement is not healthy.
F   Speak and act more neutral, less temper.

051   ANGER
A   In September, 2 years ago. I had taped some of the results of my
A   tests which I was doing for my doctor's degree. XXX erased the tape,
A   without informing me beforehand although she knew that my recordings
A   were on it. I questioned XXX and told her off. The emotion lasted
A   for some days.

B   "Why . . .?"
C   I controlled my words exactly, spoke slowly, thought exactly about
C   what I would say.
D   Shaking in my voice, "moved" tone, pressure on my head, stomach-
D   pressure, stomach-ache, no blood in my head, tingling in my hands,
D   dry mouth.
E   Tried to keep calm, to breathe calmly.
F   I would show my feelings more.

052   ANGER
A   When I wanted to see a friend, 2 days ago. We had planned to
A   meet at a certain time, to finish a report. I had hurried very
A   much to be on time. For the second time she wasn't there. After
A   15 minutes when I was just about to go, she came up the stairs
A   with a big smile on her face.
A   The emotion lasted for some hours.
B   First of all nothing. Later I said that I didn't approve,
B   because I am also expected on time.
C   Said nothing.
D   No information.
E   No information.
F   Say at once what I don't like.

062   ANGER
A   After 2 friends, whom I had invited, hadn't appeared,
A   about 2 weeks ago. After more than half an hour had passed
A   over the time when they were expected, I phoned my friends
A   and asked. I learned that they had missed, in other words,
A   forgotten the date. When I repeated my invitation they
A   answered without any positive emotion and said they couldn't
A   come. After talking to my wife, she convinced me that such
A   things can happen. She calmed me down.
A   The emotion lasted for about an hour.
B   To my wife: "They should stay away. I won't invite them any-
B   more. We can do without them."
C   I thought and tried to analyze the situation. Tried to
C   control myself.
D   Rejecting movements of my hand, facial expression around my
D   mouth, trembling, tense muscles.
E   Nothing.
F   Be more understanding, react more calmly.

064   ANGER
A   Seven years ago, in summer. I was camping with 4 friends.
A   We were just going for a walk when two elderly men, whom
A   we didn't know, came running toward us. I was the only one

A   they managed to catch and they literally beat me up
A   (for no reason). After some time, when the two men had let
A   me go, we ran back to our tent as quickly as possible.
A   The emotion lasted for some days.
B   "Let me go. I didn't do anything."
C   No information.
D   Shaking, pain, screaming, cramps.
E   No information.
F   I would hit back brutally.

070   ANGER
A   Last weekend, during a party. A guy wanted to kiss my girl-
A   friend. There were several people around. My girlfriend
A   reacted passively. I pulled him toward me by his hair and
A   shook him, then let go of him and said to him "Go away!".
A   He left. I went to him to excuse my behavior. My girlfriend
A   said that there was nothing between them, I shouldn't be
A   so excited.
A   The emotion lasted some seconds.
B   "Go away."
C   Nothing.
D   Threatening gestures, fist.
E   Shouted.
F   I would do the same again.

075   ANGER
A   3 days ago. At 7 o'clock in the morning I was standing at the
A   station, waiting for the train. I had to wait for more than an
A   hour out in the cold until the train came in at last (due to snow-
A   fall). A fellow-student was standing next to me, waiting as well, and
A   was angry too. The train came after 45 minutes, and our anger vanished
A   slowly during the ride. The emotion lasted for about 2 hours.
B   Trying to guess when the train would arrive, why the train was
B   delayed.
C   No information.
D   No.
E   No information.
F   Nothing.

088   ANGER
A   About half a year ago. An acquaintance who had always said that
A   he was my best friend but who had actually never been a friend sold
A   a car to me. He assured me that the car was in the best condition and
A   that I could be sure to have made a bargain. Through various circum-
A   stances it transpired that this person, whom I had regarded as my
A   friend, was a swindler and had consciously used my ignorance. The
A   situation was brought to court and has not come to an end yet. Emo-

A	tionally I have finished with the situation and look upon it only
A	occasionally, without caring and with great distance. The emotion
A	lasted for many days.
B	I said many bad things to him, I tried everything to hurt him or to
B	make him unsure of himself. It is impossible for me to repeat single
B	statements here.
C	No information.
D	I shouted, hit my fist on the table, ran up and down in excitement,
D	and I am sure I was making faces.
E	To demonstrate my superiority I tried to imagine my appearance
E	first. I knew that I would shout, etc.
F	If it really were the same situation with the same
F	partner, I would do the same.

APPENDIX F:
LABELS DESCRIBING
AFFECTIVE STATES IN FIVE
MAJOR LANGUAGES

English	German	French	Italian	Spanish
affectionate	voller Zuneigung	affectueux	affezionato	encarinado
afraid	verängstigt	apeuré	impaurito	atemorizado
agitated	aufgeregt	agité	agitato	agitado
amazed	verwundert	stupéfait	stupefatto	estupefacto
amused	belustigt	amusé	divertito	estar divertiéndose
angry	ärgerlich	en colère	arrabiato	enfadado
anguished	gequalt	tourmenté	angosciato	angustiado
annoyed	verärgert	agacé	seccato	fastidiado
anxious	ängstlich	anxieux	ansioso	ansioso
apathetic	apathisch	apathique	apatico	apático
ashamed	voller Scham	honteux	vergognoso	avergonzado
astonished	erstaunt	étonné	sorpreso	asombrado
at ease	wohlfühlen	(se sentir) à l'aise	a proprio agio	sentirse a gusto
bored	gelangweilt	ennuyé	annoiato	aburrido
calm	ruhig	calme	tranquillo	tranquilo
carefree	unbekümmert	insouciant	incurante	despreocupado
cheerful	fröhlich	gai	allegro	alegre, divertido(*)
compassionate	mitleidig	compatissant	pietoso	compasivo
confident	zuversichtlich	confiant	fiducioso	seguro de si mismo
confused	verwirrt	confus	sconcertato	desconcertado
contented	zufrieden	content	contento	contento
courageous	mutig	courageux	coraggioso	sentirse valiente
cowardly	feige	lâche	codardo	sentirse cobarde
curious	neugierig	curieux	curioso	tener, sentir curiosida
dejected	niedergeschlagen	abattu	abbattuto	abatido
delighted	entzückt	ravi	deliziato	encantado
depressed	bedrückt	déprimé	depresso	deprimido
desirous	begehrlich	désireux	desideroso	deseoso
desperate	verzweifelt	désespéré	disperato	desesperado
despondent	verzagt	accablé	sfiduciato	desanimado
disappointed	enttäuscht	déçu	deluso	desilusionado

English	German	French	Italian	Spanish
discontented	unzufrieden	mécontent	scontento	descontento
discouraged	mutlos	découragé	scoraggiato	descorazonado
disdainful	voller Geringschätzung	dédaigneux	disdegnoso	desdeñoso
disgruntled	missvergnügt	contrarié	contrariato	disgustado
disgusted	voller Ekel	dégouté	disgustato	asqueado
dismayed	bestürzt	consterné	costernato	consternado
distressed	bekümmert	affligé	afflitto	afligido
distrustful	misstrauisch	méfiant	diffidente	desconfiado
doubtful	zweifelnd	plein de doute	dubbioso	dubitativo
drowsy	schläfrig	somnolent	somnolento	amodorrado
dumbfounded	verblüfft	ébahi	stupito	pasmado
eager	eifrig	empressé	bramoso	emprendedor
earnest	ernst	sérieux	serio	formal
elated	hocherfreut	transporté de joie	esultante	gozoso
enthusiastic	begeistert	enthousiaste	entusiasta	entusiasmado
embarrassed	verlegen	embarrassé	imbarazzato	azorado
embittered	erbittert	aigri	amareggiato	amargado, agriado
envious	neidisch	envieux	invidioso	envidioso
exasperated	ausser sich sein	exaspéré	esasperato	exasperado
excited	erregt	excité	eccitato	excitado
exctatic	ekstatisch	extatique	estasiato	extasiado
exuberant	übermutig	exubérant	esuberante	eufórico
fascinated	fasziniert	fasciné	affascinato	fascinado
fed up	verdrossen	dépité	annoiato	estar harto
forlorn	verlassen	délaissé	abbandonato	abandonado
frightened	voller Furcht	apeuré	spaventato	aterrorizado
frolicsome	lustig	folâtre	divertente	juguetón
full of contempt	verachtungsvoll	plein de mépris	sprezzante	lleno de desprecio
full of hatred	hasserfüllt	plein de haine	pieno di odio	sentir mucho odio
full of regrets	voller Reue	plein de regrets	spiacente	arrepentido
full of reverence	ehrfürchtig	plein de révérence	riverente	reverente
furious	wütend	furieux	furioso	furioso
gloomy	düster	sombre	cupo	tristón
grateful	dankbar	reconnaissant	riconoscente	agradecido
griefstricken	voller Gram	chagriné	afflitto	apenado
guilty	schuldig	coupable	colpevole	culpable
happy	glücklich	heureux	felice	feliz
helpless	hilflos	impuissant	indifeso	indefenso
hesitant	zögernd	hésitant	esitante	vacilante
homesick	voller Heimweh	mal du pays	nostalgico	tener, sentir morrina
hopeful	hoffnungsvoll	plein d'espoir	fiducioso	esperanzado
hopeless	hoffnungslos	sans espoir	disperato	desesperanzado
horrified	voller Grauen	horrifié	terrorizzato	horrorizado
hostile	feindselig	hostile	ostile	enemistado
humble	demütig	humble	umile	humilde
ill at ease	unbehaglich	mal á l'aise	inquieto	incómodo
impatient	ungeduldig	impatient	impaziente	impaciente
impressed	beeindruckt	impressionné	impressionato	impresionado
in high spirits	ausgelassen	plein d'entrain	pieno di vita	animadisimo
in love	verliebt	amoureux	innamorato	enamorado
indecisive	unentschlossen	indécis	indeciso	indeciso
indifferent	desinteressiert	indifférent	indifferente	indiferente
indignant	entrüstet	indigné	indignato	indignado
inspired	inspiriert	inspiré	ispirato	inspirado
interested	interessiert	intéressé	interessato	interesado
intimidated	eingeschüchtert	intimidé	intimidito	acobardado

English	German	French	Italian	Spanish
intolerant	unduldsam	intolarant	intollerante	intolerante
jealous	eifersüchtig	jaloux	geloso	celoso
joyful	freudig	joyeux	gioioso	muy alegre
jubilant	jubelnd	jubilant	giubilante	jubiloso
listless	lustlos	langoureux	apatico	lánguido
lively	munter	allègre	animato	animado
lonely	einsam	(se sentir) seul	(sentirsi) solo	(sentirse) solo
melancholic	melancholisch	mélancolique	melanconico	melancólico
nervous	nervös	nerveux	nervoso	nervioso
nostalgic	nostalgisch	nostalgique	nostalgico	nostálgico
offended	gekränkt	offensé	offeso	ofendido
outraged	empört	révolté	oltraggiato	ultrajado
overexcited	aufgedreht	surexcité	sovreccitato	sobreexcita
passionate	voller Leidenschaft	passionné	appassionato	apasionado
proud	stolz	fier	fiero	orgulloso
puzzled	ratlos	perplexe	perplesso	perplejo
relaxed	entspannt	détendu	rilassato	relajado
relieved	erleichtert	soulagé	sollevato	aliviado
repelled	angewidert	répugné	provare ripugnanza	sentir repugnancia
resigned	resigniert	résigné	rassegnato	resignado
respectful	respektvoll	respectueux	rispettoso	respetuoso
sad	traurig	triste	triste	triste
satisfied	befriedigt	satisfait	soddisfatto	satisfecho
scared	voller Schrecken	effrayé	spaventato	asustado
sensual	sinnlich	sensuel	sensuale	sensual
serene	heiter	serein	sereno	sereno
shy	schüchtern	timide	timido	timido
sorry	leid tun	désolé	spiacente	pesaroso
stimulated	angeregt	stimulé	stimolato	estimulado
stubborn	trotzig	buté	ostinato	terco
surprised	überrascht	surpris	sorpreso	sorprendido
tender	zärtlich	tendre	tenero	tierno
tense	angespannt	tendu	teso	tenso
tired	müde	fatigué	stanco	cansado
touched	gerührt	touché	commosso	conmovido
triumphant	triumphierend	triomphant	trionfante	victorioso
undecided	unentschlossen	indécis	indeciso	indeciso
uneasy	beunruhigt	inquiet	inquieto	inquieto
unhappy	unglücklich	malheureux	infelice	infeliz
vengeful	rachsüchtig	vindicatif	vendicativo	vengativo
warmhearted	warm	chaleureux	caloroso	cálido
weak	schwach	faible	debole	debil
worried	besorgt	soucieux	preoccupato	preocupado

REFERENCES

Abelson, R. P. (1983). Whatever became of consistency theory? *Personality and Social Psychology Bulletin, 9*, 37–54.

Anderson, N. H. (1971). Two more tests against change of meaning in adjective combinations. *Journal of Verbal Learning and Verbal Behavior, 10*, 75–85.

Anderson, N. H. (1974). Cognitive algebra: Integration theory applied to social attribution. In L. Berkowitz (Ed.), *Advances in experimental social psychology* Vol. 7. (pp. 1–101). New York: Academic Press.

Anderson, N. H., & Jacobson, A. (1965). Effects of stimulus inconsistency and discounting instructions in personality impression formation. *Journal of Personality and Social Psychology, 2*, 531–539.

Archer, D., & Akert, R. M. (1977). Words and everything else: Verbal and nonverbal cues in social interpretation. *Journal of Personality and Social Psychology, 35*, 443–449.

Argyle, M., Alkema, F., & Gilmour, R. (1971). The communication of friendly and hostile by verbal and non-verbal signals. *European Journal of Social Psychology, 1*, 385–402.

Aristoteles (1935). In G. L. J. Tafel, E. R. Osiander, & G. Schwab (Eds.), *Griechische Prosaiker in neuen Übersetzungen.* Stuttgart: Metzler.

Arnold, M. B. (1960a). *Emotion and personality. Vol. 1: Psychological aspects.* New York: Columbia University Press.

Arnold, M. B. (1960b). *Emotion and personality. Vol. 2: Neurological and physiological aspects.* New York: Columbia University Press.

Asch, S. E. (1946). Forming impressions of personality. *Journal of Abnormal and Social Psychology, 41*, 258–290.

Asch, S. E., & Zukier, H. (1984). Thinking about persons. *Journal of Personality and Social Psychology, 46*, 1230–1240.

Asendorpf, J. B., & Scherer, K. R. (1983). The discrepant repressor: Differentiation between low anxiety, high anxiety, and repression of anxiety. *Journal of Personality and Social Psychology, 45*, 1334–1346.

Averill, J. R. (1975). A semantic atlas of emotional concepts. *JSAS Catalogue of Selected Documents in Psychology, 5*, 330.

Averill, J. R. (1982). *Anger and aggression: An essay on emotion.* New York: Springer.

Ax, A. F. (1953). The physiological differentiation between fear and anger in humans. *Psychosomatic Medicine, 15,* 433–442.

Babad, E. Y., & Wallbott, H. G. (1986). The effects of social factors on emotional reactions. In K. R. Scherer, H. G. Wallbott, & A. B. Summerfield (Eds.), *Experiencing emotion: A cross-cultural study* (pp. 154–172). Cambridge: Cambridge University Press.

Berman, H. J., Shulman, A. D., & Marwitt, S. J. (1976). Comparison of multidimensional decoding of affect from audio, video, and audiovideo recordings. *Sociometry, 39,* 83–89.

Bernstein, I. S. (1970). Activity patterns in pigtail monkey groups. *Folia Primatologica, 12,* 187–198.

Birdwhistell, R. L. (1968). Communication without words. In P. Alexandre (Ed.), *L'aventure humaine* (pp. 157–166). Genf: Kister.

Birdwhistell, R. L. (1970). *Kinesics and context.* Philadelphia: University of Pennsylvania Press.

Block, J. (1957). Studies in the phenomenology of the emotions. *Journal of Abnormal and Social Psychology, 54,* 358–363.

Borg, I. (1979). Some basic concepts of facet theory. In J. C. Lingoes, E. E. Roskam, & I. Borg (Eds.), *Geometric representations of relational data.* Ann Arbor, MI: Mathesis Press.

Borg, I. (1986). Facettentheorie: Prinzipien und Beispiele. *Psychologische Rundschau, 37,* 121–137.

Borg, I., & Lingoes, J. C. (1987). *Multidimensional similarity structure analysis.* New York: Springer.

Borg, I., Scherer, K. R., & Staufenbiel, T. (1986). Determinanten von Peinlichkeit und Scham. *Archiv für Psychologie, 138,* 53–70.

Bottenberg, E. H. (1972). *Emotionspsychologie. Ein Beitrag zur empirischen Dimensionierung emotionaler Vorgänge.* München: Goldmann.

Bruce, G. (1982). Developing the Swedish intonation model. *Working Papers of Department of Linguistics University of Lund, 22,* 51–114.

Bruce, G., & Garding, E. (1978). A prosodic typology for Swedish dialects. In E. Garding, G. Bruce, & R. Bannert (Eds.), *Nordic prosody* (pp. 219–228). Travaux de l'institut de linguistique de Lund No. 13.

Buck, R., Baron, R., Goodman, N., & Shapiro, B. (1980). Unitization of spontaneous nonverbal behavior in the study of emotion communication. *Journal of Personality and Social Psychology, 39,* 522–529.

Bugental, D. E., Kaswan, J. W., & Love, L. R., & Fox, M. N. (1970a). Child versus adult perception of evaluative messages in verbal, vocal, and visual channels. *Developmental Psychology, 2,* 367–375.

Bugental, D. E., Kaswan, J. W., & Love, L. R. (1970b). Perception of contradictory meanings conveyed by verbal and nonverbal channels. *Journal of Personality and Social Psychology, 16,* 647–655.

Bugental, D. E., Love, L. R., Kaswan, J. W., & April, C. (1971a). Verbal-nonverbal conflict in parental messages to normal and disturbed children. *Journal of Abnormal Psychology, 17,* 314–318.

Bugental, D. E., Love, L. R., & Gianetti, R. M. (1971b). Perfidous feminine faces. *Journal of Personality and Social Psychology, 17,* 314–318.

Bush, L. E. (1973). Individual differences in multidimensional scaling of adjectives denoting feelings. *Journal of Personality and Social Psychology, 25,* 50–57.

Canter, D. (1985). *Facet theory: Approaches to social research.* New York: Springer.

Carmichael, J. W., George, J. A., & Juluis, R. S. (1968). Finding natural clusters. *Systematical Zoology, 17,* 144–150.

Cline, V. B., Atzet, J., & Holmes, E. (1972). Assessing the validity of verbal and nonverbal cues in accurately judging others. *Comparative Group Studies, 3,* 383–394.

Collins, R. (1984). The role of emotion in social structure. In K. R. Scherer & P. Ekman (Eds.), *Approaches to emotion* (pp. 385–396). Hillsdale, NJ: Lawrence Erlbaum Associates.

Cooley, C. H. (1922). *Human nature and social order.* New York: Scribner's.

Crowne, D. P., & Marlowe, D. (1964). *The approval motive.* New York: Wiley.

Crystal, D. (1969). *Prosodic systems and intonation in English.* Cambridge: Cambridge University Press.

Dahl, H., & Stengel, B. (1978). A classification of emotion words. *Psychoanalysis and Contemporary Thought, 1,* 269–312.

Daly, E. M., Lancee, J. W., & Polivy, J. (1983). A conical model for the taxonomy of emotional experience. *Journal of Personality and Social Psychology, 45,* 443–457.

Darwin, C. (1872). *The expression of the emotions in man and animals.* London: Murray. (Originally published, Chicago: University of Chicago Press, 1965).

Davis, R. C. (1934). The specificity of facial expression, *Journal of General Psychology, 10,* 42–58.

De Rivera, J. (1977). A structural theory of the emotions. *Psychological Issues, 10,* Monograph 40.

Dore, F. Y., & Kirouac, G. (1986). Reliability of accuracy and intensity judgments of eliciting situations of emotions. *Canadian Journal of Behavioral Science, 18,* 92–103.

Ekman, P. (1972). Universals and cultural differences in facial expressions of emotion. In J. Cole (Ed.), *Nebraska Symposium on Motivation, 1971* (Vol. 19, pp. 207–283). Lincoln: University of Nebraska Press.

Ekman, P. (1973). Darwin and cross-cultural studies of facial expression. In P. Ekman (Ed.), *Darwin and facial expression* (pp. 1–83). New York: Academic Press.

Ekman, P. (1978). Facial signs: Facts, fantasies, and possibilities. In T. Sebeok (Ed.), *Sight, Sound, and Sense* (pp. 124–156). Bloomington: Indiana University Press.

Ekman, P. (1982). (Ed.). *Emotion in the human face* (2nd ed.). Cambridge: Cambridge University Press.

Ekman, P. (1984). Expression and the nature of emotion. In K. R. Scherer & P. Ekman (Eds.), *Approaches to emotion* (pp. 319–344). Hillsdale, NJ: Lawrence Erlbaum Associates.

Ekman, P., & Friesen, W. V. (1967). Head and body cues in the judgment of emotion: A reformulation. *Perceptual and Motor Skills, 24,* 711–724.

Ekman, P., & Friesen, W. V. (1969). Nonverbal leakage and cues to deception. *Psychiatry, 32,* 88–106.

Ekman, P., & Friesen, W. V. (1974). Detecting deception from the body or face. *Journal of Personality and Social Psychology, 29,* 188–198.

Ekman, P., & Friesen, W. V. (1976). *Pictures of facial affect.* Palo Alto, CA: Consulting Psychologists Press (series of slides).

Ekman, P., & Friesen, W. V. (1978). *Facial Action Coding System (FACS): A technique for the measurement of facial action.* Palo Alto, CA: Consulting Psychologists Press.

Ekman, P., & Friesen, W. V. (1982). Felt, false, and miserable smiles. *Journal of Nonverbal Behavior, 6,* 238–252.

Ekman, P., Friesen, W. V., & Ancoli, S. (1980). Facial signs of emotional experience. *Journal of Personality and Social Psychology, 39,* 1125–1134.

Ekman, P., Friesen W. V., & Ellsworth, P. (1982a). What are the relative contributions of facial behavior and contextual information to the judgment of emotion? In P. Ekman (Ed.), *Emotion in the human face* (2nd ed, pp. 111–127). New York: Cambridge University Press.

Ekman, P., Friesen, W. V., & Ellsworth, P. (1982b). Does the face provide accurate information? In P. Ekman (Ed.), *Emotion in the human face* (pp. 56–97). New York: Cambridge University Press.

Ekman, P., Friesen, W. F., & Scherer, K. R. (1976). Body movement and voice pitch in deceptive interaction. *Semiotica, 16,* 23–27.

Ekman, P., Levenson, R. W., & Friesen, W. V. (1983). Autonomic nervous system activity distinguishes between emotions. *Science, 221,* 1208–1210.

Elias, N. (1977). *The civilizing process.* New York: Urizen.

Ellgring, J.H., & Baenninger-Huber, E. (1986). The coding of reported emotional experiences: Antecedents and reactions. In K.R. Scherer, H.G. Wallbott, & A.B. Summerfield (Eds.), *Experiencing emotion: A cross cultural study* (pp. 39–49. Cambridge:Cambridge University Press.

Emde, R. N. (1984). Levels of meaning for infant emotions: A biosocial view. In K. R. Scherer & P. Ekman (Eds.), *Approaches to emotion* (pp. 11–108). Hillsdale, NJ: Lawrence Erlbaum Associates.

Emde, R. N., Kligman, D. H., Reich, J. H., & Wade, T. D. (1978). Emotional expression in infancy: I. Initial studies of social signaling and an emergent model. In M. Lewis & I. Rosenblum (Eds.), *The development of affect*. New York: Plenum Press.

Ertel, S. (1964). Die emotionale Natur des "semantischen" Raumes. *Psychologische Forschung, 28*, 1–32.

Everitt, B. (1974). *Cluster analysis*. London: Heinemann Educational Books.

Feleky, A. M. (1914). The expression of the emotions. *Psychological Review, 21*, 33–41.

Fernberger, S. W. (1927). Six more Piderit faces. *American Journal of Psychology, 39*, 162–166.

Fernberger, S. W. (1928). False suggestion and the Piderit model. *American Journal of Psychology, 40*, 562–568.

Fillenbaum, S., & Rapoport, A. (1971). *Structures in the subjective lexicon*. New York: Academic Press.

Foa, U. G. (1958). The contiguity principle in the structure of interpersonal relations. *Human Relations, 11*, 229–238.

Fraisse, P. (1981). Cognition of time in human activity. In G. d'Ydewalle & W. Lens (Eds.), *Cognition in motivation and learning* (pp. 233–258). Hillsdale, NJ: Lawrence Erlbaum Associates.

Frijda, N. H. (1953). The understanding of facial expression of emotion. *Acta Psychologica, 9*, 294–362.

Frijda, N. H. (1969). Recognition of emotion. In L. Berkowitz (Ed.), *Advances in experimental social psychology* (Vol. 4, pp. 167–224). New York: Academic Press.

Frijda, N. H. (1986). *The emotions*. Cambridge: Cambridge University Press.

Frois-Wittmann, J. (1930). The judgment of facial expression. *Journal of Experimental Psychology, 8*, 113–151.

Galinat, W. H., & Borg, I. (1987). On symbolic temporal information: Beliefs about the experience of duration. *Memory and Cognition, 15*, 308–317.

Gaylin, W. (1981). *Feelings: Our vital signs*. New York: Ballantine.

Gehm, T. (1987). *Interindividuelle Unterschiede im Erleben der Ähnlichkeit von Emotionen* (Interindividual differences in experiencing the similarity of emotions). (Submitted for publication).

Gellhorn, E. (1967). *Principles of autonomic-somatic integration*. Minneapolis: University of Minnesota Press.

Goldbeck, T., Bergmann, G., & Tolkmitt, F. (1986). *Neutralisierung emotionaler Äusserungen durch suprasegmentelle Parametervariationen des Sprachsignals*. Paper presented at the 28th Conference of the Experimentally Working Psychologists (TEAP), March, 1986.

Gollin, E. S. (1956). Concept formation and impressions of personality. *Journal of Abnormal and Social Psychology, 52*, 39–42.

Goodenough, F. L. (1931). The expression of the emotions in infancy. *Child Development, 2*, 96–101.

Goodenough, F. L., & Tinker, M. A. (1931). The relative potency of facial expression and verbal description of stimulus in the judgment of emotion. *Comparative Psychology, 12*, 365–370.

Goodman, L. A., & Magidson, J. (1978). *Analyzing qualitative/categorial data: Log-linear models and latentstructure analysis*. Cambridge, MA: ABT Books.

Gordon, S. L. (1981). The sociology of sentiments and emotion. In M. Rosenberg & R. Turner (Eds.), *Social psychology: Sociological perspectives* (pp. 261–278). New York: Basic Books.

Gordon, S. L. (1984). Microsociological theories of emotion. In S. N. Eisenstadt & H. Helle (Eds.), *Perspectives on sociological theory*. London: Sage.

Graham, J. A., Ricci-Bitti, P., & Argyle, M. (1975). A cross-cultural study of the communication of emotion by facial and gestural cues. *International Journal of Psychology, 10*, 57–67.

Gregor, U., & Patalas, E. (1976). *Geschichte des Films. Band 1: 1895–1939*. Reinbek: Rowohlt.

Grizzle, J. E., Starmer, C. F., & Koch, G. G. (1969). Analysis of categorical data by linear models. *Biometrics, 25*, 489–504.

Guilford, J. P. (1929). An experiment in learning to read facial expression. *Journal of Abnormal and Social Psychology, 24*, 191–202.

Guttman, L. (1959). Introduction to facet design and analysis. *Proceedings of the 15th International Congress of Psychology in Brussels*. Amsterdam: North-Holland.

Guttman, L. (1968). A general nonmetric technique for finding the smallest coordinate spaces for a configuration of points. *Psychometrika, 33*, 469–506.

Guttman, L. (1981a). What is not what in statistics. In I. Borg (Ed.), *Multidimensional data representations: When and why*. Ann Arbor, MI: Mathesis Press.

Guttman, L. (1981b). Efficacy coefficients for differences among averages. In I. Borg (Ed.), *Multidimensional data representations: When and why*. Ann Arbor, MI: Mathesis Press.

Hecker, M. H. L., Stevens, K. N., Bismarck, G., von, & Williams, C. E. (1968). Manifestations of the task-induced stress in the acoustic speech signal. *Journal of the Acoustical Society of America, 44*, 993–1001.

Heelas, P. (1985). Emotion talk, cross cultures. In R. Harré (Ed.), *Social construction of emotions*. Oxford: Basil Blackwell.

Heider, F. (1958). *The psychology of interpersonal relations*. New York: Wiley.

Hinde, R. A., & Rowell, T. E. (1962). Communication by postures and facial expressions in the rhesus monkey (Macaca mulatta). *Proceedings of the Zoological Society of London, 138*, 1–21.

Hochschild, A. R. (1979). Emotion work, feeling rules, and social structure. *American Journal of Sociology, 3*, 551–575.

Höfer, I., Wallbott, H. G., & Scherer, K. R. (1985). Messung multimodaler Stressindikatoren in Belastungssituationen: Person-Situationsfaktoren. In H. W. Krohne (Ed.), *Angstbewältigung in Leistungssituationen* (pp. 94–114). Weinheim: Edition Psychologie.

Horney, K. (1937). *The neurotic personality of our time*. New York: Norton.

Hubert, L., & Arabie, P. (1985). Comparing partitions. *Journal of Classification, 2*, 193–218.

Izard, C. (1980). Cross-cultural perspectives on emotion and emotion communication. In H. Triandis (Ed.), *Handbook of cross-cultural psychology* (pp. 95–126). Boston: Allyn & Bacon.

Izard, C. E. (1977). *Human emotions*. New York: Plenum Press.

Klineberg, O. (1938). Emotional expression in Chinese literature. *Journal of Abnormal and Social Psychology, 33*, 517–520.

Knudsen, H. R., & Muzekari, L. H. (1983). The effects of verbal statements of context on facial expressions of emotion. *Journal of Nonverbal Behavior, 7*, 202–212.

Kritzer, H. M. (1982). *Nonmet II: A program for analysis of contingency tables and other types of nonmetric data by weighted least squares*. Unpublished program description. University of Wisconsin at Madison.

Kruskal, J. B., & Wish, M. (1978). *Multidimensional scaling*. Sage Series: Quantitative applications in the social sciences, 11. Beverly Hills, CA: Sage.

Kuechler, M. (1979). *Multivariate Analyseverfahren*. Stuttgart: Teubner.

Kuechler, M., & Wides, J. W. (1981). *Economic perception and the '76 and '80 presidential votes*. Paper presented at the 1981 annual meeting of the American Sociological Association in Toronto, Canada.

Ladd, D. R. (1983). Phonological features of international peaks. *Language, 59*, 721–759.

Ladd, D. R., Silverman, K. E. A., Tolkmitt, F., Bergmann, G., & Scherer, K. R. (1985). Evidence for the independent function of intonation contour type, voice quality, and F0 range in signaling speaker affect. *Journal of the Acoustical Society of America, 78*, 335–444.

Landis, C. (1924). Studies of emotional reactions. II: General behavior and facial expression. *Journal of Comparative Psychology, 4*, 447–509.

Landis, C. (1929). The interpretation of facial expression in emotion. *Journal of General Psychology, 2*, 59–72.

Langfeld, H. S. (1918). The judgment of emotions from facial expressions. *Journal of Abnormal Psychology, 13*, 172–184.

Laver, J. (1980). *The phonetic description of voice quality.* Cambridge: Cambridge University Press.

Lazarus, R. S. (1966). *Psychological stress and the coping process.* New York: McGraw-Hill.

Lazarus, R. S. (1984). Thoughts on the relations between emotion and cognition. In K. R. Scherer & P. Ekman (Eds.), *Approaches to emotion* (pp. 247–258). Hillsdale, NJ: Lawrence Erlbaum Associates.

Lazarus, R. S., Averill, J. R., & Opton, E. M. (1970). Towards a cognitive theory of emotion. In M. B. Arnold (Ed.), *Feelings and emotions* (pp. 207–232). New York: Academic Press.

Leventhal, H., & Scherer, K. R. (1987). The relationship of emotion and cognition: A functional approach to a semantic controversy. *Cognition and Emotion, 1*, 3–28.

Levitt, E. A. (1964). The relationship between abilities to express emotional meanings vocally and facially. In J. R. Davitz (Ed.), *The communication of emotional meaning*, pp. 87–100. New York: McGraw-Hill.

Levy, R. (1984). The emotions in comparative perspective. In. K. R. Scherer & P. Ekman (Eds.), *Approaches to emotion* (pp. 397–412). Hillsdale, NJ: Lawrence Erlbaum Associates.

Levy, S. (1981). Lawful roles of facets in social theories. In I. Borg (Ed.), *Multidimensional data representations: When and why* (pp. 65–107). Ann Arbor, MI: Mathesis Press.

Liberman, P., & Pierrehumbert, J. (1984). International invariance under changes in pitch range and length. In M. Aronoff & R. Ochrle (Eds.), *Language sound structure.* Cambridge, MA: M.I.T. Press.

Lingoes, J. C. (1973). *The Guttman-Lingoes nonmetric program series.* Ann Arbor, MI: Mathesis Press.

Lutz, C. (1986). Cultural patterns and individual differences in the child's emotional meaning system. In C. Saarni & M. Lewis (Eds.), *The socialization of affect.* New York: Plenum Press.

Lynd, H. M. (1961). *On Shame and the search of identity.* New York: Science Editions.

Magnusson, D., & Stattin, H. (1981). *Situation-outcome contingencies: A conceptual and empirical analysis of threatening situations.* Reports from the Department of Psychology, University of Stockholm, No. 571.

Mandler, G. (1984). *Mind and body: The psychology of emotion and stress.* New York: Norton.

Markel, F. D., & Gray, A. H. (1976). *Linear prediction of speech.* New York: Springer.

Mead, G. H. (1934). *Mind, self, and society.* Chicago: University of Chicago Press.

Mehrabian, A., & Ferris, S. R. (1967). Inference of attitudes from nonverbal communication in two channels. *Journal of Consulting Psychology, 31*, 248–252.

Menn, L., & Boyce, S. (1982). Fundamental frequency and discourse structure. *Language and Speech, 25*, 341–383.

Mielke, P. W., Berry, K. J., & Johnson, E. S. (1976). Multi-response permutation procedures for a priori classifications. *Commun. Statistical-Theoretical Methods, A5*, 1409–1424.

Moscovici, S., & Farr, R. (Eds.) (1986) *Social representation.* Cambridge: Cambridge University Press.

Munn, N. L. (1940). The effect of knowledge of the situation upon judgment of emotion from facial expression. *Journal of Abnormal and Social Psychology, 35*, 324–338.

Nisbett, R., & Ross, L. (1980). *Human inference: Strategies and shortcomings of social judgment.* Englewood Cliffs, NJ: Prentice-Hall.

Nisbett, R. E., & Wilson, T. D. (1977). Telling more than we can know: Verbal reports on mental processes. *Psychological Review, 84,* 231–259.

O'Connor, J. D., & Arnold, G. F. (1961). *Intonation of colloquial English.* London: Arnold.

Osgood, C. E. (1966). Dimensionality of the semantic space for communication via facial expression. *Scandinavian Journal of Psychology, 7,* 1–130.

Osgood, C. E., Suci, G. J., & Tannenbaum, P. H. (1957). *The measurement of meaning.* Urbana: University of Illinois Press.

Pennebaker, J. W. (1982). *The psychology of physiological symptoms.* New York: Springer.

Piers, G., & Singer, M. B. (1971). Shame and guilt. New York: Norton.

Pike, K. L. (1945). *The intonation of American English.* Ann Arbor: University of Michigan.

Plutchik, R. (1980). *Emotion: A psychoevolutionary synthesis.* New York: Harper & Row.

Riskind, J. H. (1984). They stoop to conquer: Guiding and self-regulatory functions of physical posture after success and failure. *Journal of Personality and Social Psychology, 47,* 479–493.

Roseman, I. J. (1984). Cognitive determinants of emotion: A structural theory. In P. Shaver (Ed.), *Review of personality and social psychology: Vol. 5. Emotions, relationships, and health* (pp. 11–36). Beverly Hills, CA: Sage Publications.

Rosenthal, R. (1982). Conducting judgment studies. In K. R. Scherer & P. Ekman (Eds.), *Handbook of methods in nonverbal behavior research.* Cambridge: Cambridge University Press.

Roskam, E. E. (1975). A documentation of MINISSA. *Program Bulletin, No. 12,* Nijmegen, Department of Psychology.

Russell, J. A. (1978). Evidence of convergence validity on the dimensions of affect. *Journal of Personality and Social Psychology, 36,* 1152–1168.

Russell, J. A. (1980). A circumplex model of affect. *Journal of Personality and Social Psychology, 39,* 1161–1178.

Russell, J. A. (1983). Pancultural aspects of the human conceptual organization of emotions. *Journal of Personality and Social Psychology, 45,* 1281–1288.

Russell, J. A., & Mehrabian, A. (1977). Evidence for three-factor theory of emotions. *Journal of Research in Personality, 11,* 273–294.

Sade, D. C. (1967). Determinants of dominance in a group of free-ranging rhesus monkeys, In S. A. Altman (Ed.), *Social communication among primates* (pp. 99–113). Chicago: University of Chicago Press.

Scherer, K. R. (1974). Acoustic concomitants of emotional dimensions: Judging affects from synthesized tone sequences. In S. Weitz (Ed.), *Nonverbal communication* (pp. 105–111). New York: Oxford University Press.

Scherer, K. R. (1978). Personality inference from voice quality: The loud voice of extraversion. *European Journal of Social Psychology, 8,* 467–487.

Scherer, K. R. (1979). Nonlinguistic indicators of emotions and psychopathology. In C. E. Izard (Ed.), *Emotions in personality and psychopathology* (pp. 495–529). New York: Plenum Press.

Scherer, K. R. (1981a). Speech and emotional states. In J. Darby (Ed.), *Speech evaluation in psychiatry* (pp. 189–220). New York: Grune & Stratton.

Scherer, K. R. (1981b). Wider die Vernachlässigung der Emotion in der Psychologie. In W. Michaelis (Ed.), *Bericht über den 32. Kongress der Duetschen Gesellscharft für Psychologie in Zürich* (pp. 304–317). Göttingen: Hogrefe.

Scherer, K. R. (1981c). Vocal indicators of stress. In J. Darby (Ed.). *Speech evaluation in psychiatry* (pp. 171–187). New York: Grune & Stratton.

Scherer, K. R. (1982). Methods of research on vocal communication: Paradigms and parameters. In K. R. Scherer & P. Ekman (Eds.), *Handbook of methods in nonverbal behavior research* (pp. 137–198). Cambridge: Cambridge University Press.

Scherer, K. R. (1983). Prolegomina zu einer Taxonomie affektiver Zustände: Ein Komponenten-Prozess-Modell. In G. Lüer (Ed.), *Bericht über den 33. Kongress der Deutschen Gesellschaft für Psychologie in Mainz* (pp. 415–423). Göttingen: Hogrefe.

Scherer, K. R. (1984a). On the nature and function of emotion: A component process approach. In K. R. Scherer & P. Ekman (Eds.), *Approaches to emotion* (pp. 293–317). Hillsdale, NJ: Lawrence Erlbaum Associates.

Scherer, K. R. (1984b). Emotion as a multicomponent process: A model and some cross-cultural data. In P. Shaver & L. Wheeler (Eds.), *Review of personality and social psychology: Vol. 5*. Beverly Hills, CA: Sage Publications.

Scherer, K. R. (1986a). Vocal affect expression: A review and a model for future research. *Psychological Bulletin, 99*, 143–165.

Scherer, K. R. (1986b). Emotion experiences across European cultures: A summary statement. In K. R. Scherer, H. G. Wallbott, & A. B. Summerfield (Eds.), *Experiencing emotion: A cross-cultural study* (pp. 173–189). Cambridge: Cambridge University Press.

Scherer, K. R. (1986c). Voice, stress, and emotion. In M. H. Appley & R. Trumbull (Eds.), *Dynamics of stress* (pp. 159–181). New York: Plenum Press.

Scherer, K. R. (in press). Criteria for emotion antecedent appraisal: A review. In V. Hamilton, G. H. Bower, & N. Frijda (Eds.), *Cognitive perspectives on emotion and motivation*. Dordrecht: Nijhoff.

Scherer, K. R., Ladd, D. R., & Silverman, K. E. A. (1984). Vocal cues to speaker affect: Testing two models. *Journal of the Acoustical Society of America, 76*, 1346–1356.

Scherer, K. R., & Oshinsky, J. (1977). Cue utilization in emotion attribution from auditory stimuli. *Motivation and Emotion, 1*, 331–346.

Scherer, K. R., & Scherer, U. (1981a). Speech behavior and personality. In J. Darby (Ed.), *Speech evaluation in psychiatry* (pp. 115–135). New York: Grune & Stratton.

Scherer, K. R., & Scherer, U. (1981b). Nonverbal behavior and impression formation in naturalistic situations. In H. Hiebsch, H. Brandstätter, & H. H. Kelley (Eds.), *Proceedings of the XXIInd International Congress of Psychology, Leipzig (GDR), 1980. Social Psychology*. Amsterdam: VEB Deutscher Verlag de Wissenschaften Berlin.

Scherer, K. R., Scherer, U., Hall, J. A., & Rosenthal, R. (1977). Differential attribution of personality based on multichannel presentation of verbal and nonverbal cues. *Psychological Research, 39*, 221–247.

Scherer, K. R., Scherer, U., & Klink, M. (1979). Determinanten des Verhaltens öffentlich Bediensteter im Publikumsverkehr. In F. X. Kaufmann (Ed.), *Bürgernahe Sozialpolitik* (pp. 408–451). Frankfurt: Campus.

Scherer, K. R., Summerfield, A. B., & Wallbott, H. G. (1983). Cross-national research on antecedents and components of emotion: A progress report. *Social Science Information, 3*, 355–385.

Scherer, K. R., & Tannenbaum, P. H. (1986). Emotional experiences in everyday life: A survey approach. *Motivation and Emotion, 10*, (pp. 295–314)

Scherer, K. R., & Wallbott, H. G. (1985). Analysis of nonverbal behavior. In T. A. van Dijk (Ed.), *Handbook of discourse analysis* (pp. 199–230). London: Academic Press.

Scherer, K. R., Wallbott, H. G., & Summerfield, A. B. (Eds.) (1986). *Experiencing emotion: A cross-cultural study*. Cambridge: Cambridge University Press.

Scherer, K. R., Wallbott, H. G., Tolkmitt, F., & Bergmann, G. (1985). *Die Stressreaktion: Physiologie und Verhalten*. Göttingen: Hogrefe.

Scherer, U., & Scherer, K. R. (1980). Psychological factors in bureaucratic encounters: Determinants and effects of interactions between officials and clients. In W. T. Singleton, P. Spurgeon, & R. B. Stammers (Eds.), *The analysis of social skill* p. 315–328). New York: Plenum Press.

Schmidt-Atzert, L. (1981). *Emotionspsychologie*. Stuttgart: Kohlhammer.

Schwartz, G. E., & Weinberger, D. A. (1980). Patterns of emotional responses to affective situations: Relations among happiness, sadness, anger, fear, depression, and anxiety. *Motivation and Emotion, 4*, 175–191.

Shapiro, J. G. (1972). Variability and usefulness of facial and body cues. *Journal of Comparative Group Studies, 3*, 437–442.

Sherman, M. (1927). The differentiation of emotion responses in infants. I: Judgments of emotional responses from motion pictures views and from actual observation. *Journal of Comparative Psychology, 7,* 265–284.

Shye, S. (1985). *Multiple Scaling.* Amsterdam: North-Holland.

Simon, H. A. (1967). Motivational and emotional controls of cognition. *Psychological Review, 74,* 29–39.

Smith, C. A., & Ellsworth, P. C. (1985). Patterns of cognitive appraisal in emotion. *Journal of Personality and Social Psychology, 48,* 813–838.

Smith, W. J. (1977). *The behavior of communicating.* Cambridge, MA: Harvard University Press.

Solomon, R. C. (1976). *The passions, the myth and nature of human emotion.* Garden City, NY: Doubleday.

Späth, H. (1975). *Cluster-Analyse-Algorithmen zur Objektklassifizierung und Datenreduktion.* München: Oldenbourg.

Spence, J., & Graef, J. (1974). The determination of the underlying dimensionality of an empirically obtained matrix of proximities. *Multivariate Behavioral Research, 9,* 331–342.

Spence, J., & Ogilvie, J. C. (1973). A table of expected stress values for random rankings in nonmetric multidimensional scaling. *Multivariate Behavioral Research, 8,* 511–517.

Spignesi, A., & Shor, R. E. (1981). The judgment of emotion from facial expressions, contexts, and their combination. *Journal of General Psychology, 104,* 41–58.

Stemmler, G. (1984). *Psychophysiologische Emotionsmuster.* Frankfurt: P. Lang.

Tartter, V. C. (1980). Happy talk: Perceptual and acoustic effects of smiling on speech. *Perception and Psychophysics, 27,* 24–27.

Thayer, S., & Schiff, W. (1969). Stimulus factors in observer judgment of social interaction: Facial expression and motion pattern. *American Journal of Psychology, 82,* 73–85.

Tolkmitt, F., Bergmann, G., & Goldbeck, T. (1987). Der Einfluss prosodischer Strukturvariationen des Satzakzents auf die Emotionsattribution. In J. P. Köster & V. A. Borowsky (Eds.), *Neue Tendenzen in der angewandten Phonetik II* (pp. 191–201). Hamburg: Buske.

Tolkmitt, F., Helfrich, H., Standke, R., & Scherer, K. R. (1982). Vocal indicators of psychiatric treatment effects in depressives and schizophrenics. *Journal of Communication Disorders, 15,* 209–222.

Tolkmitt, F., & Scherer, K. R. (1986). Effects of experimentally induced stress on vocal parameters. *Journal of Experimental Psychology: Human Perception and Performance, 12,* 302–313.

Tomkins, S. S. (1962). *Affect, imagery, consciousness. Vol. 1: The positive affects.* New York: Springer.

Tomkins, S. S. (1963). *Affect, imagery, consciousness. Vol. 2: The negative affects.* New York: Springer.

Tomkins, S. S., & McCarter, R. (1964). What and where are the primary affects? Some evidence for a theory. *Perceptual and Motor Skills, 18,* 119–158.

Traxel, W., & Heide, H. J. (1961). Dimensionen der Gefühle. Das Problem der Klassifikation der Gefühle und die Möglichkeit seiner empirischen Lösung. *Psychologische Forschung, 26,* 179–204.

Trevarthen, C. (1984). Emotions in infancy: Regulators of contact and relationships with persons. In K. R. Scherer, & P. Ekman (Eds.), *Approaches to emotion* (pp. 129–162). Hillsdale, NJ: Lawrence Erlbaum Associates.

Triandis, H., & Fishbein, M. (1962). Cognitive interaction in person perception. *Journal of Abnormal and Social Psychology, 67,* 446–453.

Turhan M. (1960). Über die Bedeutung des Gesichtsausdrucks. *Psychologische Beiträge, 5,* 440–495.

Tversky, A., & Kahneman, D. (1974). *Judgment under uncertainty: Heuristics and biases.* New York: Springer.

Van Hoof, J. A. R. A. M. (1962). Facial expression in higher primates. *Symposium of the Zoological Society of London, 8,* 97–125.

Vinacke, W. E. (1949). The judgment of facial expressions by three national-racial groups in Hawaii. I: Caucasian faces. *Journal of Personality, 17*, 407–429.

Wallbott, H. G. (1986). Person und Kontext: Zur relativen Bedeutung von mimischem Verhalten und Situationsinformationen im Erkennen von Emotionen. *Archiv für Psychologie, 138*, 211–231.

Wallbott, H. G., & Scherer, K. R. (1985a). Differentielle Situations-und Reaktionscharakteristika in Emotionserinnerungen: Ein neuer Forschungsansatz. *Psychologische Rundschau, 36*, 83–101.

Wallbott, H. G., & Scherer, K. R. (1985b). Person × Reaktion × Situation: Zur Versuchsplanung in der Stressforschung. *Psychologische Rundschau, 36*, 143–152.

Wallbott, H. G., & Scherer, K. R. (1986a). How universal and specific is emotional experience? Evidence from 25 countries on five continents. *Social Science Information, 25*, 763–795.

Wallbott, H. G., & Scherer, K. R. (1986b). Cues and channels in emotion recognition. *Journal of Personality and Social Psychology, 51*, 690–699.

Warr, P. B., & Knapper, C. (1968). *The perception of people and events.* London: Wiley.

Watson, S. G. (1972). Judgment of emotion from facial and contextual cue combinations. *Journal of Personality and Social Psychology, 24*, 334–342.

Weiner, B. (1982). The emotional consequences of causal attributions. In M. S. Clark & S. T. Fiske (Eds.), *Affect and cognition: The 17th Annual Carnegie Symposium on Cognition* (pp. 185–210). Hillsdale, NJ: Lawrence Erlbaum Associates.

Weiner, B. (1985). An attributional theory of achievement motivation and emotion. *Psychological Review, 92*, 548–573.

Wicker, F. W., Payne, G. C., & Morgan, R. D. (1983). Participant descriptions of guilt and shame. *Motivation and Emotion, 7*, 25–39.

Wiggers, M. (1982). Judgments of facial expressions of emotions predicted from facial behavior. *Journal of Nonverbal Behavior, 7*, 101–116.

Williams, C. E., & Stevens, K. N. (1972). Emotions and speech: Some acoustical correlates. *Journal of the Acoustical Society of America, 52*, 1238–1250.

Williams, C. E., & Stevens, K. N. (1981). Vocal correlates of emotional states. In J. Darby (Ed.), *Speech evaluation in psychiatry* (pp. 221–240). New York: Grune & Stratton.

Wishart, D. (1978). *Clustan user manual* (3rd ed.). Program library unit, University of Edinburgh.

Woodworth, R. S. (1938). *Experimental Psychology.* New York: Henry Holt.

Wundt, W. (1905). *Grundzüge der physiologischen Psychologie* (Vol. 3). Leipzig: Wilhelm Engelmann.

Zaidel, S., & Mehrabian, A. (1969). The ability to communicate and infer positive and negative attitudes facially and vocally. *Journal of Experimental Research in Personality, 3*, 233–241.

Zuckerman, M., DeFrank, R. S., Hall, A., Larrance, D. T., & Rosenthal, R. (1979). Facial and vocal cues of deception and honesty. *Journal of Experimental Social Psychology, 15*, 378–396.

Zuckerman, M., Koestner, R., & Colella, M. J. (1985). Learning to detect deception from three communication channels. *Journal of Nonverbal Behavior, 9*, 188–194.

Zuckerman, M., Larrance, D. T., Hall, J. A., DeFrank, R. S., & Rosenthal, R. (1979). Posed and spontaneous communication of emotion via facial and emotional cues. *Journal of Personality and Social Psychology, 47*, 712–733.

Zuckerman, M., Spiegel, N. H., DePaulo, B. M., & Rosenthal, R. (1982). Nonverbal strategies for decoding deception. *Journal of Nonverbal Behavior, 6*, 171–187.

AUTHOR INDEX

SUBJECT INDEX